Sacrifice and Atonement

Sacrifice and Atonement

Psychological Motives and Biblical Patterns

Stephen Finlan

Fortress Press
Minneapolis

SACRIFICE AND ATONEMENT

Psychological Motives and Biblical Patterns

Copyright © 2016 Fortress Press. All rights reserved. Except for brief quotations in critical articles or reviews, no part of this book may be reproduced in any manner without prior written permission from the publisher. Visit http://www.augsburgfortress.org/copyrights/ or write to Permissions, Augsburg Fortress, Box 1209, Minneapolis, MN 55440.

Cover image: Crown of Thorns, 2015 (photograph), Lions, Joy / Private Collection / Bridgeman Images

Cover design: Laurie Ingram

Library of Congress Cataloging-in-Publication Data

Print ISBN: 978-1-5064-0196-6

eBook ISBN: 978-1-5064-0197-3

The paper used in this publication meets the minimum requirements of American National Standard for Information Sciences — Permanence of Paper for Printed Library Materials, ANSI Z329.48-1984.

Manufactured in the U.S.A.

This book was produced using Pressbooks.com, and PDF rendering was done by PrinceXML.

Contents

Abbreviations	vii
Introduction	xi
Why Atonement Is Compelling	xiii
Revelation to the Wounded	xv
The Approach Used Here	xviii
1. Atonement as Purification	**1**
Functions of Ritual	1
Atonement Ideas in the Hebrew System	5
Spiritualizing or Metaphorical Understandings	12
The Psychology of Purity	14
2. Atonement as Compensation or Reciprocity	**23**
The Nature of Sacrifice in the Old Testament	24
Theories of Atonement Arising from Guilt	32
Sacrifice as a Part of Reciprocity Systems	37
No Inducement in the Kingdom	56
3. Attachment, Cruelty, and Coping	**59**
Attachment Theory	60
The Legacy of Cruel Punishing	66
Ideologies of Payment through Suffering	69
Not Your Fault	71
A Case of Ambivalent Attachment	73

4. Rescue and Disgust in Paul — 75
   - The Abstraction of Sacrifice in Paul's Theology — 75
   - Other Atonement Images in Paul — 90
   - The Trouble with Images — 99
   - Paul's Psychology — 102
   - The Problem with Atonement — 109

5. Answers to Atonement — 113
   - Paul Is "Participationist" — 113
   - Paul Is "Restorative" — 115
   - Paul Is "New Covenantal" — 117
   - The Son Was Not Intended to Be Killed — 118
   - Luke-Acts Is Not Cross-Centered — 122

6. Fear and Loathing in the Epistle to the Hebrews — 129
   - Hebrews' Dilemma about Sacrifice — 129
   - Innocent Blood and a Fury of Fire — 140
   - Another Soteriology in Hebrews — 145

7. Atonement Played Out — 149
   - Chronology of Theories of Atonement — 149
   - Anxiety, Guilt, and Shame — 162
   - Luther and Calvin — 166
   - Ritual Murder — 173
   - Without Price — 180

Conclusion — 183
- Wrestling with Propitiation — 183
- What We Can Say about Christ's Death — 185
- No Need to Manipulate — 187

Bibliography — 191

Index of Names — 211

Index of Scripture and Pre-Modern Sources — 219

Abbreviations

AB	Anchor Bible
ABD	*Anchor Bible Dictionary*. Edited by David Noel Freedman. 6 vols. New York: Doubleday, 1992
AcBib	Academia Biblica
Adv. haer.	Irenaeus, *Adversus haereses*
AnBib	Analecta Biblica
ANTC	Abingdon New Testament Commentaries
ANRW	*Aufstieg und Niedergang der römischen Welt: Geschichte und Kultur Roms im Spiegel der neueren Forschung*. Part 2, *Principat*. Edited by Hildegard Temporini and Wolfgang Haase. Berlin: de Gruyter, 1972–
BAG	*A Greek-English Lexicon of the New Testament and Other Early Christian Literature*. Translated and adapted by William F. Arndt and F. Wilbur Gingrich. 2nd ed. Chicago: University of Chicago Press, 1979
BCE	Before Common Era
BZAW	Beihefte zur Zeitschrift für die alttestamentliche Wissenschaft
BZNW	Beihefte zur Zeitschrift für die neutestamentliche Wissenschaft
CBQ	*Catholic Biblical Quarterly*
CC	Continental Commentaries
CE	Common Era
ConBNT	Coniectanea Biblica: New Testament Series
CSIR	Cambridge Studies in Ideology and Religion
DSS	Dead Sea Scrolls
EJL	Early Judaism and its Literature

1 En.	1 Enoch
ESV	English Standard Version
FOTL	Forms of Old Testament Literature
HBM	Hebrew Biblical Monographs
Eph.	Ignatius of Antioch, *Letter to the Ephesians*
Inc.	Athanasius, *De incarnatione*
JAPA	*Journal of the American Psychoanalytic Association*
JBL	*Journal of Biblical Literature*
JSSR	*Journal for the Scientific Study of Religion*
JSNTSup	Journal for the Study of the New Testament Supplement Series
JSOTSup	Journal for the Study of the Old Testament Supplement Series
JTS	*Journal of Theological Studies*
KJV	King James Version
LCL	Loeb Classical Library
LXX	Septuagint, the Greek translation of the Jewish Scriptures (Old Testament)
LSJ	Liddell, Henry George, Robert Scott, Henry Stuart Jones. *A Greek-English Lexicon*. 9th ed. with revised supplement. Oxford: Clarendon, 1996
Mor.	Gregory the Great, *Expositio in Librum Job, sive Moralium libri xxv*
MT	Masoretic Text
NAB	New American Bible
NASB	New American Standard Bible
NICNT	New International Commentary on the New Testament
NIV	New International Version
NRSV	New Revised Standard Version, the default translation used in this book
NT	New Testament
NTL	New Testament Library
NTS	*New Testament Studies*
OT	Old Testament
OTL	Old Testament Library
OTP	*Old Testament Pseudepigrapha*. Edited by James H. Charlesworth. 2 vols. New York: Doubleday, 1983–1985

ABBREVIATIONS

P.Oxy.	Oxyrhynchus papyri
PTMS	Princeton Theological Monograph Series
RBS	Resources for Biblical Study
SBL	Society of Biblical Literature
SBLECL	Society of Biblical Literature Early Christianity and Its Literature
SBLSCS	Society of Biblical Literature Septuagint and Cognate Studies
SHR	Studies in the History of Religions (supplements to Numen)
SJLA	Studies in Judaism in Late Antiquity
Smyrn.	Ignatius of Antioch, *Letter to the Smyrnaeans*
SNTSMS	Society for New Testament Studies Monograph Series
TDNT	*Theological Dictionary of the New Testament*. Edited by Gerhard Kittel and Gerhard Friedrich. Translated by Geoffrey W. Bromiley. 10 vols. Grand Rapids: Eerdmans, 1964–1976
TynBul	*Tyndale Bulletin*
VT	*Vetus Testamentum*
VTSup	Supplements to *Vetus Testamentum*
WA	*D. Martin Luthers Werke* [Weimarer Ausgabe]. Weimar: Böhlau, 1883–1993
WBC	Word Biblical Commentary
WUNT	Wissenschaftliche Untersuchungen zum Neuen Testament
WW	*Word and World*
ZNW	*Zeitschrift für die neutestamentliche Wissenschaft*

Introduction

Atonement has its origins in ritual sacrifice, so most biblical scholars who write about Christian atonement begin with a survey of sacrifice. But biblical scholars usually resist the application of psychology to biblical texts, possibly with good reason. No one wants to see the Bible explained away as a disguised fear of Daddy or yearning for Mommy. And yet, almost every biblical scholar and theologian brings *some* psychology to bear on the subject, without identifying it as such. John Goldingay writes of atoning sacrifices as a reconciling type of gift, "parallel to the gift of flowers in human relationships."[1] This asserts something about the psychology of sacrifice: that its motivation is similar to that of a pleasant and familiar custom. It suggests that sacrifice is about love and reconciliation, that it is thoroughly sensible and charming, with no thought of plying God with gifts in order to get something in return.

Even the most rigorous of biblical scholars resort to some psychological explanations. It is time to acknowledge that we are already using psychological categories to interpret ancient texts. We might then become more responsible for, and self-critical about, our psychological interpretations.

How could we *not* use psychology, when we are talking about religious traditions and practices that involved deep feelings, and may involve such feelings for the scholar, as well? What a writer asserts

---

1. John Goldingay, "Old Testament Sacrifice and the Death of Christ," in *Atonement Today*, ed. John Goldingay (London: SPCK, 1995), 4.

about psychology needs to be tested for coherence, as do all assertions. The reader must judge whether the psychological theories utilized in this study coordinate well with biblical studies, and seem to help us in understanding atonement in Jewish and Christian thinking.

But first we must study the Bible. Christian atonement is, generally, the idea that "Christ died for our sins" or died as a "sacrifice." In the New Testament, this idea mostly occurs in the Epistles and in Revelation. The subject is best introduced by providing some New Testament atonement passages, holding off on extensive commentary at this point. I give four texts from the apostle Paul and four from the successors to Paul.

> Our paschal lamb, Christ, has been sacrificed. (1 Cor. 5:7 NRSV, the default translation used in this book)

> I handed on to you . . . what I . . . received: that Christ died for our sins in accordance with the scriptures, and that he was buried, and that he was raised on the third day in accordance with the scriptures. (1 Cor. 15:3-4)

> While we still were sinners Christ died for us. Much more surely then, now that we have been justified by his blood, will we be saved through him from the wrath of God. For if while we were enemies, we were reconciled to God through the death of his Son, much more surely, having been reconciled, will we be saved by his life. (Rom. 5:8-10)

> Christ redeemed us from the curse of the law by becoming a curse for us. (Gal. 3:13)

> For there is one God; there is also one mediator between God and humankind, Christ Jesus, himself human, who gave himself a ransom for all. (1 Tim. 2:5-6)

> When he had made purification for sins, he sat down at the right hand of the Majesty on high. (Heb. 1:3)

> If the blood of goats and bulls, with the sprinkling of the ashes of a heifer, sanctifies those who have been defiled so that their flesh is purified, how much more will the blood of Christ, who through the eternal Spirit offered himself without blemish to God, purify our conscience from dead works. (Heb. 9:13-14)

INTRODUCTION

He has appeared once for all at the end of the age to remove sin by the sacrifice of himself. (Heb. 9:26)

Of course, Christ dying as a sacrifice is metaphorical, but the metaphors turn out to contain a number of basic Jewish sacrificial concepts, such as the notion that sacrificial blood purifies (see chapter 1) and the idea that sacrifice provides a "ransom" or "redemption" (see chapter 2).

Much more informally than in the biblical studies chapters, I would like now to introduce some of my views on the psychology of atonement.

Why Atonement Is Compelling

We need to ask why atonement has been so compelling in religious thought (whether monotheistic or not). I think it is partly because it corresponds to common beliefs about "the way life is": that there is "no pain, no gain," and "no free lunch." People have experienced that, on the material level, nothing is free, and they assume that the same principle operates on the divine level as well: a "ransom" had to be paid (1 Tim. 2:6; 1 Pet. 1:18). In ancient cultures, people tended to deal with their gods in the same ways they dealt with each other, practicing inducement, ingratiation, appeasement, and manipulation in their religion, as they did in their social lives. Gift-giving and praise were techniques for eliciting divine attention.

> I will offer in his tent
>   sacrifices with shouts of joy. . . .
> Hear, O Lord, when I cry aloud! . . .
>   Do not hide your face from me. (Ps. 27:6–7, 9)

Self-interest is quite apparent in Psalm 20.

> May he remember all your offerings,
>   and regard with favor your burnt sacrifices.
> May he grant you your heart's desire,
>   and fulfill all your plans. (Ps. 20:3–4)

The goal of sacrifice here is to get God to grant one's desires, which happens if God is pleased with the offering (regards it "with favor"). It is a kind of prosperity gospel!

But there were those who rejected this way of seeking God's favor, asking,

> Has the Lord as great delight in burnt offerings and sacrifices,
>   as in obedience to the voice of the Lord?
> Surely, to obey is better than sacrifice. (1 Sam. 15:22)

From a very early time, there were theological arguments about sacrifice.

Some of the prophets were upset with public displays of piety and sacrifice meant to impress God, to win God's favor. Micah asked,

> Will the Lord be pleased with thousands of rams,
>   with tens of thousands of rivers of oil? (Mic. 6:7)

Grandiose piety is manipulative. Jesus offers a radically different view by teaching that people should *trust* God, who need not be persuaded to give every good thing to God's children (Matt. 6:30–33; 7:7–11). God *cannot* be manipulated. (That was Micah's point as well; see Mic. 6:8; 3:11.)

The perceived need to butter up God, or to placate God's anger, has its psychological origin in childhood strategies for placating moody parents. The harsh God derives from harsh parenting, and the latter is reinforced by beliefs about God as violent and punishing. Our God-concept and our approach to parenting have a reciprocal effect on each other. We project our earthly experience onto God, and our understanding of God affects how we approach parenting. The good news is that, as parents become less frightening, God becomes less frightening. The message becomes "come, let us reason together" (Isa. 1:18) rather than "a fire is kindled by my anger" (Deut. 32:22). Our concepts of God would never make any progress if we had parents who would rather give their child a stone than a loaf of bread (Matt. 7:9), but Jesus chooses to use that illustration because he assumes that most parents are better than that. He is saying that most parents would provide *good* things, not a stone. And—*of course*—God is kind: "How much more will your Father in heaven give good things to those who ask him!" (Matt. 7:11; cf. Luke 11:13). Jesus proclaims that the Father gives *freely*, and not because sacrifice has been made or obeisance given. The Father does not want the children to grovel.

Revelation to the Wounded

There are many themes, ideas, and values that undergo reflection, debate, and struggle in the development of religion in any culture. But the single most important struggle, the great ideological battle of the ages, is the conflict between love and fear in believers' attitudes toward God. I understand God to be actively involved in the struggle in the heart of each believer, revealing love to us, and trying to help love to win out over fear. It is a long, slow process. I speak of "revelation" to refer to any revealing of divine reality or truth by God or by Spirit to humans. Unfortunately, the human mind is a very dense filter, and every revelation is adapted, assimilated, and distorted by the individual receiving it. As soon as revelation enters the human mind and heart, it is altered to one degree or another, domesticated to fit the beliefs the person already holds. Too often, we insist on pouring new wine into old wineskins that cannot "stretch." Old ways of thinking cannot hold the new truth (the point in Mark 2:22). And yet it also helps us to change our thinking.

Religion operates on our wounds, our loves, our fears, hopes, and yearnings. But unless revelation succeeds in clarifying religious values, they will remain poorly conceived, still attached to primitive origins and expressing more of woundedness than of healing, more of fear than of love. Religion carries a long heritage of fear. Divine revelation communicates a message of trust (and "perfect love casts out fear," 1 John 4:18), but it takes a long time for the new message to sink in. In Judaism and Christianity (and in other religions, to one degree or another, I would argue), the fear legacy of ancient religion has been *partly* replaced by the trust inspired by revelation. Fear and anxiety dominate ancient religion. One is always in danger of breaking some taboo or angering some spirit. This can even be seen in biblical religion. The Lord can lash out in anger at even the unintended transgression of sacred boundaries, as he did at Uzzah, who reached out to steady the ark of the covenant, "for the oxen shook it. The anger of the Lord was kindled against Uzzah; and God struck him there because he reached out his hand to the ark; and he died there beside the ark of God" (2 Sam. 6:6–7). Fear is the operative emotion: "David was afraid of the Lord that day" (6:9). Perhaps the original readers of this text experienced some of the same horror that most of us experience when reading this. But, hopefully, we find it much harder to accept the idea that God is a holy terror.

It should be obvious that, if one's relationship with God is characterized by fear, one's theology and thinking will be distorted. But to this day, many people are taught a message of mingled love and fear, as we see in the Epistle to the Hebrews: God is "faithful" and we are "to love" and be "encouraging" (Heb. 10:23–25), but "if we willfully persist in sin after having received the knowledge of the truth, there no longer remains a sacrifice for sins, but a fearful prospect of judgment, and a fury of fire" (10:26–27). Would not fear overwhelm love here? Every promise in Hebrews seems to carry a threat: "How can we escape if we neglect so great a salvation?" (2:3). "Since we are receiving a kingdom that cannot be shaken, let us give thanks ... for indeed our God is a consuming fire" (12:28–29). How confident can our love be then?

The idea of God as a punishing presence reflects dynamics learned in childhood. We tend to think about God in the ways we learned to think about our parents. A major thesis of this book is that atonement theology is largely based on childhood strategies for satisfying moody and explosive parents by "paying for" infractions (or having someone else pay for them). It would be a big mistake always to reduce religion to child psychology, but it would also be a mistake to deny the connection when there is good reason to notice it. We need to ask why brutal symbolism and mythology are common in our religions—not just in Christianity.

INTRODUCTION

The mixture of love and fear, forgiveness and threat, is nothing new in the history of religious symbols. The really effective religious symbols have a mysterious socializing power, since they combine divergent levels of human thought and draw together people of different backgrounds. The fact that the blending is illogical may actually *increase* its religious potency. Religious ideas are embraced for their vividness, their unconsciously compelling power. That which arouses the passions corresponds to something in early childhood experience evoking those things that have most harmed us, as well as those that have most helped us. They speak of what has cut most deeply into us—fear and love.

Bossy and impatient parenting styles were common in ancient societies. Doctrines of hell, payment in blood, and sacrificial substitution ring true for those who have been taught to consider violent retribution and punishment to be normal parental behaviors. As the sixth-to-seventh-century pope Gregory the Great wrote, "The rust of vice can only be purged by the fire of torment."[2] Tragically, people have sought repair by returning to the matrix of brutality that damaged them in the first place. It takes a long time to unlearn the idea of payment through suffering.

Atonement doctrines correspond closely with the strategies for handling emotional trauma and surviving in families where the parents put conditions on their love. Teachers of atonement claim that salvation was purchased by a sacrifice made "once for all" (Heb. 9:26; 10:10), but in fact atonement thinking reflects *chronic* stress, manifesting in repeated cycles of sinning, bingeing, getting caught, confessing, repenting, and being told to "make good" by paying a certain penance or penalty. Restoration is not free, but is purchased through suffering. The psychology of atonement is constantly dramatized in a cycle of guilt, confession, and forgiveness. The message that the innocent Son of God was nailed to the cross to pay for one's sins does not reduce anxiety but deepens it.

---

2. Gregory the Great, *Moralia on Job* 3.14; quoted in L. W. Grensted, *A Short History of the Doctrine of the Atonement* (Manchester, UK: Longmans, Green, 1920), 98.

Real repair from the matrix of damage caused by brutal parenting requires recognizing the psychopathology of cruelty, and repudiating it. This will affect our religious beliefs and our social living; there is a link between what people believe about God and how they treat each other.

Christian atonement is a paradoxical mixture of noble hopes and religious fear. The surface of atonement theology involves the love of God, but the underlying (unconscious) pattern involves coping with parental rage. Therefore, atonement doctrine is fueled by anxiety, even while it also embodies love, although love that is frustrated and hedged about with conditions. Atonement thinking is complex, commingling personal need, fear, and ideal hope based on the assumption of a God both violent and loving. The sacrificial interpretation of the death of Jesus takes ancient ideas of ritual purification and ransoming, and spiritualizes them with ideas of transformation and grace. The result is a complicated mixture of anxiety, guilt, and love. To the extent that it focuses on ransom or substitutionary atonement, it reflects the dynamics of a dysfunctional home. To the extent that it emphasizes attunement with the will and the love of God, it reflects healthy psychology within a healthy family.

The Approach Used Here

Cultic metaphors are particularly important in Paul and Hebrews. When cultic language is used metaphorically, there is some *continuity* and some *discontinuity* with the preceding cult. Given the importance of both continuity and discontinuity between Old Testament ideas and New Testament images, and between New Testament images and subsequent Christian beliefs, there must be a chronological dimension to this study, examining the ancestry and development of atonement ideas. But a merely chronological study would not necessarily highlight psychological factors. To uncover the psychological dimension, one must study the *functions* of atonement, the needs that people believed atonement was meeting. If we look at the reasons and explanations that believers have given for sacrifice and atonement, psychological factors will be illuminated. Even if the real motives are partially disguised or even unconscious, the rationalizations will give clues to the hidden motives. Thus this study must have both a chronological and a functional dimension, which complicates the matter of organization.

I will begin with two chapters on the two main functions of sacrifice in the Old Testament, purification and compensation. These chapters will include some sections on psychology where relevant. Chapter 3 is entirely devoted to psychological ideas, including attachment theory. Chapters 4 through 6 will be on Paul and Hebrews, the main sources of Christian atonement thinking. Chapter 7 looks at the development of atonement concepts in Christian history. Psychological theories will be brought in at appropriate points. The final section of each biblical or historical chapter will concern the teachings and approach of Jesus, and how they differ from the beliefs and practices just discussed.

Biblical scholars often object to the mixing of biblical studies with later popularizing interpretations because they find the latter to distort the Bible rather than illuminate it. But the study of the Bible must extend beyond the biblical text itself. The community that receives the text also shapes it and transmits it through time. The relevance of the Bible includes how it was received and interpreted, even distorted. The latter is certainly the case with atonement doctrines that exaggerate and distort a few statements of Paul while ignoring the rest of what he said. The doctrine of penal substitution exaggerates the element of substitution that *is* present in Paul, adds ideas that are not found in Paul at all (such as that Christ was *rightly* punished when he bore our sins, since, at that moment, he become "a transgressor .... rebel, blasphemer"),[3] and ignores much of what Paul taught (about the ability to do God's will [Romans 12], to imitate Christ [Phil. 2:5; 1 Thess. 1:6], and to be transformed and divinized [Rom. 8:29–30]). Still, the seeds of later popular ideas are usually found to have been planted by the biblical authors.

---

3. Martin Luther, *Commentary on Galatians* 3.13; in John Dillenberger, *Martin Luther: Selections from His Writings* (Garden City, NY: Doubleday, 1961), 135.

I will utilize some existing psychological theories about patterns of psychic injury and coping. My own addition is the assertion that some concepts of atonement are psychologically based on a pattern of assuaging or soothing angry parents through a strategy of payment through suffering.

1

Atonement as Purification

The emphasis in this book will be on Christian atonement ideas and patterns of thinking, but this requires some knowledge of origins. Atonement originates primarily from sacrifice; therefore, we must look into the concepts of sacrifice that early Christians would have known mainly from Jewish, but also from gentile, sources.

Functions of Ritual

Before talking about sacrifice specifically, a few views on the function of ritual in society may be helpful. One view has ritual playing the role of restoring order: "Ritual recognizes the potency of disorder. . . . Danger is controlled by ritual."[1] In Jewish culture, sacrificial ritual provides for the expiation (cleansing) of impurity, and thus the restoration of order. Further, ritual helps to solidify the group and its values: "Ritual as a restricted code. . . . enables a given pattern of values to be enforced and allows members to internalise the structure of the group and its norms."[2] Walter Burkert says that ritual's "function

---

1. Mary Douglas, *Purity and Danger: An Analysis of Concepts of Pollution and Taboo* (1966; repr., New York: Routledge, 1991), 95, 97. In the original 1966 edition, these were on pages 94 and 96.
2. Mary Douglas, *Natural Symbols: Explorations in Cosmology* (New York: Pantheon, 1982), 54.

normally lies in group formation, the creation of solidarity, or the negotiation of understanding."³

David Janzen has a similar understanding: "Rituals function as a kind of rhetoric to convince their participants to lend their allegiance to the worldview and moral system of one social group in particular."⁴ Janzen is talking about P, the hypothetical priestly author and editor of a large portion of the first four books of the Bible, including Leviticus 1–16, which contain the most concentrated set of sacrificial instructions.

Mary Douglas points out that "doctrines of atonement" are most prominent in "high group, high grid" (rigidly structured and controlled) societies.⁵ The priests in postexilic Judah (after about 530 BCE) became the ruling class, and were in charge of all sacrificing. The class structure in classical Greece was also reinforced by sacrificial ritual but usually not through a priestly class. In Athens, all free men performed priestly roles for certain periods.⁶ Participation in the ritual was determined by one's social status; distribution of animal parts was metaphoric for the distribution of rights.⁷ Sacrificial ritual reflects and inscribes the lines of power in both Israel and Greece, despite their having very different kinds of priesthood.

Religious ritual, therefore, seems to be responding to a human anxiety about order. People were anxious about the real and constant dangers to life and limb, as well as the perceived threat from hostile spirits or demons, many of whom would visit them in their dreams. "Fear of the supernatural, divine beings or demons, was a natural part of life in the ancient world."⁸ The priests had the monopoly on handling sacred substances, and so protecting the community.

Moshe Halbertal believes that ritual helped to reduce anxiety about

---

3. Walter Burkert, *Greek Religion: Archaic and Classical*, trans. John Raffan (Oxford: Blackwell, 1985), 54.
4. David Janzen, *The Social Meanings of Sacrifice in the Hebrew Bible: A Study of Four Writings*, BZAW 344 (Berlin: de Gruyter, 2004), 4.
5. Mary Douglas, *In the Active Voice* (London: Routledge & Kegan Paul, 1982), 211.
6. Stanley K. Stowers, "Greeks Who Sacrifice and Those Who Do Not: Toward an Anthropology of Greek Religion," in *The Social World of the First Christians: Essays in Honor of Wayne A. Meeks*, ed. L. Michael White and O. Larry Yarbrough (Minneapolis: Fortress Press, 1995), 310, 317, 322, 325.
7. Ibid., 306, and throughout.
8. Thomas Kazen, *Issues of Impurity in Early Judaism*, ConBNT 45 (Winona Lake, IN: Eisenbrauns, 2010), 25.

the danger of God rejecting a sacrifice, as happened to Cain's sacrifice in Gen. 4:3–5. The "detailed routine" of ritual provides consistency, perhaps even a kind of insurance: "Ritual is thus a protocol that protects from the risk of rejection. . . . The establishment of ritual [is] an effort to overcome the anxiety of rejection."[9]

Ritual identifies a society, and helps to *bind* society together. It provides coded behavior understood only by insiders, and enforces conformity on insiders. But the socialized religious mentality is stifling to those who seek justice or truth beyond conventional habits and beliefs. No good deed, if it transgresses the boundaries, goes unpunished. Jesus seems to have been profoundly ill at ease with purity boundaries, as is shown by his arguing with purity rules, and his disrupting the sacrificial trade at the temple (Matt. 15:1–20; 23:23–27; Mark 7:1–21; 11:15–17; John 2:14–19). Even if some of these texts may be shaped by disputes between the church and the rabbis of fifty years later, there is enough "smoke" to affirm the "fire" of Jesus' resistance to purity barriers. He also rejected any kind of religious snobbery, as is shown by his associating with gentiles and Samaritans (including women), and with "tax collectors and sinners" (Mark 2:15). Jesus' altogether independent prophetic stance was profoundly threatening to the priestly monopoly.

Another function of purity systems seems to be to help the human mind make distinctions. The Israelites are told, "You shall therefore make a distinction between the clean animal and the unclean. You shall be holy to me" (Lev. 20:25–26). The fundamental, ancient meaning of "holy" is "separate," and its basic mandate is to separate what is common from what is *qōdeš* (holy). God's separateness and superiority must always be honored. Horror stories occur amid the sacrificial instructions to reinforce this point. When two of Aaron's sons light up some "unholy fire" in their censers, "fire came out from the presence of the Lord and consumed them, and they died before the Lord" (Lev. 10:1–2). When there was rebellion against Moses over who could perform priestly functions, God had the earth swallow up some of the

---

9. Moshe Halbertal, *On Sacrifice* (Princeton: Princeton University Press, 2012), 15, 18.

rebels, and sent fire "and consumed the two hundred and fifty men offering the incense" (Num. 16:23–35). Let *that* be a warning! Priestly prerogatives are surrounded by threats of violence.

Boundaries, rules, and strictures are fundamental to purity and to holiness. Ritual helps to define and enforce the boundaries. "The priests act like God in their role of 'separating (*hbdyl*) between the holy and the profane and between the impure and the clean' (Lev 10:10)."[10] "The notion of separation carried over to priestly thinking about holy place (sanctuary), holy times (sabbath, rites of passage . . .), holy persons (. . . priests, Levites)."[11]

The first half of Leviticus is heavily focused on sacrificial rituals. The second half of Leviticus has some sacrificial instructions, but also rules about forbidden sexual behaviors, family and marriage ethics (chaps. 18–21), economic instructions (do not harvest your fields fully; leave some gleanings for the poor, 19:10; 23:22), prohibitions of idolatry, rules on holy days, and warnings about infractions that can result in banishment (being "cut off," as in 17:4, 9; 18:29; 20:6, 18) or death (20:2, 13, 27; 24:16–17, 21). God gave them the land, but God can just as easily drive them out (20:22–26), especially for murder, idolatry, and certain sexual sins, which "pollute the land" (Num. 35:33; cf. Lev. 18:13–28; Ps. 106:38).

Ritual comes increasingly to reflect ideas about order and reliability in the spiritual universe, even the ideas of spiritual law and of sin, which is a breaking of the law. If there are laws, then there is a certain reliability in the spiritual level, so that one can learn to please God. Two ideas emerge, in some tension with each other: the notion of maintaining order through correct ritual procedure in worship and devotion, and the idea of living in loyalty to spiritual law through the ethics of the covenant, the moral commandments. Either one, or both, of these principles could be meant by "keep the law" (1 Chron. 22:12; Prov. 28:4; Acts 15:5; Rom. 2:27). The Bible reflects differing views of what this meant.

---

10. Janzen, *Social Meanings of Sacrifice*, 113.
11. John G. Gammie, *Holiness in Israel* (1989; repr., Eugene, OR: Wipf & Stock, 2005), 43.

Speaking in terms of developmental psychology, purity systems help people engage in classification, differentiation, and separation. Socially speaking, purification is a control trip: purity inscribes social stratification and separation. In Judaism, the high priest is more holy than ordinary priests, and can go places they cannot go. He also is more vulnerable to impurity, in a way, since he is barred from access if he has become impure. Ordinary priests are holier than laypeople. Within the lay population, men have more access and higher status than women. Finally, all the people within the Israelite culture are more holy than foreigners. In many ways, purification systems can be seen to reflect, to inscribe, and to defend social structures. Nancy Jay argues that sacrificial systems create an imagined male lineage, assigning men their place in a holy community. "Membership in patrilineal descent groups is identified by rights of participation in blood sacrifice. . . . Sacrificing can identify membership in groups with no presumption of actual family descent."[12] (See the rights of male "descendants of Aaron" as described, for instance, in Lev. 6:15–18.)

Atonement Ideas in the Hebrew System

The Hebrew sacrificial system, as described primarily in Leviticus, had whole or burnt offerings, purification or sin offerings, reparation or guilt offerings, peace offerings, and cereal offerings. However, rather than organizing this study by *types* of sacrifice, I am approaching it through the main atoning *functions* or outcomes.

Atonement concepts can become complex or composite, but it is important to begin with the simpler and foundational concepts. As I see it, biblical sacrifice had two fundamental purposes (some sacrifices seem to point to one or the other, thus I use the conjunction *or*): to purify or to compensate. These foundational ideas of sacrificial atonement in the Bible, then, are as follows:

1. Atonement as *purification*: In priestly thinking, God resides in the tabernacle, which needs to be ritually cleansed to ensure God's

---

12. Nancy Jay, *Throughout Your Generations Forever: Sacrifice, Religion, and Paternity* (Chicago: University of Chicago Press, 1992), 36–37.

continuation there; along with purification goes the restoration or "forgiveness" (Lev. 4:20; 5:10) of persons in society. It is not the mere death of the animal, but the application of the blood and the burning of the fat, that accomplishes atonement. Purity will be the main subject of this chapter.

2a. Atonement as *compensation* or reparation (including the notion of feeding God with offerings): This is expressed *formally* in the reparation or guilt sacrifice (Lev. 7:1–7), and *functionally* in any sacrifice that is understood to secure benefit (Ps. 54:5–7) or in noncultic activities such as prayer (Psalm 141) or even violent retribution (2 Samuel 21). Compensation is the subject of chapter 2.

2b. Atonement as *redemption*: This is a variation of compensatory atonement, and overlaps with the noncultic realm. Being a crucial soteriological (saving) metaphor for the apostle Paul, redemption will be examined in chapter 4.

In the first of his two "purity" books, Jonathan Klawans argues that there seem to be two kinds of impurity in Israel: ritual impurity and moral impurity.[13] "Ritual" and "moral" impurity are scholarly terms (the topic is hotly debated). The Bible does not have these separate terms, but it does show the differing consequences and significations that have led scholars to make these distinctions. "Ritual impurity in all its forms is natural";[14] it is not sinful. It simply needs to be eliminated through purifications or sacrifices, and no blame attaches to those impurity-causing acts (like being in the vicinity of a corpse) that are unrelated to sin. It is physically contagious.[15] Moral impurity *is* blameworthy, is not contracted by physical touch, and has serious consequences: causing the temple and the whole land to be polluted. (The Pentateuch, speaking of Moses' time, mentions only *tabernacle*, not *temple*, but most scholars believe tabernacle stands for temple,

---

13. Jonathan Klawans, *Impurity and Sin in Ancient Judaism* (Oxford: Oxford University Press, 2000), 22–31. His second purity book is *Purity, Sacrifice, and the Temple: Symbolism and Supersessionism in the Study of Ancient Judaism* (Oxford: Oxford University Press, 2006). Walter Houston finds Klawans's "neat distinction" inadequate (Walter J. Houston, review of *Impurity and Sin in Ancient Judaism*, by Jonathan Klawans, *JTS* 52 [2001]: 724).
14. Klawans, *Impurity and Sin*, 24.
15. Ibid., 22–26.

since the texts were written during the times of the Jerusalem temple.) The main three sins (or groups of sins) that produce moral impurity are idolatry, homicide, and sexual sins;[16] Hannah Harrington adds certain cultic violations as a fourth category of moral impurity.[17] The danger of moral impurity is that "defilement of the land will vomit out Israel as it vomited out its previous inhabitants (Lev. 18:28; 20:22)."[18] Only moral impurity is called תועבה, *tôʿēbâ*, an "abomination," although both ritual and moral impurity can be called טמא, *tāmēʾ*, "impure."[19]

No ritual can cleanse the "pollution that is generated by apostasy (Lev 20) ..., sexual misconduct (Lev 18), and murder (Deut 19:13; 21:8). These three classes of impurity pollute both the people and the land," and ultimately lead to "be[ing] נכרת ('cut off')"[20] or exiled.

Really there are not two different kinds of impurity but two different *causes* of impurity; one sinful, one not. Menstruation, nocturnal emissions, and skin disease are not considered sinful. All impurity has its dangers. One must never bring impurity into the temple, or into contact with anything deemed holy: "Anyone who brings impurity into contact with holiness is in danger of כָּרֵת [*kereth*], death by divine agency (Lev 7:20–21).... Deliberate mixing of impurity and holiness is the most dangerous of all combinations."[21] All impurity threatens the temple if purification rites are not maintained. (In the last section of this chapter, "The Psychology of Purity," I will say something about impurity itself, its possible origins, and how people reacted to it.)

From the seventh century BCE, Judah's ritual system was centralized at the Jerusalem temple. For the priestly author, "P," the focus of the ritual system is the removal of impurity. Whenever sin is committed anywhere in Israel, impurity settles on the temple furnishings; "sin

---

16. Ibid., 26–31; Susan Haber, *"They Shall Purify Themselves": Essays on Purity in Early Judaism*, edited by Adele Reinhartz, EJL 24 (Atlanta: SBL, 2008), 163.
17. Hannah K. Harrington, "Clean and Unclean," in *The New Interpreter's Dictionary of the Bible*, ed. Katharine Doob Sakenfeld (Nashville: Abingdon, 2006), 1:682.
18. Jacob Milgrom, "Kipper," *Encyclopaedia Judaica*, vol. 10 (New York: Macmillan, 1971), 1043.
19. Haber, *They Shall Purify Themselves*, 27–28; the last point cites Klawans, *Impurity and Sin*, 26.
20. Haber, *They Shall Purify Themselves*, 23; she is drawing on Tikva Frymer-Kensky, "Pollution, Purification, and Purgation in Biblical Israel," in *The Word of the Lord Shall Go Forth*, ed. Carol L. Meyers and M. O'Connor (Winona Lake, IN: Eisenbrauns, 1983), 404, 407–9.
21. Harrington, "Clean and Unclean," 682.

is a miasma which wherever committed is attracted to the sanctuary. There it adheres and accumulates until God will no longer abide in it."²² Hence the necessity for ritual purification. The main verb used for sacrificial purification is the *piel* verb *kipper* (כִּפֶּר), and the main purifying sacrifice is the חַטָּאת, *ḥaṭṭā't* (the "sin sacrifice" or "purification offering").

The impurity caused by the worst sins—"presumptuous sins"—lodges on the כַּפֹּרֶת, *kappōrēt* (cognate with כִּפֶּר), the lid of the ark of the covenant.²³ If the impurity is not cleansed, God will abandon the temple.²⁴ The ark cover is often referred to as the "mercy seat" in English. "Mercy seat" may not be the most accurate translation of *kappōrēt*, but it has become a recognized technical term, so I use it.²⁵

On Yom Kippur, the Day of Atonement, the high priest goes into the Most Holy Place and sprinkles the blood of the *ḥaṭṭā't* sacrifice on various holy objects. "Only the 'most sacred' areas are purged: the adytum, the shrine, and the outer altar (16:14–19)."²⁶ Most importantly, the impurity caused by presumptuous sins is cleansed when the high priest sprinkles the *ḥaṭṭā't* blood on the mercy seat, ensuring that the Lord will continue to reside there.²⁷ The blood expiates (cleanses) the temple furnishings. This is the only time in the whole year that *anyone* is allowed to enter the Most Holy Place, a particularly holy—and dangerous—place, and a particularly solemn and important day (Lev. 16:29–34).

For most Jews, the *kappōrēt* was always a figure of imagination, known from the teachings imparted, not from the thing being seen. The mercy seat is the golden lid of the ark of the covenant, carved into

---

22. Milgrom, "Kipper," 1040.
23. David P. Wright, "Day of Atonement," in *ABD* 2:73–75.
24. Jacob Milgrom, *Studies in Cultic Theology and Terminology*, SJLA 36 (Leiden: Brill, 1983), 76, 80.
25. "Mercy seat" first appears in Tyndale's translation; see Daniel P. Bailey, "Jesus as the Mercy Seat: The Semantics and Theology of Paul's Use of *Hilasterion* in Romans 3:25" (PhD diss., Cambridge University, 1999), 6 §7, 174–76. Tyndale seems to be echoing Luther's German term *Gnadenstuhl* (Hastings Rashdall, *The Idea of the Atonement in Christian Theology* [London: Macmillan, 1919], 130). For more on the mercy seat in Rom. 3:25, see chapter 4.
26. Jacob Milgrom, *Leviticus 1–16*, AB 3 (Garden City, N.Y.: Doubleday, 1991), 393.
27. Milgrom, *Studies in Cultic Theology*, 73, 81; Wright, "Day of Atonement," 73; Daniel Stökl Ben Ezra, *The Impact of Yom Kippur on Early Christianity: The Day of Atonement from Second Temple Judaism to the Fifth Century*, WUNT 163 (Tübingen: Mohr Siebeck, 2003), 30.

the image of two winged cherubim. Priestly theology claimed that God (or God's *presence*) dwelt between the cherubim. It is "from above the mercy seat, from between the two cherubim" (Exod. 25:22; cf. Num. 7:89), that God speaks with Moses. "I appear in the cloud upon the mercy seat" (Lev. 16:2). To Moses alone does God appear here. Having God dwell at the mercy seat appears to be aimed at legitimizing the sacrificial ideology.

What Jacob Milgrom succeeded in making clear is that sacrifice, in the Levitical texts, is *not* punitive or substitutionary, it is purificatory. The blood of the ḥaṭṭā't sacrifice is sprinkled in particular places in the temple, cleansing impurity from all the furnishings. The sacrificial blood acts as a kind of "ritual detergent"[28] on the temple installations. (Nehemia Polen criticizes this phrase as "too mechanical" and downplaying relational issues.[29] Milgrom does overemphasize the "mechanical" aspect of cleansing, but we will see below that he also deals with forgiveness.) This function can be seen in purification rituals in other cultures. The Hittite rite of Ulippi has a sheep's blood being smeared "on the god's statue, the wall of the edifice, and cultic utensils. The text explicitly says this application renders the god and its temple pure."[30] Also useful is the metaphor of electricity, which conveys something of the instantaneous and magic-like power of sacrificial blood, which draws off the sin charge from the temple sancta like a lightning rod drawing lightning to itself. This is not a punitive operation, but a cleansing or discharging operation. It is not a punishment of the animal that brings about atonement, but the magical power of blood. By *magical*, I mean the belief that acting on the community's temple will have an effect on the community, the belief that blood sprinkled on the *kappōrēt* will *actually* cleanse the people. The temple seems to be an analogue to the community; purity changes happening to one are reflected in the other.

Milgrom refocused scholarly attention to the cleansing of the temple

---

28. Milgrom, *Leviticus 1–16*, 254.
29. Nehemia Polen, "Leviticus and Hebrews . . . and Leviticus," in *The Epistle to the Hebrews and Christian Theology*, ed. Richard Bauckham et al. (Grand Rapids: Eerdmans, 2009), 218.
30. Wright, "Day of Atonement," 74.

from impurity, but he resisted saying that the sacrifice correlates with the "forgiveness" of persons (Lev. 4:20–35; 5:10–18) and a restoration of relationships. He insists "in the context of the ḥaṭṭā't, kipper means 'purge' and nothing else. . . . Ritual texts also support this meaning, for they regularly couple kipper with ṭihar 'purify' and ḥiṭṭē' 'decontaminate.'"[31] Roy Gane allows that the ḥaṭṭā't sacrifice purges the sanctuary on Yom Kippur, but vehemently argues that it has a different function throughout the year, where the ḥaṭṭā't cleanses *persons*, not the sanctuary.[32] It seems that Gane offers a somewhat extreme thesis (the ḥaṭṭā't throughout the year cleanses persons and *not* the sanctuary) in response to what seems like an extreme thesis by Milgrom (the ḥaṭṭā't cleanses the sanctuary and not persons). Gane at least partially wins his point, since forgiveness is indeed seen in Lev. 4:20, 26, 31; 5:5–6, 10. But there is also blood daubing and sprinkling at certain installations in the temple on these days (Lev. 4:17–18, 25, 30, 34; 5:9). Really, both temple and persons are in view, both on Yom Kippur and throughout the year. It may be that Gane has considered the ḥaṭṭā't in isolation. Christian Eberhart points out that atonement in those texts is accomplished by "combined blood and burning rites," and indeed, Lev. 4:19, 26, 31, does speak of burning the ḥaṭṭā't animal's fat, while 5:10 has a second animal as a burnt offering; in both cases, forgiveness is mentioned *after* the burning. Thus Gane "neglects the fact that atonement is accomplished through two distinct ritual components: a blood rite and a burning rite. . . . Blood rites do purge the sanctuary and its components, while burning rites accomplish forgiveness for sins that the offerer bears."[33] Clearly, the complexity of sacrificial texts requires some scholarly humility and willingness to revise theories in light of new studies. In any case, Milgrom's scholarship regarding Yom Kippur is relevant for New Testament studies, since both Paul and Hebrews speak of the death of Christ

---

31. Milgrom, *Leviticus 1–16*, 255, 1079.
32. Roy E. Gane, *Cult and Character: Purification Offerings, Day of Atonement, and Theodicy* (Winona Lake, IN: Eisenbrauns, 2005), 142, 176–77, 273–75.
33. Christian A. Eberhart, review of *Cult and Character: Purification Offerings, Day of Atonement, and Theodicy*, by Roy E. Gane, *Review of Biblical Literature*, July 1, 2006, 4, http://www.bookreviews.org/pdf/5068_5341.pdf.

metaphorically as a kind of new Yom Kippur (Rom. 3:25; Heb. 9:6–15, 21–10:3).

Purification is not concerned only with the temple's condition; cult is not an end in itself. Temple purification stands for both the restoration of the community sanctuary and for the forgiveness of persons, not just the purification of a building. Most scholars affirm something like the view of Daniel Stökl Ben Ezra: "The temple ritual serves simultaneously to atone for the people and to purify the temple."[34] Only a few scholars would say, as Stanley Stowers does, that "the person did not receive forgiveness for a sinful act itself but dealt only with the consequences of such acts on the temple. . . . The sacrifices on that day [Day of Atonement] provide a complete purification of the temple, not an atonement or forgiveness of the people's sin."[35] This is refuted by cases where *kipper* actually is translated "forgive" (Deut. 21:8; Pss. 65:3 [MT 65:4]; 78:38; 79:9; Ezek. 16:63).[36] Stowers is leaning here on Milgrom's emphasis on temple purification at the expense of the effect of the ritual on individuals. But, in fact, Milgrom wanted to stress that something *more* than forgiveness is involved; the person "hopes to repair the broken relationship. He therefore seeks more than forgiveness."[37] Both Milgrom's critics and supporters seem to miss this passage, which is understandable, given that his commentary is over two and a half thousand pages long.

It is interesting to notice that the rabbis understood atonement and forgiveness to be equivalent, as seen "from the way in which 'atone' and 'forgive' can interchange" in rabbinic texts,[38] although, of

---

34. Daniel Stökl Ben Ezra, "Atonement. Judaism: Second Temple Period," in *Encyclopedia of the Bible and Its Reception*, vol. 3, *Athena-Birkat ha-Minim*, ed. Hans-Josef Klauck et al. (Berlin: de Gruyter, 2011), 43. See similar observation by Wright, "Day of Atonement," 73.
35. Stanley K. Stowers, *A Rereading of Romans: Justice, Jews, and Gentiles* (New Haven: Yale University Press, 1994), 208, 210.
36. Sharon L. Baker, *Executing God: Rethinking Everything You've Been Taught about Salvation and the Cross* (Louisville: Westminster John Knox, 2013), 116–17; Jarvis J. Williams, *Maccabean Martyr Traditions in Paul's Theology of Atonement: Did Martyr Theology Shape Paul's Conception of Jesus' Death?* (Eugene, OR: Wipf & Stock, 2010), 45.
37. Milgrom, *Leviticus 1–16*, 245.
38. E. P. Sanders, *Paul and Palestinian Judaism* (Philadelphia: Fortress Press, 1977), 161.

course, their views are postbiblical, and do not prove anything about the biblical period.

Another purification rite is the scapegoat ritual. On the Day of Atonement, the priest lays his hands on the goat's head, confessing all the peoples' sins, and "the goat shall bear on itself all their iniquities to a barren region" (Lev. 16:22). It is not a sacrifice; it is not offered to the Lord. It is a quasi-physical sin bearer. This becomes a very important metaphor for the apostle Paul, so it will be discussed in chapter 4.

Spiritualizing or Metaphorical Understandings

A metaphorical version of purification occurs in the New Testament epistles. A "washed" and "holy" church is held up in Eph. 5:26–27; Jesus will "purify for himself a people" in Tit. 2:14. "The blood of Christ" is said to "purify our conscience" (Heb. 9:14), or it "cleanses us from all sin" (1 John 1:7). The purifying function of blood in the cult is here extended to the conscience or the innocence of Christians. This intense metaphorical application of the "sacrifice" of Christ is a major feature in the Epistles and Revelation, but is nearly absent from the Gospels, except for the eucharistic passages (Matt. 26:28; Mark 14:24; regarding Luke, see the section "Luke-Acts Is Not Cross-Centered" in chapter 5).

The Gospels have a unique attitude toward impurity; it is not treated metaphorically, but neither do the Gospels reflect a priestly viewpoint. Jesus touches and heals many "unclean" people; he is never infected by their impurity, as the purity system would indicate; rather, Jesus' life and health are transmitted to them. On one or two occasions, Jesus makes use of the purity ideas that people have. After healing the ten lepers, he tells them, "Go and show yourselves to the priests"; undoubtedly they would have started thinking about purification as they walked; "and as they went, they were made clean" (Luke 17:14).[39] Forever after, such recipients of healing would not think of purification as a *ritual* category so much as a *Jesus* category, because of what he did for them.

---

39. See also Luke 5:14, where he tells a healed leper, "Show yourself to the priest, and, as Moses commanded, make an offering for your cleansing, for a testimony to them."

Purity and impurity words are used metaphorically by Paul and by the anonymous author of Hebrews. Paul will sometimes give a moralizing meaning to purity or impurity (2 Cor. 6:6; Gal. 5:19), but he is more renowned for his soteriological metaphors. I look at only one of those here, and at others in chapter 4. In the Letter to the Romans, Paul refers to Christ as a purification offering: "What the Law could not do, weak as it was through the flesh, God did: sending His own Son in the likeness of sinful flesh and as an offering for sin, He condemned sin in the flesh" (Rom. 8:3 NASB). The NASB is better than the NRSV here, since Paul uses the Septuagint term for the purification sacrifice, περὶ ἁμαρτίας, *peri hamartias*,[40] which the NRSV translates in a generalizing way as "to deal with sin" (although "as a sin offering" is given as a marginal alternative). Paul refers to Christ, metaphorically, as a sin offering, but does not go into any of the sacrificial procedural details, nor develop the theme of purification.

More closely attached to cultic details and to purification is the usage of Hebrews. (As many other scholars, I refer to the unknown author of Hebrews as "Hebrews." So "Hebrews" can mean either the epistle or the author.) Hebrews thinks of Jesus as having "made purification for sins" (1:3) in a way very close to the original cultic meaning: "He entered once for all into the Holy Place, not with the blood of goats and calves, but with his own blood . . . offered himself without blemish to God . . . to remove sin by the sacrifice of himself" (9:12, 14, 26).

Hebrews takes quite literally the concept of Christ's death as the final and perfect "sacrifice for sins" that opened the way to God "for us through the curtain (that is, through his flesh)" (10:12, 20). Access to God's forgiveness required the proper ritual. For Hebrews, there had to be purification with blood in the new covenant because there was purification with blood in the *old*: "Under the law almost everything is purified with blood, and without the shedding of blood there is no forgiveness of sins. Thus [οὖν] it was necessary for the sketches of the

---

40. N. T. Wright, *The Climax of the Covenant: Christ and the Law in Pauline Theology* (Edinburgh: T&T Clark, 1991), 222.

heavenly things to be purified with these rites" (9:22–23). Hebrews is committed to that "thus"—to the necessity for sacrifices (first the literal ones, then the metaphorical one)—to a greater degree than Paul is.

But both Paul and Hebrews claim more for sacrifice (*Christ's* sacrifice, that is) than the Old Testament ever claimed, since Christ's sacrifice not only purifies but also *saves* (Rom. 5:9; Heb. 7:25–27).

The Psychology of Purity

What gives origin to the psychology of purity itself? Beyond the need for order, mentioned at the beginning of the chapter, what is the perceived *need* for purification? Richard Beck argues that the psychology of disgust underlies the experience of impurity, the same emotion that causes a reaction of recoil from certain foods, smells, or animals.[41] Thomas Kazen speaks of *three* emotions connected with impurity: disgust, fear, and the sense of justice.[42] In my view, the sense of justice is not causative here, while disgust and fear are fundamental to cult. Justice emerges because it *always* emerges in the course of social life. Given that we are social creatures and we have a sense of justice and fair play, we *will* develop a discourse about justice, touching all realms of social life, including what is done in ritual, which gives different privileges and duties to different people. I leave aside the justice issue since it is not one of the *causes* of ritual behavior. I am more interested in uncovering some of the ancient *motives* of ritual behavior.

Contamination and Disgust

Clinical researcher Paul Rozin has cowritten several important articles on disgust. In one paper, he and his colleagues borrow the definition of Andras Angyal that "core disgust . . . . is 'Revulsion at the prospect of (oral) incorporation of an offensive object.'"[43] There seems to be

---

41. Richard Beck, *Unclean: Meditations on Purity, Hospitality, and Mortality* (Eugene, OR: Cascade, 2011), 37, 42–51.
42. Kazen, *Issues of Impurity in Early Judaism*, 13.

a "law of contagion . . . . [:] once in contact, always in contact"; in clinical experiments, Rozin and his colleagues showed that "Americans are inclined to reject foods that have contacted a disgusting entity, such as a . . . cockroach [even] if the disgusting contaminating agent is sterilized. The intuition here, even for educated Westerners, is that when a cockroach touches their mashed potatoes . . . the potatoes have been 'cockroached' and take on some cockroach properties."[44] The same result occurred when he dipped a sterilized cockroach into some juice; most students would not touch the juice, even when they were assured that the bug had been sterilized and the juice boiled and filtered.[45] Even in modern, educated people, emotional judgments about contamination easily overrule logic; "sympathetic magic" takes over: "once in contact, always in contact."[46] Touching a disgusting object renders something *permanently* contaminated.

The particular things that elicit disgust can change; the objects of disgust are culturally determined. This can be seen in the recent growth of hostility to, and disgust with, cigarette smoke and smokers. This is suggestive of what evolutionary biologists call "preadaptation," where a new function develops for "an existing system" of reaction.[47]

Even moral evil was judged to have quasi-physical properties. In another study, Rozin and colleagues look at the expansion of disgust beyond "core disgust" to reactions against "inappropriate sexual acts, poor hygiene, death, and violations of the ideal body 'envelope.' . . . Research . . . has shown a strong connection between disgust and the fear of death."[48] Beyond this comes "interpersonal disgust," as when one would rather not wear an article of clothing worn by a stranger, even when one knows it has been sanitized; this is followed by "moral disgust," wherein people will use the word *disgust* to signify moral

---

43. Paul Rozin et al., "Disgust: Preadaptation and the Cultural Evolution of a Food-Based Emotion," in *Food Preferences and Taste: Continuity and Change*, ed. Helen Macbeth (Oxford: Berghahn, 1997), 68.
44. Ibid., 69.
45. Paul Rozin, Jonathan Haidt, and Clark R. McCauley, "Disgust," in *Handbook of Emotions*, ed. Michael Lewis, Jeannette M. Haviland-Jones, and Lisa Feldman Barrett, 3rd ed. (New York: Guilford, 2008), 760; Beck, *Unclean*, 22–23.
46. Beck, *Unclean*, 24–25.
47. Rozin, Haidt, and McCauley, "Disgust," 763–64; see also Rozin et al., "Disgust: Preadaptation," 65.
48. Rozin, Haidt, and McCauley, "Disgust," 761.

outrage,[49] for instance, regarding child abuse.[50] Most people were disgusted with the suggestion that they try on a sweater that Hitler once wore; some were uncomfortable even being in the same room with it; this shows how "evil is sticky and contagious."[51]

Beck calls this "magical thinking" because it makes "causal judgments that defy the laws of physics."[52] Beck sees magical thinking in the Pharisees' reaction to Jesus' contact with sinners: "This worry over *proximity* is symptomatic of the magical thinking imported into the religious domain through the psychology of disgust."[53] The psychology of disgust is accompanied by a sociology of exclusion (excluding impure people), an attitude of contempt, and a mentality of superiority and pride. That is how the Pharisees are depicted in Matthew, and often in the other Gospels, although the others show some scribes or Pharisees being receptive to Jesus (Mark 12:32–34; Luke 23:50; John 3:1). The danger in Beck's approach is that he fails to mention that *Christian* religious authorities have often been as bigoted and exclusionary as anyone. The point is really not about the Pharisees but about human beings: exclusivism and pride are a *human* problem. I will return to this issue after looking at some more biblical passages.

Decay and Ooze

Fear plays a key role in impurity and disgust. The "common denominator" in purity systems, according to Thomas Kazen, is "a negative emotional response to threatening stimuli, a reaction of disgust towards revolting or objectionable substances and toward states associated with such substances"; disgust is triggered not just by the thought of death, but by the decaying things that *suggest* death: "Disgust is rather directed towards death in the form of decayed life."[54] Disgust is a reaction against that which seems to be "threatening

---

49. Ibid., 762; Rozin et al., "Disgust: Preadaptation," 71–75.
50. Michael Owen Jones, "What's Disgusting, Why, and What Does It Matter?," *Journal of Folklore Research* 37 (2000): 57.
51. Beck, *Unclean*, 25.
52. Ibid., 27.
53. Ibid., 26.
54. Kazen, *Issues of Impurity in Early Judaism*, 17–18.

society with dirt, disorder, decay and death."[55] In many cultures, the moral sense becomes linked with the sense of disgust. In Leviticus 11, unclean animals are said to be *"tame'* and *sheqetz* (unclean and detestable)."[56] A strategy of avoidance of uncleanness is usually tried first; if that is insufficient, "a strategy of removal is found instead": scraping off a skin disease, removing moldy bricks from a house, burning "leprous" cloths.[57] A number of sexual and cultic behaviors evoked disgust and were believed to generate impurity that would infect the nation's sanctuary.

Kazen looks at certain texts in Leviticus that evoke fear by threatening death or being "cut off" from the community.[58] Some of these texts are as follows: "You shall keep the people of Israel separate from their uncleanness, so that they do not die in their uncleanness by defiling my tabernacle" (Lev. 15:31); "Tell your brother Aaron not to come just at any time into the sanctuary inside the curtain before the mercy seat that is upon the ark, or he will die" (16:2); "Do not defile yourselves in any of these ways, for by all these practices the nations I am casting out before you have defiled themselves" (18:24); "If a man lies with a woman having her sickness and uncovers her nakedness, he has laid bare her flow and she has laid bare her flow of blood; both of them shall be cut off from their people" (20:18).

In these four passages, we see anxiety about ritual purity, hyperseriousness about boundaries, fear of being treated like a despised alien, and disgust about being bloodied by having sex with a woman during her period. Disgust and fear show themselves in the rule about "the cry of the skin diseased person ('impure, impure') ... (Lev 13:45–46)."[59] Kazen also sees a fear of demons (common in the ancient world) in a number of purification rites, even when they have been successfully "integrate[d] within a priestly sacrificial system."[60] Demonology can persist, even when it is not officially accepted. It

---

55. Ibid., 19.
56. Ibid., 20.
57. Ibid., 21.
58. Ibid., 23, with n64.
59. Ibid., 30.
60. Ibid., 25.

shows up in the second-century writer Origen, who sees the deaths of Christian martyrs as combating demons: "One righteous man dying voluntarily for the community may avert the activities of evil daemons by expiation, since it is they who bring about plagues or famines or stormy seas."[61] The notion of fighting off demons can occur even when only metaphorical "sacrifice" or "purity" are present.

The God of the purity system is a God to be feared, even in the New Testament. The Epistle to the Hebrews frequently speaks of purity (Heb. 1:3; 9:13–14, 22–23; 10:22), and right after exhorting believers to "give thanks" to their benefactor, says, "We offer to God an acceptable worship with reverence and awe; for indeed our God is a consuming fire" (Heb. 12:28–29). "It is a fearful thing to fall into the hands of the living God" (Heb. 10:31). Paul says, "The wrath of God is revealed from heaven against all ungodliness" (Rom. 1:18), just before discussing the impure activities of the gentiles.

Impurity thinking can go back and forth between an abstract idea and a physical concept, as seen in the "tendency to link physical cleansing with moral cleansing" or in the "socio-moral disgust"[62] with the person who is seen as unclean: the leper, the menstruant woman, the gentile. The ritual system develops boundaries to isolate impurity. Some forms of impurity are temporary and can be cleansed. The gentiles, however, are a permanent problem, so certain boundaries are drawn against them. The sharp dichotomy between clean and unclean seems to help society to develop its sense of identity.

The Jesus Response

Both core disgust (about foods) and sociomoral disgust (against certain social groups) were in play in the Jewish society in which Jesus found himself. Jesus allowed the "unclean" to be part of his fellowship, not making divisions and separations.[63] It is hard for us to imagine how radical was Jesus' inviting people to step over these boundaries and

---

61. Origen, *Contra Celsum* 1.31, quoted in Frances M. Young, *The Use of Sacrificial Ideas in Greek Christian Writers from the New Testament to John Chrysostom* (1979; repr., Eugene: Wipf & Stock, 2004), 182.
62. Beck, *Unclean*, 43, 19.
63. Ibid., 80–81.

join the "kingdom" family. "Disgust *erects* boundaries while love *dismantles* boundaries," Beck argues. "Love is, at root, the suspension of disgust."[64]

Love and healing work against the exclusions that a purity system demands. Insofar as purity is the purpose of the sacrificial system, and purity requires exclusion, sacrificial purity works against mercy and inclusiveness. Beck sees Jesus creating the notion of "purity *via inclusion*," undermining the exclusiveness of the purity system.[65] When Pharisees rebuke him for sitting with "tax collectors and sinners," he says that he calls sinners and "those who are sick," and says, "Go and learn what this means, 'I desire mercy, not sacrifice'" (Matt. 9:12–13).

Beck says, "Mercy and sacrifice are *intrinsically* incompatible, due largely to psychological factors."[66] Or one could say "spiritual factors," since deliberate expansion of the circle of people to be loved and included in the "family" is really a spiritual idea. But the factors are "psychological" insofar as an attitude of welcome is incompatible with an attitude of disgust and exclusion.

Jesus extends fellowship and welcome, not fear and disgust, to those on the margins. The invitation into God's family is open to *everyone*. "Anyone who comes to me I will never drive away" (John 6:37). Ungenerous attitudes are inconsistent with this advice: "Whoever is not against you is for you" (Luke 9:50). Jesus is not the only Jew to show openness to gentiles. First Enoch hints at such openness; the promised "Son of Man" is called "the light of the gentiles" (1 En. 48.4; citing Isa. 42:6), and judgment is directed not against whole nations but against "the kings and the mighty ones . . . the mighty landowners" (1 En. 46.4; 48.8).[67] But the openness to the gentiles attributed to Jesus in the Gospels is much more explicit.

Beck has an intriguing concept of the Eucharist: "By universalizing kinship language the Lord's Supper is actively pushing against the

---
64. Ibid., 88.
65. Ibid., 89, 193.
66. Ibid., 79.
67. 1 Enoch passages are taken from E. Isaac, trans., "1 (Ethiopic Apocalypse of) Enoch," in *OTP* 1:34–36.

sociomoral fissures of disgust and contempt. . . . [It] dismantles the psychic fissures within the heart."[68] Beck argues that Jesus created the Eucharist in order to confront and overcome feelings of social disgust; it is a "psychological *intervention*."[69] The Eucharist asks us to include more people in the category of "us." The act of eating his body and drinking his blood summons up a disgust reaction, which we then have to suspend by consciously including "tax collectors and sinners" (or whatever group *we* consider disgusting). Beck does not use the word "suspend"; that was my attempt to make sense of his argument. This part of Beck's thesis is really unfinished, even embryonic, but is very interesting. I want to ask, Why would Jesus arouse disgust emotions, if they suggest bad theology? Is the Eucharist meant to arouse theological debate? Beck's position implies a yes answer, but he does not directly address the question. I would welcome a sequel from Beck wherein he pursues his thesis about the negation of disgust being the founding purpose of the Eucharist. I am interested in the psychological implications. Is it really true that Jesus intended the Eucharist to be disgust-experiencing and then disgust-transcending? Is this a therapeutic pattern that we can discern in other religions or cultures? The classic view of the value of live theater is that it helps people experience and *purge* strong emotions, including negative ones. I have some misgivings about thinking of the Eucharist as a kind of therapeutic theater, but I would be willing to listen to a theologian who can present a good argument for it. I am not yet convinced. I offer a different idea about the original Eucharist in the section "Luke-Acts Is Not Cross-Centered" in chapter 5.

Whether or not the Eucharist does all the things Beck suggests, Jesus and Paul *did* push against the social disgust that is connected with purity thinking, and all who asked for healing from Jesus also received social acceptance and love. Jesus would have people recognize that they are already accepted within the family of God, and that "your faith has saved you" or "your faith has made you well" (Matt. 9:22; Mark

68. Beck, *Unclean*, 113.
69. Ibid., 114.

5:34; 10:52; Luke 7:50; 8:48; 17:19; 18:42), which implies that every act of honest faith *reaches* God and brings salvation. Jesus made people *whole*: healed them physically, restored them socially, took away their shame. Jesus was *always* healing people from shame and feelings of impurity. He affirmed that people *can* do the will of God, can be good,[70] and this without any reference to atonement or a substitutionary death. No transaction was needed, but only trust.

Why were the ideas of a transaction with God, of a sacrificial cleansing, so appealing? Beck thinks it is due to our unconscious magical thinking: "*Moral failings* stimulated a need for *physical cleansing*. When we *sin* we like to take *showers*. We all act like Lady Macbeth,"[71] who tried to clean off guilt by hand-washing. The concept of "penal substitutionary atonement might be so popular" because it draws on the magical idea of being *washed*; there is a "psychological connection between salvation and washing"; penal substitution is "psychologically sticky: more memorable."[72] It also puts up new social barriers (after Jesus and Paul had deconstructed the old ones); penal substitution enables the in-crowd to see itself as special, and to categorize people as "Justified versus Condemned and Pure versus Impure."[73]

Let us state the issue very starkly: Is salvation a spiritual reality or a magical reality?

---

70. Matt. 5:5–9 ("the meek," "the pure in heart"); 12:33–36 ("make the tree good," "the good person"); Luke 6:45 ("the good person"); 8:21 ("those who do the will of God"); 10:27–28, 37 ("love the Lord . . . show mercy"); 11:42 ("practice justice and the love of God"); 16:10 ("faithful in a little").
71. Beck, *Unclean*, 44.
72. Ibid., 42.
73. Ibid., 40.

2

Atonement as Compensation or Reciprocity

Atonement as compensation, gift, or payment is one of the underlying concepts in the Hebrew sacrificial system. The עוֹלָה, ʿōlâ, burnt offering or whole offering, is thought of as a gift to God. Except for the skin, which is retained by the priests, the animal is wholly burnt: "The priest shall turn the whole into smoke on the altar as a burnt offering, an offering by fire of pleasing odor to the Lord" (Lev. 1:9; cf. Num. 28:6).

The sacrifice described in Lev. 7:1–7 is the ’āšām (אָשָׁם), formerly called the "guilt offering," but now frequently translated "reparation offering."[1] This sacrifice is performed "when you have sinned and realize your guilt, and would restore what you took . . . you shall repay the principal amount and shall add one-fifth to it" (Lev. 6:4–5). The *function* of reparation is also secondarily present in other sacrifices, which have *primary* functions different from reparation. I use "reparation" in its usual English meaning, according to *Webster's New Collegiate Dictionary*: "making amends for a wrong . . . compensation."

---

1. Jacob Milgrom, "Further on the Expiatory Sacrifices," *JBL* 115 (1996): 513.

The Nature of Sacrifice in the Old Testament

Even in the present day, the abstract usage of "sacrifice" is understood to have payment value. On any Veterans Day, we can hear speeches about how freedom was "purchased" by the "sacrifice" made by soldiers. Freedom is not free, we are told, but must be paid for with heroic self-sacrifice. *To whom* the payment is made need not be spelled out; the need to pay is perceived to be inherent in reality itself; the concept "rings true."

Even though there are multiple purposes for sacrifice, even within a single culture such as the Hebrew culture,[2] there has always been a suggestion of *payment* connected with sacrifice, and sometimes even of *payback*, associated with a concept of justice as retribution.

Commenting on sacrifices cross-culturally, Jacob Milgrom says there seem to be "four possible purposes behind ... sacrifice: (1) to provide food for the god ... (2) to assimilate the life force of the sacrificial animal ... (3) to effect union with the deity ... and (4) to induce the aid of the deity by means of a gift (Tylor 1873). The first three purposes are not to be found in Israel."[3] He does allow that sacrifice to induce the deity's aid is present in the Hebrew system, where "the quintessential sacrificial act, then, is ... making a gift to the deity.... The *'ōlâ* and *minḥa* are gifts to God to obtain his blessing or forgiveness."[4] The gifts offered are the culture's most valuable foodstuffs.

Milgrom resists admitting that feeding the god was a theme in Hebrew religion, but he concedes that the notion is found in "some sacrificial idioms of the Bible: 'my table' (Ezek 44:16), 'the food of his God' ([Lev] 21:22 ... Num 28:2)"; however, these are "only fossilized vestiges from a dim past."[5] But to call something a "vestige" is to say that it *does* lie in the background. I think it better to admit that feeding God is an idea that exists in the ancestry of Hebrew sacrifice. (The nearby Hittite and Akkadian cultures thought "of sacrifice as a

---

2. One of the main points made in Kathryn McClymond, *Beyond Sacred Violence: A Comparative Study of Sacrifice* (Baltimore: Johns Hopkins University Press, 2008).
3. Jacob Milgrom, *Leviticus 1–16*, AB 3 (Garden City, NY: Doubleday, 1991), 440.
4. Ibid., 441.
5. Ibid., 440.

provisioning of the gods."[6]) The authors of Leviticus did not believe the Deity was *literally* eating the smoke, but by that time the idea had coalesced into a fixed expression that the authors of Leviticus allowed to stand, so that "of pleasing odor to the Lord" (Lev. 1:9, 13, 17; 2:2, 9; 23:13; Num. 15:10) meant that the Lord accepted the sacrifice.

Sacrifice as Payment

As in gentile cultures, it is likely that Hebrew sacrifice was originally for *appeasement*, placating God with gifts. The theme is still strongly present in the Bible; Yahweh demands from Moses "my offering, the food for my offerings by fire, my pleasing odor, you shall take care to offer to me at its appointed time" (Num. 28:2). The "pleasing odor" (רֵיחַ נִיחֹחַ, *rēyaḥ niḥōaḥ*) occurs eleven times in just this and the following chapter of Numbers, and forty-two times throughout the Pentateuch. Frances Young allows that the phrase may have "originally referred to propitiation."[7] The "pleasing odor" can be used metaphorically, as in Ezek. 20:41 and Phil. 4:18.

The idea of sacrifice as a payment in food has parallels in other cultures, as in Zoroastrianism, where Ahura Mazda (the Creator) demands that more sacrifices be brought to the demigod Tistrya, who would be "strengthened by the sacrifice."[8]

Some suggestion of *payment* or *gift* seems to underlie Hebrew sacrifice in all its phases. Some early texts indicate that sacrifice, to be effective, must be costly. In 2 Samuel, David seeks to use sacrifice to persuade God to avert a plague he has sent against Israel. When a certain Araunah wants to give David some animals to sacrifice, David insists on buying them, saying, "No; I will buy them for the full price. I will not take for the Lord what is yours, nor offer burnt offerings that cost me nothing" (1 Chron. 21:24; an emphatic restatement of 2 Sam.

---

6. Dennis J. McCarthy, "Further Notes on the Symbolism of Blood and Sacrifice," *JBL* 92 (1973): 206.
7. Frances M. Young, *The Use of Sacrificial Ideas in Greek Christian Writers from the New Testament to John Chrysostom* (1970; repr., Eugene, OR: Wipf & Stock, 2004), 39n23. She cites Gen. 8:21; Num. 28:2; and 1 Sam. 26:19 as examples of Yahweh being propitiated by the odor.
8. *Yasht* 8.58, cited in Albert de Jong, "Animal Sacrifice in Ancient Zoroastrianism: A Ritual and Its Interpretation," in *Sacrifice in Religious Experience*, ed. Albert I. Baumgarten, SHR 93 (Leiden: Brill, 2002), 144.

24:24). Costliness was *necessary* to the sacrificial gift being effective. It was only *after* "David built there an altar to the Lord, and offered burnt offerings.... The Lord answered his supplication for the land, and the plague was averted from Israel" (2 Sam. 24:25). In 1 Chronicles, David pays "six hundred shekels of gold" for the site, and the Lord shows his approval when "he answered him with fire from heaven on the altar of burnt offering" (1 Chron. 21:26).

Sacrifice was always seen to have an *exchange* value. Money could sometimes be offered in place of an *'āšām*, or guilt offering, suggesting the gift or payment idea.[9] The necessity of sacrifices *costing* the giver also occurs in Mal. 1:10 (MT 1:8), although it is disguised in NRSV: "So that you would not kindle fire on my altar in vain!" Jonathan Klawans points out that what is really said is "so that you would not kindle fire on my altar *at no cost* (חנם)!"[10] The only translation I could find that retained that idea was an old Catholic one: "kindle the fire on my altar gratis?" (Mal. 1:10 Douay-Rheims).

Ephesians picks up on the "pleasing odor" in its Greek form, and adds two more sacrificial terms: "Christ ... gave Himself up for us, an offering and a sacrifice [προσφορὰν καὶ θυσίαν, *prosforan kai thysian*] to God as a fragrant aroma [ὀσμὴν εὐωδίας, *osmēn euōdias*]" (Eph. 5:2 NASB, which follows the Greek word order closely). Here it is the *idea* rather than the practice of sacrifice that is important. Author and readers are sharing a typological mode of interpretation: the sacrificial cult serves as a *type*, a prefiguration, of the death of Christ. But even in such an abstract interpretation, sacrifice is pictured as a pleasing offering to God.

In Exodus, God insists, "No one shall appear before me empty-handed" (Exod. 23:15), but if the Israelites follow instructions, he promises to "blot out" the Amorites (23:23). This is a God made in the image of acquisitive, conquest-oriented men. He wants to be fed good food, and he offers military backing in exchange.

The key sacrificial verb, *kipper* (כִּפֶּר), is linked with the idea of

---

9. Young, *Use of Sacrificial Ideas*, 38.
10. Jonathan Klawans, *Purity, Sacrifice, and the Temple: Symbolism and Supersessionism in the Study of Ancient Judaism* (Oxford: Oxford University Press, 2006), 87 (emphasis original).

payment. Cognate with *kipper* is the noun *kōper* [כֹּפֶר], which is a "ransom" payment or "atonement money." When the Lord orders a census, Moses is told that each person "shall give a ransom for his life to the Lord.... Half a shekel.... To make atonement for your lives.... Atonement money" (Exod. 30:12–13, 15–16 ESV). The verb *kipper* occurs in verses 10 and 15. The same conjunction of *kipper* and *kōper* is found in Num. 35:31–33, where it is said that no *kōper* can pay for a murder. Even though there is no *kōper* payment there, the grammatical point is supported, for it has to be explicitly stated that *kipper*ing through a *kōper* does *not* apply. We see the usual sense of *kōper* in Gen. 32:20, where Jacob seeks to mollify Esau, to "appease him with the present [*kōper*]."[11] There are also places, such as 1 Sam. 12:1–5; Amos 5:12; and Prov. 6:35, where *kōper* means "bribe."[12]

Milgrom says, "The ransom principle is clearly operative [in] Exod 30:12–16 ... 21:30.... There exists a strong possibility that all texts that assign to *kipper* the function of averting God's wrath have *kōper* in mind."[13] Uncongenial though it may be to advancing monotheistic philosophy, God's wrath is averted through a payment, although not in the case of murder (Numbers 35). It really seems that *kipper* has two main meanings: "'to ransom' in sin contexts and 'to purify/effect purgation' in cleansing or consecration contexts.... Deciding between 'to ransom' and 'to purify' is not always easy."[14]

Another key sacrificial word, מִנְחָה, *minḥâ*, the grain offering, shows a link with payment. First we must notice that the grain offering is called a sacrifice, because it is burned on the altar. Christian Eberhart points out, "Since all rituals that feature this burning rite are called an 'offering for Yhwh,' this rite can be interpreted as the *constitutive element of sacrifice*."[15] But in noncultic usage, *minḥâ* simply means a

---

11. Gen. 32:20 also contains the verb *kipper*, where it means "to appease, to mollify" (Jay Sklar, *Sin, Impurity, Sacrifice, Atonement: The Priestly Conceptions*, HBM 2 [Sheffield: Sheffield Phoenix, 2005], 73).
12. Ibid., 56, 58.
13. Milgrom, *Leviticus 1–16*, 1082.
14. Sklar, *Sin, Impurity, Sacrifice, Atonement*, 7.
15. Christian A. Eberhart, *The Sacrifice of Jesus: Understanding Atonement Biblically*, Facets (Minneapolis: Fortress Press, 2011), 98. The grain offering is as much a part of the sacrificial system as are the animal sacrifices (ibid., 76).

SACRIFICE AND ATONEMENT

gift.[16] In 2 Kgs. 8:8–9, *minḥâ* is a "present . . . all kinds of goods of Damascus, forty camel loads," a gift given in exchange for a prophecy.

Another word that simply means "gift" in secular usage, שַׁי, *šay*, is used for offerings brought to the Lord in Ps. 68:30 and Isa. 18:7. Sacrifices, then, are grammatically and practically linked to social acts of exchange, payment, and tribute. A common scholarly comment is something along these lines: "Sacrifices were not offered to attain God's mercy but to retain it,"[17] but this is a quibble, since it implies propitiation or payment to *retain* favor.

Sacrifice as payment is even more blatant in non-Jewish cultures, as in popular Greek religion. Passages in Aeschylus remind the god that "'pleasing offerings' will be discontinued unless the speaker or the speaker's city is preserved."[18] A number of inscriptions on Greek statues indicate that the monument is "in return for good deeds," or are a way of "paying back a favour."[19]

Let us look at another sacrificing culture. The Muslims have a Feast of Sacrifice, which in some localities is still accompanied by animal sacrifice. A study of ritual among the Gayo people of the Sumatran countryside finds them sharing the sacrificial meat because "giving meat to the poor brings benefit to the sacrificers."[20] An educated, urban religious teacher among the Gayo gives a more intellectual and spiritual understanding: "The sacrifice of any animal to him can give us merit, but only if done for the sake of God and not for a worldly reason; it depends entirely on our intention."[21] But both the rural and the urban Gayo see the basic purpose of the sacrifice as "to free us [the sacrificers] from torment after we die by increasing our merit."[22]

Advancing monotheistic thought finds the idea of appeasement

---

16. Baruch A. Levine, *Leviticus: The Traditional Hebrew Text with the New JPS Translation* (Philadelphia: Jewish Publication Society, 1989), xxiv.
17. J. S. Whale, *Victor and Victim: The Christian Doctrine of Redemption* (Cambridge: Cambridge University Press, 1960), 52.
18. *Choephoroi* 255–57; 791–93 ; Robert Parker, "Pleasing Thighs: Reciprocity in Greek Religion," in *Reciprocity in Ancient Greece*, ed. Christopher Gill et al. (Oxford: Oxford University Press, 1998), 108.
19. Parker, "Pleasing Thighs," 110–11.
20. John R. Bowen, *Muslims through Discourse: Religion and Ritual in Gayo Society* (Princeton: Princeton University Press, 1993), 277.
21. Ibid., 280.
22. Ibid., 281.

abhorrent and tries to shift the focus from propitiating (manipulating) the deity to expiating (cleansing) the sin. But popular belief tends to think of atonement as compensation: a ritual that is also a payment, or a payment that is also a solemn ritual. A successful transaction results in *propitiation*: soothing or satisfying God's anger. Ethical monotheists have regularly come to the uncomfortable realization that this makes God look like a moody king who can be mollified by payments, and they make vigorous, rationalizing moves to forestall this impression, but the logic of sacrifice and ransom ensure that these subethical images keep returning, like a nightmare. Atonement draws on sacrificial notions: ritual cleansing of the effects of sin (a magical idea), and offering gifts that satisfy God (a manipulative idea). Even today, our prayers are supplicatory and manipulative: "Lord have mercy, Lord have mercy, look kindly upon these our gifts." Bargaining and magic remain underlying intuitions even when the more moral atonement ideas (nowadays attached to the term *reconciliation*) are emphasized.

In Old Testament atonement texts, violence is never far away. In Numbers 25 and Psalm 106, the Lord is angry with Israel and sends a plague among them because of their consorting with gentile women. The priest Phinehas then skewers an Israelite and his foreign girlfriend with a spear (Num. 25:7-8), and the Lord announces that this "has turned back my wrath.... He ... made atonement for the Israelites" (Num. 25:11, 13). "Phinehas interceded," says a psalmist,

> and the plague was stopped.
> And that has been reckoned to him as righteousness.
> (Ps 106:30–31)

It almost sounds like an understatement to say that "the *kipper* word group is often used in relation to God's wrath."[23]

Sacrifice as Payback

That sacrifice has "payback" value in the crudest sense can be shown

---

23. Timothy Gorringe, *God's Just Vengeance: Crime, Violence and the Rhetoric of Salvation*, CSIR 9 (Cambridge: Cambridge University Press, 1996), 38.

through some acts of massacre that are described with sacrificial terms in the Hebrew Bible. The greatest reforming king of Judah, Josiah, "sacrificed all the priests of the high places" (2 Kgs. 23:20 ESV). It really does use the verb for sacrificing, זָבַח, *zebaḥ*, although most translations say "slaughtered," so as to disguise this unpleasant notion.[24] Deuteronomy 13:13–15 commands that, if the inhabitants of a town induce people to go worship other gods, they are to be massacred, and "then burn the town and all its spoil with fire, as a whole burnt offering to the Lord your God" (Deut. 13:16).[25] So here sacrificial language is used for the חרם, *ḥerem*, or ban, which involved the slaying of entire populations. Jason Tatlock sees sacrificial connections in another *ḥerem* passage, where the common sacrificial phrase "before (*lifnē*) the Lord" is used: Samuel "hewed Agag in pieces before the Lord" (1 Sam 15:33).[26]

Some would want to dismiss these violent passages of the sacrificial slaughtering of humans as a survival from a primitive layer in the tradition. But the main verb used for atonement throughout the Old Testament has a connection with violent outcomes. The atonement word *kipper* can refer to the ritual cleansing of impurity or to the conciliation of an aggrieved party. When uses of *kipper* outside of Leviticus are examined, we see strong suggestions of a transaction being made, even revenge transactions. When David asks the Gibeonites how he can "make expiation" (*kipper*) for the late King Saul's violence against them, they answer, "Let seven of his sons be handed over to us, and we will impale them before the Lord at Gibeon" (2 Sam. 21:6), and David complies with this request. After the deed is done, David sees to it that the bones of the seven, and also of Saul and Jonathan, are properly buried. "After that, God heeded supplications for the land," lifting the famine (21:14). God is very much involved in these affairs. The story begins with God sending a famine on the land, then telling David that it is because "there is bloodguilt on Saul and on his house" (21:1). God would not take pity on Israel until both a violent

---

24. Jason Tatlock, "The Place of Human Sacrifice in the Israelite Cult," in *Ritual and Metaphor: Sacrifice in the Bible*, ed. Christian A. Eberhart (Atlanta: SBL, 2011), 40.
25. Ibid., 43.
26. Ibid., 42.

payback for Saul's violence *and* a respectful burial of the victims had taken place. Full atonement, apparently, requires violent payback ... and a respectful burial afterward!

Another example shows the Lord thoroughly implicated in savage violence. Angry with Israel, the Lord "incited David" to hold a census, after which "the Lord sent a pestilence on Israel" (1 Sam. 24:1, 15). When David buys a threshing floor, refusing the offer to accept the threshing floor free of charge, builds an altar there, and offers sacrifice, then "the Lord answered his supplication for the land, and the plague was averted from Israel" (24:25). The Lord provokes the evil, punishes the evil, offers atonement for the evil, and lifts the punishment. Surely this Lord is the source of good and evil. One can fear such a God, one can appease, propitiate, and grovel before such a God, but it is not easy to *love* such a God.

In Deuteronomy, the descendants of Joseph are promised "the favor of the one who dwells on Sinai," for

> His [Joseph's] horns are the horns of a wild ox;
> with them he gores the peoples,
>   driving them to the ends of the earth. (Deut. 33:16–17)

God's favor is proved by the violent destruction of one's enemies. On the Deuteronomistic Historian, David Janzen writes, "Sacrifice in Dtr most clearly stands as recognition of the authority of YHWH and the law.... The perfect slaughter of the sacrificial victim mirrors the perfect slaughter of Israel's enemies."[27] Deuteronomy and the Deuteronomistic Historian are not as interested in holiness and purity as P is, but they give a political significance to sacrifice: it stands for obedience to God, and for the threat of violence that accompanies the mandate to obey:

> You shall present your burnt offerings, both the meat and the blood, on the altar of the Lord your God. ...

---

27. David Janzen, *The Social Meanings of Sacrifice in the Hebrew Bible: A Study of Four Writings*, BZAW 344 (Berlin: de Gruyter, 2004), 182.

Be careful to obey all these words that I command you today, so that it may go well with you and with your children after you. (Deut. 12:27–28)

The relationship of sacrificial thinking to violence is more apparent in the Vedic system of ancient India. The texts abound in stories of violence preceding, interrupting, or following the sacrifice. "The proceedings, from the initial invitation to the distribution of food and gifts, is imbued with conflict. By offering an arena apart from normal life sacrifice calls forth and intensifies competition and conflict."[28] Many sacrificial rituals are accompanied by dicing games or riddling games, and sometimes the loser is killed. "The disturbing and destabilizing effect of sacrifice makes itself manifest in its fiercely agonistic character."[29]

Theories of Atonement Arising from Guilt

Before examining more biblical material, it will be helpful to look at two very intriguing psychological approaches to atonement. These psychologists' remarks are relevant even though they are not speaking of the Levitical cult but of "atonement" in normal usage, where it means conciliating, making up, repairing, making good again.

Erikson on Atonement and Regret

Many psychologists, from Freud onward, have seen the roots of atonement in conflict and the overwhelming feelings of guilt that follow. We could start with Erik Erikson, who finds that "our thoughts and feelings have described a constant . . . seesaw" between "fantasies of omnipotent control" and distress about "what we ought to have done instead of what we did do."[30] We feel crippling regret for having "antagonized quite well-meaning people," which leads to "fantasied atonements"; because we can swing between extremes of self-

---

28. J. C. Heesterman, *The Broken World of Sacrifice: An Essay in Ancient Indian Ritual* (Chicago: University of Chicago Press, 1993), 44.
29. Ibid., 42.
30. Erik H. Erikson, *Childhood and Society*, 2nd ed. (New York: Norton, 1963), 189.

awareness and of unconsciousness, we are caught in "cycles of usurpation and atonement."[31]

He points to the North American Dakota tribe's ritualized self-punishment as evidence for chronic regret. When nursing children start biting, the mother pushes them away. Children feel rage at the mother, and then feel regret about this rage, and this has led to the ritual practice of turning rage "back against themselves by making their own chests the particular focus of their self-torture."[32] This is the ritual where men pierce themselves with skewers, "ripping the flesh of their chests open."[33] Erikson says every culture has its "particular brand of inner damnation" that is felt by all but is ritually enacted by only a few.[34] He suspects that regret and manipulation lie at the bottom of it: "We suspect that the cycle of usurpation and atonement represents a collective magic means of coercing nature. . . . Primitive religions, the most primitive layer in all religions, and the religious layer in each individual, abound with efforts at atonement which try to make up for vague deeds against a maternal matrix."[35]

The "maternal matrix" refers not just to the literal mother, but to the natural environment, which also must be appeased: "The Supernatural Providers of food . . . must be appeased by prayer and self-torture."[36] Whether or not one accepts Erikson's theories, one can hardly deny that the thought of "mother" arouses feelings of love, rage, frustration, and guilt in many people.

Irwin Rosen, a therapist with many years of experience, discusses a personality type he calls the "atoner," the one who "feels guilty, alone, vulnerable, exiled" in relationship to the "lost victim-parent."[37] In therapeutic sessions, this author encountered various affects of "atoners," ranging from feelings of "righteous and entitled revenge, [holding] the moral high ground," to "the dreaded *retaliation* that the

---

31. Ibid., 190.
32. Ibid., 149.
33. Ibid., 148.
34. Ibid., 149.
35. Ibid., 191, 251.
36. Ibid., 251.
37. Irwin C. Rosen, "The Atonement-Forgiveness Dyad: Identification with the Aggressed," *Psychoanalytic Inquiry* 29 (2009): 415.

atoner fears at the hands of an outraged and vengeful retributory force."[38] The latter type can manifest "the magical belief that masochistic suffering ... can undo and repair the" relationship.[39] Rosen "wondered if revenge and atonement were not obverse sides of the same very thin coin.... The revenger attacks that object, the atoner ... wards off fear of his fantasized reprisal with sacrifice and placation"; both involve rage and cruelty (directed against the self, in the case of the atoner).[40] I cannot accept certain parts of his theory, but I think his experience-backed observations are intriguing.

The extreme anger often exhibited by scholars when debating sacrifice or atonement is (anecdotal) evidence of the high degree of rage that exists in atonement thinking. I have actually lost friends over this issue.

Rado: Atonement as Manipulation

Sandor Rado was a follower of Freud who departed from his teacher's theories in a number of ways, primarily by striving to develop a more holistic psychological theory in place of one that treated Libido, Ego, and Superego as three nearly independent entities in conflict with each other. Rado wrote a number of articles discussing the process of "atonement," which he saw as the attempt by children to "atone" for deeds that "incur the parents' disapproval"; this "reparation takes place on the psychic plane,"[41] as the child seeks to win back parental approval.

Rado sees melancholia developing from repeated self-punishments, and he even observed melancholia in children. The melancholiac "begins *unconsciously* to reproduce within his mind the punishments anticipated from his parents and, in doing so, he unconsciously *hopes to win love*.... Self-punishment takes place in the hope of absolution....

---

38. Ibid., 416–17.
39. Ibid., 422.
40. Ibid., 423.
41. A summary of Rado's work is given by Myer Mendelson, *Psychoanalytic Concepts of Depression*, 2nd ed. (Flushing, NY: Spectrum, 1974), 46–47.

The close connection between *guilt, atonement, and forgiveness* [is] deeply rooted in our mental life."[42]

Thus atonement is self-punishment with a purpose: "It is by means of punishing himself that he hopes to regain his mother."[43] This is not a trivial matter. Retaining parental love and approval is a survival measure. The child feels deeply threatened by parental rage.

> His *guilty* fear of inescapable punishment ... is a signal that his security is endangered. It brings into play the reparative procedure of expiatory behavior taught him by his parents: he is reprimanded, must make a confession, take his punishment, promise never to do it again and ask for forgiveness.... Parental reproach gives rise to self-reproach, parental punishment to self-punishment, parental forgiveness to self-forgiveness.[44]

This cycle of self-punishment and perception of (temporary) forgiveness is really a "pathology of conscience."[45] It derives from "the mechanisms of the stern punishment system"—a system vastly inferior to one in which "parental reward" is emphasized and where "self-respect and moral pride" are facilitated in the child.[46] However, a rational reward system "steers clear from indiscriminate 'permissiveness' ... resorted to by parents who are both frightened and misguided."[47]

Rado also speaks of a pathology of conscience that is a kind of moral masochism, where "the patient is forced to maintain his emotional security, his self-respect and moral pride, by a self-sacrificing way of life, turning himself, often enough, into a martyr—without a cause ... incessantly atoning ... not for their sins, but for their temptations, their imagined sins."[48] Who of us has not met (or *been*) such a person? We have read of such persons, especially in the books of Dostoevsky,

---

42. Sandor Rado, "The Problem of Melancholia," in *Psychoanalysis of Behavior: The Collected Papers of Sandor Rado*, vol. 1, *1922-1956* (New York: Grune & Stratton, 1956), 51.
43. Sandor Rado, "Hedonic Control, Action-Self, and the Depressive Spell," in *1922-1956*, 287.
44. Sandor Rado, "Rage, Violence, and Conscience," in *1922-1956*, 148-49.
45. Ibid., 149.
46. Ibid.
47. Ibid., 150.
48. Sandor Rado, "Contribution to a Discussion on Masochism," in *Psychoanalysis of Behavior: The Collected Papers of Sandor Rado*, vol. 2, *1956-1961* (New York: Grune & Stratton, 1962), 86.

whom Rado calls "the finest literary expert in the pathology of conscience."[49]

One aspect of Rado's theory that I want to heighten in developing my own theory is that self-punishment is a manipulative strategy designed for self-protection: "Guilt makes him desirous of undergoing the punishment he fears because he wishes to propitiate his parents and be again loved and cared for by them."[50] Underneath atonement, Rado writes, is rage at the parent who has withdrawn her love, but the guilty conscience will not allow direct expression of this rage, so there is "dispersed rage" or "enraged atonement," which manifests as irritability, restlessness, and "agitated depression."[51] Its most extreme expression is suicide, "the extreme form of expiatory self-punishment.... Its motivation" was an "illusory expectation that by giving his life the patient will break his mother's heart."[52] I think all of this shows the manipulative nature of atonement, although Rado does not use that word.

Potentially devastating in both the fields of psychology and theology is Rado's conclusion that "rage, retroflexed [inward-directed] rage, fear, fear of conscience, and guilty fear are the chief emotional forces of which the atonement pattern is composed."[53]

Many of these patterns could be perceived in the biblical materials: the need for (self-)punishment and reparation, the perception of a judging parental God who sometimes withholds love, the belief that atoning acts lead to forgiveness. We should not be surprised that this psychological pattern leads to melancholia. Rado "saw the melancholic process as a love drama, as a grand attempt at reparation."[54] Self-punishment as "an expiation undertaken in order to win back love"[55] would be as much at home in a study of biblical sacrifice as in a psychology book (or a nineteenth-century novel). There is a

---

49. Rado, "Rage, Violence, and Conscience," 149.
50. Sandor Rado, "The Automatic Motivating System of Depressive Behavior," in *1956–1961*, 168.
51. Ibid., 171.
52. Ibid., 172.
53. Ibid., 176.
54. Mendelson, *Psychoanalytic Concepts*, 48.
55. Ibid., 48.

connection between common psychological patterns and themes in traditional religions.

The pattern could be studied with less attention to its possible origin in the mother-child relationship, and with more attention to the guilt-inducing power of certain religious ideas. Donald Capps speaks of some "religious ideas as inherently tormenting."[56] Some of the "most common ... traumatizing effects of religious ideas are ... repression ... withdrawal of feeling ... loss of confidence in the testimony of one's own perceptions."[57] But Jesus stretched out his hand to bless and to welcome children, "the same hand that other adults have used to strike their children."[58] Jesus confronted alienation with love.

I think these theorists' findings support my thesis that atonement arises out of the perceived need to appease angry parents, to mollify their anger. With these theories in mind, we can return to biblical exegesis and see if the psychological theories provide any explanatory power.

Sacrifice as a Part of Reciprocity Systems

I will begin with Greek and Hellenistic cultures, and then move to Judaism, including Hellenistic Judaism.

Mundane Exchange and Patronage

Ancient people related to the gods or to God in ways similar to how they related to each other, seeking to secure the maximum benefit for themselves. Since gift-giving, gestures of respect, and outright bargaining were techniques for dealing with people, they became ways to deal with the divine as well. Reciprocity systems that prevailed in social life were reflected in religion.

Scholars have described reciprocity as a "universal norm" by which people are expected to help those who have helped them.[59] Stanley

---

56. Donald Capps, "Religion and Child Abuse: Perfect Together," *JSSR* 31 (1992): 7.
57. Ibid., 8.
58. Ibid., 13.
59. From Jason A. Whitlark, *Enabling Fidelity to God: Perseverance in Hebrews in Light of the Reciprocity*

Stowers argues that, with all Middle Eastern ethnic groups, "Through sacrificial practices the productivity of the land was interpreted in terms of reciprocity with God or the gods."[60] Sacrifice is simply "generalized reciprocity ... mundane exchange" with the gods; "mutual gift giving" was really a way of "maintain[ing] the relationship" with the deity.[61]

The economic basis for sacrifice can be seen even in the history of the symbolic sacrifice that is the Roman Catholic Eucharist: in fifteenth-century Germany, Communion wafers were pressed with images to "resemble coins.... An economy of sacrifice is at the heart of the predominant doctrine of sacrifice."[62]

Sacrifice is part of a system of relationships. Speaking of the exchange of favors (χαριτής) in Greek society, Robert Parker cautions: "An exchange of *kharites* is not an exchange of goods ... it is an exchange of favours, a voluntary, if socially prescribed, expression of a relationship of friendship.... Reciprocity [is not] trade."[63] Parker wants to emphasize the *relationship* that the exchange system enables, but he does recognize the problem "of all the talk of gifts and counter-gifts and *kharis* in relations with the gods. This is the language that mortals use to one another.... The language of *kharis* sustains, indeed creates, the fiction that the relation between human and god can be assimilated to that between human beings."[64] The Hebrew prophets and Plato criticized people who thought of their relationship to the divine in earthly, materialistic terms, using sacrifice to get the best deal possible from God or the gods. It is problematic when mundane give-and-take is applied to a Deity who is supposed to be infinite.

Of course, a distinction needs to be made between gift exchange

---

Systems of the Ancient Mediterranean World (Milton Keynes, UK: Paternoster, 2008), 17, who is summarizing the positions of S. Joubert and A. Gouldner.
60. Stanley K. Stowers, "Does Pauline Christianity Resemble a Hellenistic Philosophy?," in *Paul Beyond the Judaism/Hellenism Divide*, ed. Troels Engberg-Pedersen (Louisville: Westminster John Knox, 2001), 86.
61. Stanley Stowers, "The Religion of Plant and Animal Offerings versus the Religion of Meanings, Essences, and Textual Mysteries," in *Ancient Mediterranean Sacrifice*, ed. Jennifer Wright Knust and Zsuzsanna Várhelyi (Oxford: Oxford University Press, 2011), 37, 39, 40.
62. Dennis King Keenan, *The Question of Sacrifice* (Bloomington: Indiana University Press, 2005), 11–12.
63. Parker, "Pleasing Thighs," 118–19.
64. Ibid., 120.

between social equals in which "the bestowal of a gift places the recipient under an obligation to reciprocate,"[65] and benefaction between "a noble ... giver and groups of people"[66] of lower status, who are then, as Zeba Crook points out, "obligated to reciprocate by conferring honour, praise, gratitude and loyalty to a patron or benefactor."[67] This exchange between unequal parties is called general reciprocity.[68] Concepts of relating to Deity are often modeled on general reciprocity.

In classical Greece and in the Hellenistic societies that followed, sacrifice is linked with, and parallel to, the social systems of gift exchange and patronage. These social systems involved the balancing of self-interest with the interests of others, often more powerful others (patrons). Gods are patrons as well. Theophrastus notes the selfish motivation in religion when he says that "people sacrifice to honor the gods, to thank them, and to get something in return."[69] Plato critiqued the selfish motive in sacrifice; he has the shallow-minded aristocrat Euthyphro say, "It seems to me that reverence or piety is that kind of rectitude which is concerned with tendance of the gods," which Socrates ridicules by asking if it is the same as animal husbandry: "And in the same way not everyone knows how to tend dogs, but only the dog-trainer.... Isn't the effect of all tendance the same?"[70] Euthyphro is using the language of benefaction[71] when he says that sacrifice is a matter of "honour and esteem and ... gratitude."[72] Aristotle reasons that honor is that which humans prize most highly, so honor is what we give to the gods.[73] Aristotle (who is fundamentally a scientist, not a religious thinker) here articulates the common (but materialistic)

---

65. Zeba A. Crook, *Reconceptualising Conversion: Patronage, Loyalty, and Conversion in the Religions of the Ancient Mediterranean*, BZNW 130 (Berlin: de Gruyter, 2004), 64.
66. Ibid., 61.
67. Ibid., 64.
68. Ibid., 57–58.
69. Referring to Theophrastus, Περὶ εὐσέβειας 24.1-5, is Whitlark, *Enabling Fidelity to God*, 44n80.
70. Plato, *Euthyphro* 12E–13B; in *Plato: The Last Days of Socrates*, trans. Hugh Tredennick (Harmondsworth, UK: Penguin, revised, 1969), 36–37.
71. Whitlark, *Enabling Fidelity to God*, 44.
72. Plato, *Euthyphro* 15A; in *Plato: Last Days*, 40. The passage is rendered "honour and recognition and kharis" by Parker ("Pleasing Thighs," 121).
73. Aristotle, *Nicomachean Ethics* 1123 B17-21; Whitlark, *Enabling Fidelity to God*, 44.

religious reasoning of the ancient world. Socrates and Plato were more radical, trying to get people to realize that a *real* divinity would not have merely human motivations.

God's Favor in Jewish Culture

For the sacrificial mentality, when there is proper order and compensation, then one may hope to actually gain God's favor. Biblical characters and authors frequently worry whether they have found favor in God's sight (see Exod. 33:16; 34:9; Ps. 119:58). God tells the people,

> You shall keep my sabbaths and reverence my sanctuary. . . .
>
> If you follow my statutes and keep my commandments. . . . I will look with favor upon you. . . .
>
> But if you will not obey me . . . I will bring terror on you; consumption and fever that waste the eyes. (Lev. 26:2–3, 9, 14, 16)

The withdrawal of God's favor is fatal, and there is no middle ground; one is either favored or disfavored. Moses asks the Lord how he could know "that I have found favor in your sight, I and your people, unless you go with us? In this way, we shall be distinct, I and your people, from every people on the face of the earth" (Exod. 33:16). This is a request for God to favor Israel over other peoples, to take Israel as his "inheritance," to perform "marvels" such as driving out "the Amorites, the Canaanites, the Hittites" (Exod. 34:9–11).

Sacrifice is often the means for gaining that favor. This is seen much more clearly in the folksy Psalms and historical books than in the intellectualizing instructions in Leviticus, where motives and expectations are hardly mentioned. The Psalms are particularly useful for seeing the emotions and hopes that accompany sacrifice, and so will be the focus for this part of the study. This is another example of popular religion revealing more than strict orthodoxy does. The popularizing results of an official theology tell us how that theology was received and interpreted by the common people. Some of the

ATONEMENT AS COMPENSATION OR RECIPROCITY

Psalms reflect official and priestly views, but many of them frankly show the popular religion of Judah.

Sacrifice and God's Favor in the Psalms

The quest for God's favor is front and center in the Psalms. But it is more than just *favor*. It is God's *favoritism* that is sought. It is not everyone, but the "righteous" who receive God's favor:

> For you bless the righteous, O Lord;
> you cover them with favor [רָצוֹן, *rātsôn*] as with a shield. (Ps. 5:12)

Many psalms depict God taking sides, securing vengeance for those he favors.

> raise me up, that I may repay them.
> By this I know that you are pleased [חָפֵץ, *ḥāpaṣ*] with me. (Ps. 41:10–11)

There is anxiety about God's favor.

> Will the Lord spurn forever,
> and never again be favorable? (Ps. 77:7)

And those who benefit from God's favor must demonstrate their gratitude with public praise: "I will thank you in the great congregation" (35:18; cf. 111:1). More than that, it seems to be implied that worship helps to *secure* God's favor:

> Happy are the people who know the festal shout . . .
> they exult in your name all day long. . . .
> For you are the glory of their strength;
> by your favor our horn is exalted. (89:15–17)

Offering sacrifice, which demonstrates piety, helps to secure favor from God. The author of Psalm 26 lists the things he has done right, such as avoiding evildoers and circling the sacrificial altar (26:5–6). Sacrifice, then, is part of what qualifies him to ask that God

> Vindicate me. . . .
> Do not sweep me away with sinners" (26:1, 9)

41

The psalmist reminds God of his worshiping in the temple in verses 6, 7, 8, and 12. Ritual worship is one of his grounds for claiming to be innocent.[74] God should "be gracious [חָנֵּנִי, ḥannēni] to me" because "in the great congregation I will bless the Lord" (vv. 11–12).

The sentiment in Psalm 43 is similar. He pleads with God against his enemy (43:1–2), and then describes his worshiping in the temple, as though to establish the *right* to plead. Led to the altar by God's light and truth, he says, "I will praise you with the harp" (43:3–4). Worship empowers confidence in results, although the need to exhort his soul to "hope in God" (43:5) implies that the soul is not sufficiently hopeful yet. Prayer can signal both a perceived need for self-correction and a confidence that such correction will come, with God's help.

The author of Psalm 27 is more confident, even cocky.

> Though an army encamp against me,
>   my heart shall not fear. (27:3)

He desires above all else

> to behold the beauty of the Lord,
>   and to inquire in his temple. (27:4)

He is so full of confidence he seems to gloat:

> Now my head is lifted up
>   above my enemies all around me,
> and I will offer in his tent
>   sacrifices with shouts of joy. (27:6)

In a number of psalms, sacrifice is linked to deliverance, past and (hopefully) present. While pleading for protection from enemies (54:3), the author of Psalm 54 promises, "With a freewill offering [נְדָבָה, nədābâ] I will sacrifice to you" (54:6), and reminds God of past rescue (54:7).

Another psalmist recites God's rescuing actions, then vows:

---

74. This likely indicates that the author is a priest, according to Leopold Sabourin, *The Psalms: Their Origin and Meaning*, 2nd ed. (New York: Alba House, 1974), 323.

> I will come into your house with burnt offerings ['ōlâ];
>   I will pay you my vows [nēder],
> those that my lips uttered
>   and my mouth promised when I was in trouble. (66:13–14)

Deliverance is connected with fulfilling the vow. The occasion in Psalm 66 is public praise,[75] and sacrifice is central. The sacrificial promise made in verse 13 is reiterated in verse 15 with a twofold repetition of the verb 'ōlâ and five nouns: fatlings, smoke, rams, bulls, and goats. This is bragging; who could afford such exorbitant sacrifices?[76] It is a grandiose narrative that assumes that the more expensive the sacrifice, the more certain its effectiveness. But the moral ingredient is still important; deliverance is not contingent on sacrificing, but on his not "cherish[ing] iniquity in my heart" (66:18).

Another factor is the notion that human worship "will *add to the honour of Yahweh.*"[77] The promises with which some psalms finish, such as "In the presence of the faithful I will proclaim your name" and "All day long my tongue will talk of your righteous help" (Pss. 52:9; 71:24), show this perceived power of "blessing" God, which assumes a mutually beneficial relationship between God and worshiper. "'To bless' is to impart mental power, and is communicated in gift and greeting," Sigmund Mowinckel observes.[78] God is thought to need and desire this obeisance. The implicit agreement is that God will help the ardent worshiper. This adding to the honor of God could echo the behavior of the inferior party in a patronage arrangement, or the conciliatory strategy of a child who lives under the threat of moody parents.

We should consider the possibility that, in some psalms, sacrifices are based solely on gratitude, and are not seen as contributing to a

---

75. Erhard S. Gerstenberger, *Psalms, Part 2, and Lamentations*, FOTL 15 (Grand Rapids: Eerdmans, 2001), 30.
76. The expensive animals "transcends normal private capacities," and burnt offering, which leaves no meat to eat, "does not fit a private context" (Gerstenberger, *Psalms, Part 2*, 29).
77. Sigmund Mowinckel, *The Psalms in Israel's Worship*, trans. D. R. Ap-Thomas (Grand Rapids: Eerdmans, 2004), 1:233–34. The proclaiming of the name (52:9), the giving of thanks "in the great congregation," the tongue telling of "your righteousness . . . all day long" (35:18, 28) are examples of how the psalmists, unlike the priests, "rank the hymn above the sacrifice" (1:234).
78. Ibid., 2:33.

beneficial outcome. Are there some cases where sacrifice was not to *gain* God's favor but was rather to pour out thanksgiving after receipt of God's favor? The thanksgiving sacrifices of 107:22 and 116:17 arise from gratitude *after* God has healed and delivered (107:20–21; 116:16), has shown "his steadfast love" (107:15) or his "bounty" (116:12). The psalmist's assertions of past deliverance in Ps. 116:6–8, 12, are followed by the promise to pay his sacrificial vows, which is broadcast as publicly as possible:

> I will pay my vows to the Lord
> in the presence of all his people. (116:14; repeated in v. 18)

God did his part, now the worshiper does *his*.

> What shall I return to the Lord
> for all his bounty to me? . . .
> You have loosed my bonds.
> I will offer to you a thanksgiving sacrifice. (vv. 12, 16–17)

Although the deliverance precedes the sacrifice, the implication is that sacrifice goes along with deliverance.

The reforming Psalm 4 has noble aspirations. The hearer is admonished,

> When you are disturbed, do not sin;
> ponder it on your beds, and be silent.
> Offer right [ṣedeq] sacrifices,
> and put your trust in the Lord. (4:4–5)

It makes sense to see "right sacrifices" as consistent with patience, reflection, silence, and trust. These lead to the following culmination:

> You have put gladness in my heart. . . .
> [You] make me lie down in safety. (4:7–8)

Ritual is part of the life of faith for this author. Sacrifice is *parallel* to other expressions of faith. It does not persuade God; rather God uses the ritual to move the worshiper toward right and trustful attitudes. I call this a "reforming" psalm because "right sacrifices" are part of the quest for right living. This is not manipulative. John Eaton says, "Right sacrifices" means "sacrifices for making things right, for seeking peace."[79]

Critique by Prophets and Psalmists

I would return to some cross-cultural observations for a moment. Sacrifice often has self-interest at its base, but it is self-interest that is embedded in a system of customs, which includes concepts of fairness. At the crudest level, people use sacrifice as a way to buy favors or to placate temperamental gods; but as society increases in complexity, its theology develops beyond self-interest. There arise critics of this usage of sacrifice, who insist that the god cannot be manipulated. Under pressure of critique, the sacrificial concept undergoes reinterpretation.

It is precisely the notion of persuading God through gifts that was most offensive to religious intellectuals in Greek and Hebrew culture. Plato is disgusted with those who think that the gods "are influenced by sacrifices and supplications and can easily be won over."[80] These are the "worst and most numerous category—who hold that in return for a miserable sacrifice here and a little flattery there, the gods will help them to steal enormous sums of money."[81]

The most vivid critics are the Hebrew prophets. Amos has God saying,

> I hate, I despise your festivals. . .
> Your burnt offerings [*ōlôt*] and grain offerings [*minhōt*]. (Amos 5:21–22)

In fact, he attacks the whole idea that the sacrificial system originated with God: "Did you bring to me sacrifices and offerings the forty years in the wilderness? You shall take up Sakkuth your king, and Kaiwan your star-god" (Amos 5:25–26). He ends with a note of sarcasm.

Micah mocks the flamboyant practice of sacrifice, the quest for

---

79. John Eaton, *The Psalms: A Historical and Spiritual Commentary with an Introduction and New Translation* (London: T&T Clark, 2003), 71.
80. Plato, *Laws* 10.885C; in *Plato: The Laws*, trans. Trevor J. Saunders (Harmondsworth, UK: Penguin, 1975), 411; cf. *Republic* 390E–391A.
81. Plato, *Laws* 12.948C, Saunders, 498.

greater and more showy offerings, from "calves a year old" to "thousands of rivers of oil" to the costliest offering of all: "my firstborn for my transgression" (Mic. 6:6–7). The first chapter of Isaiah bitterly rejects the idea of God needing sacrifices. "I do not delight in the blood of bulls." "Bringing offerings is futile." "Your hands are full of blood" (1:11, 13, 15). Instead, you should

> cease to do evil,
>   learn to do good . . .
> defend the orphan,
>   plead for the widow. (1:16–17)

Good deeds are set in *contrast* to sacrificing.

Jeremiah matches the intensity of these critiques, saying it does no good to chant, "the temple of the Lord, the temple of the Lord," if one is oppressing the orphan and the widow (7:4–10). In fact, "in the day that I brought your ancestors out of the land of Egypt, I did not speak to them or command them concerning burnt offerings and sacrifices. But this command I gave them, 'Obey my voice'" (Jer. 7:22–23). He sets sacrificing in *opposition* to obeying. Further, he is critiquing the whole cult: "burnt offerings and sacrifices" stand for the cult as a whole.[82]

This rebellion against ritual is an expression of the prophets' moral and reforming zeal. Even such a defender of ritual as Mary Douglas admits that ritual is socially conservative, and that any "new viewpoint produces a revulsion against dead ritual. . . . Every conversion generates some anti-ritual feeling."[83]

What Rainer Albertz says seems obvious to me: "Amos, Micah and Isaiah fundamentally reject the cultic practice of their time because it covers up the social injustice."[84] Of course, the dispute in the texts is not *primarily* about ritual, but about reverence, ethics, and God's will. When a prophet or psalmist attacks the use of sacrificing as a cover-up for wrong behavior, the issue is the *wrong behavior*, but the immediate

---

82. Gary Anderson, "Sacrifice and Sacrificial Offerings (OT)," in *ABD* 5:882.
83. Mary Douglas, *Natural Symbols: Explorations in Cosmology* (New York: Pantheon, 1982), 145.
84. Rainer Albertz, *A History of Israelite Religion in the Old Testament Period*, vol. 1, *From the Beginnings to the End of the Monarchy*, trans. John Bowden, OTL (Louisville: Westminster John Knox, 1994), 171.

target is the cover-up. Hosea mocks the priestly consumption of the sin sacrifice, saying,

> They feed on the sin of my people;
>   they are greedy for their iniquity.
> חַטַּאת עַמִּי יֹאכֵלוּ וְאֶל־עֲוֺנָם יִשְׂאוּ נַפְשׁוֹ [ḥaṭṭaʾt ʿammî yōʾkēlû wəʾel-ʿăwōnām yiśəʾû napšô] (4:8)

But the reason is

> Swearing, lying, and murder,
>   and stealing and adultery. (4:2)

"The Lord does not accept" their sacrifices because of "their sins" (Hos. 8:13). God says,

> Though I write for him the multitude of my instructions,
>   they are regarded as a strange thing. (8:12)

Clearly, these are not *sacrificial* instructions that are being ignored.

When divine giving is understood as divine generosity, and not as God reciprocating what God supposedly *owes* people because of their offerings, there is usually no objection from religious intellectuals. It is selfish patronage, where the client *expects* payback for his sacrificial gifts, that arouses the objections of religious intellectuals in both the Greek and Hebrew traditions. The greatest minds have always been aware of the problem of conceiving of the gods in terms of selfish human relationships, where people act with manipulative motivations.

Manipulation is probably more well documented in Greece. Votive offerings were (and still are, in rural Greece) a highly visible way of expressing thanks for divine favors. "Hymnic praise ... was understood to place the deity under further obligations."[85] People wanted something in exchange for their expensive offerings. A frequently encountered phrase in the literature of votive offerings is *anth' hōn*, "ἀνθ' ὧν, 'in exchange for these things.'"[86] But Plato is

---

85. Whitlark, *Enabling Fidelity to God*, 46.
86. Ibid., 45.

outraged by those who think the gods "can be bought off," who "take everybody for fools ... promising to influence the gods through the alleged magic powers of sacrifices and prayers and charms."[87] He condemns those who are "calculating to win the favour of the gods on the quiet by sacrifices and prayers."[88]

Developmental psychology would suggest that all people fall somewhere along a *spectrum* of moral, social, and psychological development. One should not expect to find *either* entire honesty nor thoroughgoing dishonesty and disguising of motives. Biblical theology sometimes accepts all biblical texts as fully honest and their reports as undistorted. A psychological perspective can swing to the other extreme, assuming that all texts disguise selfish motives. Better to take a balanced approach, to recognize a range of motivations.

One could argue that a twenty-first-century person should not criticize the theology of a psalmist. But we can read *psalmists* who criticize the religious assumptions of other psalmists. In Psalm 40, receptivity to God is contrasted to sacrifice:

> Sacrifice and offering you do not desire,
>   but you have given me an open ear.
> Burnt offering and sin offering
>   you have not required. . . .
> I delight to do your will, O my God. (40:6, 8)

Psalm 50 ridicules a naturalistic God-concept.

> I will not accept a bull from your house. . . .
> If I were hungry, I would not tell you. . . .
> Do I eat the flesh of bulls,
> or drink the blood of goats?
> Offer to God a sacrifice of thanksgiving. (50:9, 12–14)

Here thanksgiving [תּוֹדָה, *tōdâ*] functions *in place* of sacrifice.

Psalm 51 is remarkable for its generosity; there is no attack on any enemies. The psalm is an ardent prayer for spiritual qualities: "truth

---

87. Plato, *Laws* 10.909B, Saunders, 445.
88. Plato, *Laws* 10.910A, Saunders, 446.

in the inward being," a "clean heart," a "right spirit," and a "willing spirit" (51:6, 10, 12). The author wants to "teach transgressors your ways" (51:13). The real sacrifice is a spiritual attitude, not a ritual action.

> if I were to give a burnt offering, you would not be pleased.
> The sacrifice acceptable to God is a broken spirit. (51:16–17)

The final verse of this psalm (v. 19) is almost certainly from a different author, as it contradicts the antisacrificial focus of verses 15–17.[89]

The main theme that accompanies antisacrificial expression in Psalms 40, 50, and 51 is a plea for spiritual receptivity, renewal, and joy. There is some minor attention to divine retribution in Psalms 40 and 50 (40:14; 50:16, 22), and more of it in Psalm 69 (vv. 4, 6–12, 18–28), but there is no retribution in Psalm 51. Psalms 40, 50, 51, and part of 69 are exceptional. Even the psalms near them do not follow their spiritual view, but represent the majority opinions: God chastises mortals (39:11); the righteous will gloat over the evildoer and take refuge in the temple (52:6–8), God will strike out at Zion's enemies and scatter their bones (53:5–6). But it is the minority voices that move theological thought forward, and the Bible preserves them for us.

> I will magnify him with thanksgiving.
> This will please the Lord more than an ox
>   or a bull with horns and hoofs.
> Let the oppressed see it and be glad. (Ps. 69:30–32)

Spiritual living can replace sacrificial thinking. In Ps. 51:17, a contrite heart *becomes* the sacrifice. In Ps. 141:2, prayer stands *in the place of*, or *amounts to*, sacrifice.

> Let my prayer be counted as incense before you,
>   and the lifting up of my hands as an evening sacrifice.

The implication is that sacrifice is demoted, since something *else* is able

---

89. Erhard S. Gerstenberger, *Psalms, Part 1, with an Introduction to Cultic Poetry*, FOTL 14 (Grand Rapids: Eerdmans, 1988), 214.

to do what the sacrifice was thought to do. "Surely, to obey is better than sacrifice" (1 Sam. 15:22).

Sometimes we cannot be sure of whether an author is anticultic. Paul's remark that he is being "poured out as a libation over the sacrifice and the offering of your faith" (Phil. 2:17) does not tell us anything about whether he believes in the literal practice of libations or offerings. It only shows that he thinks it makes a useful metaphor. Sirach's saying "One who keeps the law makes many offerings" (35:1) does not tell us what he thinks about literal oblations. But one can hardly fail to notice that the literal priesthood is *reduced* by the remark "You shall be to me a kingdom of priests" (Exod. 19:6). If priestly sanctity is spread throughout the population, then the priests have no exclusive holiness. To create a kingdom of priests is to publish the trade secrets of the priesthood.

The Debate about Sacrifice

It is not only modern intellectuals who dare to assert that some religious ideas and behaviors are more moral, more *true*, than others. Isaiah mocked the "familiar spirits that chirp and mutter" (Isa. 8:19), but when

> a spirit from on high is poured out on us. . . .
> Then justice will dwell in the wilderness,
>   and righteousness abide in the fruitful field. (32:15–16)

There is a constant debate going on between ritual correctness and moral values.

> When Ephraim multiplied altars to expiate sin,
>   they became to him altars for sinning. (Hos. 8:11)

> Sow for yourselves righteousness;
>   reap steadfast love . . .
> . . . seek the Lord. (Hos. 10:12)

In Greece, Israel, Iran, and India, we can see the emergence of critics, prophets, and sages who challenge the attempt to manipulate God with ritual. Hosea and Isaiah attack dishonesty; Zarathustra and Lao Tse question dominant religious practices; Socrates and Euripides attack shallow religious thinking. Many scholars today are dead set against allowing these teachers to be recognized as nonconformists. Writing from their secure positions, they do not want to hear that institutions can be a millstone around the neck of moral progress. It is as true today as it was centuries ago: a priestly Amaziah cannot tolerate a critical Amos; a politician like Creon cannot understand a rebellious Antigone, who would rather die than betray a religious principle.

In Israel and Judah, the debate goes on between different authors of the Psalms, and between some prophets and priests. Some authors attempt to synthesize competing ideas; the priestly prophet Ezekiel adds spiritual meanings to the idea of a temple-based religion (Ezek. 36:25–32; 40:5–47:14), and Joel uses numerous temple-related images in his buildup toward God pouring out spirit upon all flesh (1:13–14; 2:13–16, 28). By the time of Jesus and Paul, most Jews have a composite concept that joins some priestly cult-supportive values and some prophetic cult-critical viewpoints.

For some Jews, the debate became internalized, with cultic and prophetic values in dynamic tension with each other. We see this in the writings of the apostle Paul. He repeatedly uses cultic metaphors: "our paschal lamb, Christ, has been sacrificed. Therefore, let us celebrate the festival" (1 Cor. 5:7–8); he himself is "a minister of Christ Jesus to the Gentiles in the priestly service of the gospel of God, so that the offering of the Gentiles may be acceptable" (Rom. 15:16). Paul uses the cult metaphorically, but he never quotes an antisacrificial passage, and never lets on whether he supports the literal cult practice. He understands his own calling to be that of a prophet, alluding to Jer. 1:5 and Isa. 49:1 when he says that God "set me apart before I was born and called me" (Gal. 1:15).

In any sacrificing culture, it is a minority position that dares to criticize the practice of using sacrifice to gain God's favor. What is intriguing is that the minority view, after significant adaptation, can become the majority one, and this happened with the prophetic view.

The mainstream adopts the insight that what matters is not the ritual but the uprightness of the person. Deuteronomy adapts and recasts much prophetic thought, and many prophetic insights become standard by talmudic times. This demonstrates the ordinary progress of religious thought, a deepening that comes with centuries of reflection. Individual prophets give expression to a thought centuries before it will be generally accepted—actually, accepted *in part*. Prophetic thought is able to *partially* transform the mainstream religion, but it is also partially muffled when it is adapted, as when the book of Jeremiah is edited to support the Deuteronomistic project.[90]

The radical psalms encounter resistance even from scholars who appreciate what they are saying. For instance, Frederick Gaiser says that Psalm 50 indicates God "will not be controlled by manipulative sacrifice." Yet he says, "Never is sacrifice per se denounced in these psalms."[91] Is there no denunciation in the mocking remark, in Ps. 50:13,

> Do I eat the flesh of bulls
> or drink the blood of goats? (Ps. 50:13)

There is a widespread refusal to allow these psalms to be actually antisacrificial. Many professionals of today cannot tolerate the sharp prophetic attack on the religious professionals of another day. Sigmund Mowinckel claims that all the Psalms were uttered by cultic prophets, but this would make priest and prophet indistinguishable, John Hilber argues.[92]

The standard academic line now is that the sacrifice-critical remarks in psalms and prophets only criticize *wrong attitudes*, not sacrifice itself. This is correct as regards the *priestly* prophets, Ezekiel and Malachi, but it does not account for those attitude who say that God does not need sacrifice *at all* (Ps. 51:16; Isa. 1:13; Jer. 7:22), and it fails to appreciate the cutting remarks of Hosea, Micah, and Jeremiah. We need to let the

---

90. Rainer Albertz, *A History of Israelite Religion in the Old Testament Period*, vol. 2, *From the Exile to the Maccabees*, trans. John Bowden, OTL (Louisville: Westminster John Knox, 1994), 382–87.
91. Frederick J. Gaiser, "The David of Psalm 51: Reading 51 in Light of Psalm 50," WW 23 (2003): 391.
92. John W. Hilber, *Cultic Prophecy in the Psalms*, BZAW 352 (Berlin: de Gruyter, 2005), 7. The radical passages really are examples of "the prophetic rejection of sacrifice" (Hans-Joachim Kraus, *Theology of the Psalms*, trans. Keith Krim [Minneapolis: Fortress Press, 1992], 97).

individual writers have their own views. Regarding sacrifice, they do not all agree.

One of the more recent attempts to sweep the prophets into priestly service is that of Klawans, who argues that the prophets' use of symbolic actions (Jeremiah's wearing a yoke, Isaiah going naked and barefoot) proves that they were not antiritual: "A repeated symbolic action is hardly all that different from a ritual. This suggests to me that it is indeed unlikely that prophets categorically opposed ritual in general"; it is "biased" when there is any "distinction made between priestly 'ritual' and prophetic 'symbolic action.'"[93] But there is a *huge difference* between officially sponsored, institutional rituals, and nonconformist, socially critical actions. Klawans insists that the apparently radical passages are not antisacrificial, but only antiexploitation: "A number of the classic statements erroneously taken as 'rejections of sacrifice' are in context juxtaposed with expressions of concern over the economic exploitation of the poor," and he cites Amos 5:10–11; Isa. 1:17.[94] This is a false dichotomy. By no means does a concern with justice preclude hostility to the cult.

Klawans insists that cultic metaphor entails an affirmation of cult. He claims that Paul's use of sacrificial themes indicates "affirm[ation] of the fundamental theological tenets upon which ancient Jewish sacrificial worship is based. . . . Paul also speaks of the pleasing aroma of sacrifice sent up to God (2 Cor. 2:15; Phil. 4:18). . . . Paul affirms and even praises these notions."[95] This fails to distinguish between the literal and the metaphorical. When Paul speaks of a pleasing aroma sent up to God, he is using a recognizable image, but we do not know whether he believes that sacrificial smoke *really* rises to God. If I said that a certain actress casts a spell on the audience, putting people under her magical control, I am using a recognizable image (a spell)

---

93. Klawans, *Purity, Sacrifice, and the Temple*, 83, 98.
94. Ibid., 87.
95. Ibid., 220. See the critique in Stephen Finlan, "Spiritualization of Sacrifice in Paul and Hebrews," in *Ritual and Metaphor: Sacrifice in the Bible*, ed. Christian A. Eberhart, RBS 68 (Atlanta: SBL, 2011), 89–91.

with an associated a detail (magical control), but it does not mean that I literally believe in the magical power of spells.

Klawans presents much sound analysis and helpful clarifications, especially in his earlier purity book, *Impurity and Sin*. But his second purity book engages in lengthy and one-sided attacks on all "evolutionist" views,[96] condemning scholars who "insert ... distinctions between ritual and ethics" and "interiority and exteriority."[97] But to avoid any shade of evolutionist construction means refusing to notice the changes that occurred over time, and ignoring the debates that are taking place within the texts themselves.

The attempt to assimilate all of the prophets to the temple system is implausible. It is very misleading to speak of "the prophets' fidelity to both the temple and sacrifice"[98] (unless one specifies that one means Ezekiel, Joel, Haggai, First Zechariah, and Malachi). Klawans may be right to complain that some scholars still "place Jesus *against* ancient Judaism instead of *within* ancient Jewish disputes on matters cultic and moral," but here Klawans slips up by admitting that there really were cultic and moral disputes, even that there are "conflicts between disparate parties—priests and prophets in any age,"[99] and so he undermines his earlier denial of any real difference between priest and prophet.

I do not wish to deny that the prophetic texts eventually came to be used in Second Temple ceremonies, that texts written with "provocative sharpness" by "an outsider" could come to be recited "by the whole community assembled in worship,"[100] and so eventually become part of synagogue services as well. But the First Temple–period prophets really were as radical as they sound, and if their voices have not been muted by the editing to which they have been subjected, they will certainly not be tamed by modern scholars. You cannot turn Amos into an altar boy, or Hosea into a hierophant.

---

96. Klawans, *Purity, Sacrifice, and the Temple*, 29–32, 145–46, 247–48.
97. Ibid., 82.
98. Ibid., 226.
99. Ibid., 223.
100. Albertz, *From the Exile to the Maccabees*, 380.

ATONEMENT AS COMPENSATION OR RECIPROCITY

Reciprocity in the Hellenistic Period

"Hellenistic" refers to the Greek superculture that emerged after Alexander's conquests in the fourth century BCE, when Greek became the international language and Greek thought suddenly became available to numerous local cultures. The idea of being a "citizen of the world"[101] and "of humanity as a single family"[102] began to be discussed, thanks to the popular philosophies Cynicism and Stoicism. Even cultures that resisted Hellenism, or partly resisted it, like Jewish culture, were forever changed by their contact with Hellenism.

Reciprocity thinking is heightened in the Hellenistic period. The notion of "God who fulfills [גָּמַר, gāmar] his purpose for me" in Ps. 57:2 becomes in the Septuagint, "God who benefits/favors ... me [εὐεργετήσαντα με, euergetēsanta me]."[103] In contact with Hellenistic culture, Jewish texts take on more of the language of patronage and benefaction.[104] Χάρις and its cognates designate the ingredients of the patronage system: general beneficence, concrete favors, and grateful response, all of which can be seen in Rom. 5:2, 15, 20; 6:17; 7:25.[105] Paul would have "looked" like a "philosopher patron,"[106] a broker of salvation, to his gentile converts.

To some degree, the Bible reflects the patronage system, and to a very important degree it rejects patronage and offers a different ideology. Seth Schwartz argues that the Torah was opposed to reciprocity in human relationships; Israelites should be "slaves only to God."[107] Schwartz develops some interesting ethical implications of this, but leaves untouched the problem with simply transferring patronage to the God level, and thinking of God as a patron who receives gifts. It is likely that many people considered their expensive

---

101. Diogenes of Sinope, as recorded in Diogenes Laertius 6.63; in *Diogenes Laertius II*, ed. Jeffrey Henderson, LCL (Cambridge, MA: Harvard University Press, 1931), 65.
102. Rex Warner, *The Greek Philosophers* (New York: Mentor, 1958), 170.
103. Crook, *Reconceptualising Conversion*, 80.
104. Ibid., 79–80.
105. Ibid., 124, 134–43.
106. Ibid., 192. Crook agrees with scholars who see connections between Paul and Stoicism, and Paul and Cynicism (187–88).
107. Seth Schwartz, *Were the Jews a Mediterranean Society? Reciprocity and Solidarity in Ancient Judaism* (Princeton: Princeton University Press, 2010), 26.

SACRIFICE AND ATONEMENT

sacrificial offerings to be their "dues" or repayments to God, which would yield a return from God. Schwartz downplays the extent to which the Hebrew God is often treated as a patron who gives benefits, which is what causes the ethical "slippage" toward reciprocity that he notices.[108]

No Inducement in the Kingdom

When we read Jesus' advocacy for "justice and mercy and faith," for "mercy, not sacrifice," or his promise to "bring good news to the poor," are we aware that he is quoting the radical prophets (Matt. 23:23 [Mic. 6:8]; 9:13 [Hos. 6:6]; Luke 4:18–19 [Isa. 61:1–2; 35:5; 42:7])? In fact, I find him quoting twelve passages from Isaiah, Jeremiah, Hosea, and Micah (not counting duplications in the Synoptic Gospels).[109] These prophets and Jesus advocated a mature relationship with God that involved no inducement, no sacrificial magic. Love characterizes the relationship. The Old Testament contained wonderful invitations like "seek me and live" (Amos 5:4) and promises, such as that God "crowns you with steadfast love and mercy" (Ps. 103:4). But Jesus goes further, preaching God's love and kindness with unparalleled intensity. God is available to every widow, every child, every tax collector, every gentile, and need not be persuaded, "for it is your Father's good pleasure to give you the kingdom" (Luke 12:32).

And yet, Christian prayers continue to plead for mercy. We still seem to want to *persuade* God to be what Jesus said God *is*. We seem to constantly backslide from the prophetic insight that the "heart" is what matters. To what extent is Christian soteriology infected with the preprophetic thought that God's favor had to be induced with sacrifice, even with the "supreme sacrifice"? How hard is it to accept the fact that God never needed to be persuaded, that God is a loving parent who only wants us to grow and prosper, as any healthy parent does?

These are glass-half-empty questions, radical questions. Glass-

---
108. Ibid., 18.
109. Matt. 9:13 (Hos. 6:6); 10:35–36 (Mic. 7:6); 12:7 (Hos. 6:6); 21:13 (Isa. 56:7; Jer. 7:11); 23:23 (Mic. 6:8); Mark 11:17 (Isa. 56:7; Jer. 7:11); Luke 4:18–19 (Isa. 61:1–2; 35:5; 42:7); 8:10 (Isa. 6:9); John 6:45 (Isa. 54:13).

half-*full* questions would be these: Are we aware of how insistent was the evolution of Hebrew ritual away from manipulative motives, away from concepts of gift exchange, and—however gradually—toward the idea of worshipful communion with the God who needs no gifts, no dramatizations, no posturing, but only the enlightened appreciation of free and responsible worshipers? Are antisacrificial radicals like myself aware of how steady was the evolution in Jewish thought, both before and after the destruction of the Second Temple, toward the cultivation of "a broken and contrite heart" (Ps. 51:17)? Am I being fair to the sacrificial religion of Judah/Judea, recognizing that it *was* in process of changing, evolving?

3

Attachment, Cruelty, and Coping

It is necessary to pause between the exegetical chapters and spend a chapter on the basic psychological theories with which I am interacting, including my own theory, that of payment through suffering. If we gain some understanding of how people grow and adapt, how they learn to trust or to mistrust, we can begin to understand how people develop theologies that are based on trust or mistrust of God. Mistrust is usually unconscious and disguised through complicated theology, since the person usually cannot admit to mistrusting God. In Christianity, mistrust of God is often concealed beneath a theology that attributes all stern judgment and authority to the Father, and all mercy and kindness to the Son. But such topics will be put off until the chapters on New Testament authors. First we must look at the psychological theories.

I noted the likely presence of disgust as a psychological underpinning of purity systems, and of self-interested manipulation as the underpinning of sacrifice as compensation or payment. These underlying motivations play a big role, but they do not provide the whole story. Purity and sacrificial systems involve many symbolic and procedural details, which are developed through the religious imagination of the cultures concerned. Further, I would recall that Thomas Kazen speaks of a threefold emotional basis to purity systems: disgust, fear, and a sense of justice. The latter is not one of the causes of ritual behavior, in my opinion; it will always emerge in any social realm. But disgust and fear are psychological factors that help to *cause* ritual systems. And so I keep my antennae up to detect the presence of disgust or fear when I look at atonement-related texts. It is not that I am indifferent to justice, but justice represents a separate area of study.

At the end of the previous chapter, I said that Christians were still sometimes inclined to think that God's favor has to be induced, that God has to be persuaded. Where does this come from? I would say that it is a universal pattern, the product of uncertainty about parental love and reliability. This leads me to a discussion of attachment theory.

Attachment Theory

Attachment theory does not intend to be a separate field of study, or a theory in competition with other theories. From the very beginning, it sought to be an integrated theory that could adjust and adapt as new data and better suggestions emerged from clinical studies and experience. Attachment theory is really akin to, and possibly a subset of, developmental psychology, which also aims to be a broad-based and adaptable system of study of how humans grow and adapt. Many of the current leaders in attachment theory had their specialties in other fields: ethology (primate behavior), chemistry, language development theory, psychoanalysis, and child maltreatment psychology.[1]

Attachment theory focuses on the early child-parent relationship. The style of attachment, the *feeling* that develops in the child's experience, the level of trust and confidence the child develops, depends on the quality of attachment, the pattern of parental responses. Adult character and confidence owes an enormous amount

---

1. Mary Dozier, Melissa Manni, and Oliver Lindhiem, "Lessons from the Longitudinal Studies of Attachment," in *Attachment from Infancy to Adulthood: The Major Longitudinal Studies*, ed. Klaus Grossmann, Karin Grossmann, and Everett Waters (New York: Guilford, 2005), 316.

to the habits learned in infancy. But it is not a deterministic theory; it does not say that adult character is wholly determined by the infant environment. Nevertheless, the initial shaping of the child is highly influential on the character and emotional tone that develops in the child's life, and that helps to shape the relationships that the teenager and young adult will have.

Parents who are consistently available and interactive in a relaxed way create a pattern of *secure* attachment in their children. When there is secure attachment, "the infants showed a notable absence of anxiety in their mothers' presence.... They used their mothers as 'secure bases' for exploration."[2] "The availability of a secure base is the antidote to fear and anxiety."[3]

Parents who are inconsistently available and reliable, who are moody and unpredictable, create a pattern of *ambivalent* attachment in their children. Parents who are cruel and threatening cause the child to develop a more severe condition: *avoidant* attachment, where the child learns, "in the course of interaction with the mother," to be "angry, resistant" toward the mother; thus "infants can be classified as *securely* ... or *anxiously* ... attached to their mothers ... the anxiously attached infants can be further classified as *avoidant* ... or *ambivalent*."[4] A frequent and extremely harmful behavior by parents of avoidant children is their threatening to abandon the child as an attempted means of controlling the child's behavior. Parents who use such threats turn out to have been the victims of several kinds of threats in their childhood, threats of "separation.... Threats to kill the child, or threats that the child's behavior would lead to death of the parent."[5] The child who is thus threatened will feel extreme anger, but may

---

2. Mary Main, Erik Hesse, and Nancy Kaplan, "Predictability of Attachment Behavior and Representational Processes at 1, 6, and 19 Years of Age: The Berkeley Longitudinal Study," in *Attachment from Infancy to Adulthood: The Major Longitudinal Studies*, ed. Klaus Grossman, Karin Grossmann, and Everett Waters (New York: Guilford, 2005), 261–62.
3. Lee A. Kirkpatrick, *Attachment, Evolution, and the Psychology of Religion* (New York: Guilford, 2005), 65.
4. Mary D. Salter Ainsworth, "Attachment: Retrospect and Prospect," in *The Place of Attachment in Human Behavior*, ed. Colin Murray Parkes and Joan Stevenson-Hinde (New York: Basic, 1982), 7, with n2.
5. Pauline P. DeLozier, "Attachment Theory and Child Abuse," in Parkes and Stevenson-Hinde, *Place of Attachment in Human Behavior*, 105, 108.

learn to suppress any expression of anger for fear of precipitating the threatened abandonment.[6] Such suppression of feeling is extremely damaging, emotionally and psychologically.

Another study reports that children who develop avoidant attachment often grow into adults who habitually suppress and deny distress. They "'learned' that inhibiting attachment behavior ... was the best strategy for maintaining relationships with their own parents."[7] As adults, they may pretend that they do not need love.

The first founding figure of attachment theory was John Bowlby. "It was crucial to John to know what *really* went on between mother and child.... He takes issue with psychoanalysis for starting with a clinical symptom," and then hypothesizing about causes.[8] To this day, attachment theory is very much informed by observation and experience, and not driven by abstract hypotheses. The second key founding figure was Mary Ainsworth. Bowlby and Ainsworth observed the different patterns of adaptation that emerge, depending on whether there is secure attachment, ambivalent attachment, or avoidant attachment to the parents. Mary Ainsworth developed a "three-part classification system (secure, avoidant, and resistant/ambivalent)," to which some current authors have added a fourth category, "disorganized/disoriented."[9] Instead of "resistant/ambivalent," I use "ambivalent," as does Daniel Siegel: "I prefer to use the term 'ambivalent,' because it denotes the mixed and anxious feelings often associated with this form of relationship."[10] It is not as alienated and distant as avoidant attachment. Once again, regarding the causes: "The two insecure forms of attachment organization—detached *avoidance* and overtly anxious *resistance/ambivalence*—were related respectively to maternal rejection and unpredictability."[11]

6. Ibid., 109.
7. Main, Hesse, and Kaplan, "Predictability of Attachment Behavior," 292.
8. Robert A. Hinde, "Ethology and Attachment Theory," in Grossmann, Grossmann, and Waters, *Attachment from Infancy to Adulthood*, 3.
9. Main, Hesse, and Kaplan, "Predictability of Attachment Behavior," 250.
10. Daniel J. Siegel, *The Developing Mind: Toward a Neurobiology of Interpersonal Experience* (New York: Guilford, 1999), 100.

Mary Main wrote that in 2000. More recently, and while looking at the Adult Attachment Interview (AAI) and what it shows about adult psychology, she and some colleagues claim, "Following the advent of the disorganized infant attachment category and its AAI equivalent, unresolved/disorganized, the ambivalent category ... ha[s] become rare. This is because many individuals previously classified as insecure-ambivalent in infancy or preoccupied in adulthood have been found to be disorganized or unresolved."[12] I have not been converted to this view. It seems to me that "disorganized" is much more dysfunctional than "ambivalent." They show the weakness of their conflation of categories at the end of the quoted passage, when they admit to a distinction between "disorganized" and "unresolved," which, whether in plain English or in their technical terminology, are two *very* different categories. Someone who is fundamentally disorganized or disoriented is barely functional in real life, but someone who is unresolved may be highly functional but still struggling to find whom to trust and how to live. In their last sentence, "unresolved" corresponds to "ambivalent," in my view, which needs to be retained as a category separate from "disorganized." The ambivalent category is characterized by anxiety, and needs to be distinguished from "disorganized," which borders on dissociation and psychotic states. Alan Sroufe and his colleagues say that childhood "disorganized attachment predicted ... dissociation" in adulthood.[13] Further, Main was part of the team that observed some parents of disorganized children falling into "dissociative or quasi-dissociative states."[14]

I think the reason that Main and her colleagues are edging out the ambivalent category is they have shifted their attention to adult mental health. It is true that ambivalence does not usually remain throughout a lifetime; an adult tends to either gradually evolve toward

---

11. Mary Main, "The Adult Attachment Interview: Fear, Attention, Safety and Discourse Processes," *JAPA* 48 (2000): 1057.
12. Main, Hesse, and Kaplan, "Predictability of Attachment Behavior," 259.
13. L. Alan Sroufe, Byron Egeland, Elizabeth Carlson, and W. Andrew Collins, "Placing Early Attachment Experiences in Developmental Context," in Grossmann, Grossmann, and Waters, *Attachment from Infancy to Adulthood*, 53.
14. Main, Hesse, and Kaplan, "Predictability of Attachment Behavior," 282.

a secure mentality or to degrade toward a disorganized mentality. The young person develops an "internal model of attachment," but this changes in the course of living; "new relationship experiences have the potential to move individuals toward a more secure state of mind with respect to attachment."[15] Still, I think "ambivalence" remains useful for understanding anxiety in adults. It can be observed as an underlying attachment pattern that persists in life, manifesting in romantic and other social relationships, despite the many ways that these relationships differ from relationship to a parent.

Ambivalent and avoidant forms of attachment turn out to be extremely common from ancient times to the present. I had an ambivalent attachment to my mother, and consequently have experienced considerable anxiety in my life. My attachment to my father was fundamentally secure, but he was not present as often in my early life, so he is a *secondary* attachment figure. As is the case for most people, my primary attachment figure was my mother. My attachment to my father did act as a partial counterbalance to my mother's relative unreliability as an attachment figure. The social and peer relationships that come later in life are important but different, and need to be considered separately from the original attachment experience. My relationship with my father, like *all* important relationships in my life, had a big effect in shaping who I am. And my own reflection and choices play a huge role as well. But there is something uniquely influential about the first attachment experience.

What is the key factor in healthy parenting (what enables "secure attachment")? A recent study finds that the key is the parents having a concept of parenting as a sacred responsibility. Whether the parents are liberal or conservative, if they think of parenting as a "sanctified" calling, they will be able to interact in healthy ways with their children.[16] The key factor in parenting effectiveness is not doctrine, but the *spiritual* and *personal* attitude of the parents. A toxic attitude can

---

15. Siegel, *The Developing Mind*, 75.
16. Aaron Murray-Swank, Annette Mahoney, and Kenneth I. Pargament, "Sanctification of Parenting: Links to Corporal Punishment and Parental Warmth among Biblically Conservative and Liberal Mothers," *International Journal for the Psychology of Religion* 16 (2006): 284, 271.

lie behind a neglectful parenting style as surely as behind a style that involves threats and punishment.

Not surprisingly, parental ideas about God, as well as parental nurturing practices (or lack thereof), play a role in shaping children's God concepts. Research shows a correlation of "rejecting, authoritarian child-rearing practices" and the belief in a "more malevolent" deity.[17] Mothers with "a distant God concept" tended toward "more strict child-rearing practices, which in turn led to children's punishing God concept."[18] "Power-oriented discipline" moved girls to believe in a punishing God; punishment was "more detrimental for women's than for men's God concepts."[19] Interestingly, a boy's "sense of closeness to God" increases "when coupled with high levels of nurturance," even if the mother tends to be "punishing/judging."[20] It seems that the girl child is more affected by the mother's parenting style, while the boy child is more affected by the mother's *stated* expression of religious belief: "The child's interest in God is proportional to the mother's religious interest, particularly for boys."[21]

Intriguingly, and for both genders, "respondents with rejecting mothers (avoidant attachment) were most religious"; God was serving as a kind of "substitute attachment figure," according to some attachment theorists.[22] Similarly, God may be conceived in terms of the father who is "not as involved in their children's lives," perhaps because the child idealizes the less involved parent.[23] Attachment theory allows for God concepts to develop either from "correspondence" with beneficial parenting or from "compensation" for harmful parenting.[24] Thus conceptual development is complex.

---

17. Simone A. De Roos et al., "Influence of Maternal Denomination, God Concepts, and Child-Rearing Practices on Young Children's God Concepts," *JSSR* 43 (2004): 522.
18. Ibid., 531.
19. Jane R. Dickie et al., "Mother, Father, and Self: Sources of Young Adults' God Concepts," *Journal for the Scientific Study of Religion* 45 (2006): 59.
20. Ibid., 67–68.
21. Kalevi Tamminen et al., "The Religious Concepts of Preschoolers," in *Handbook of Preschool Religious Education*, ed. Donald Ratcliff (Birmingham, AL: Religious Education Press, 1988), 68.
22. Jane R. Dickie et al, "Parent-Child Relationships and Children's Images of God," *Journal for the Scientific Study of Religion* 36 (1997): 26.
23. Ibid., 42.
24. Dickie et al., "Mother, Father, and Self," 69.

Concepts can develop in response to a lack, or can grow out of an ideal (which itself was developed out of a mixture of parental presence and absence).

This is important to keep in mind as we turn our attention to an ideology of harsh parenting that increases the likelihood of children having to develop ambivalent or avoidant attachment.

The Legacy of Cruel Punishing

Psychiatrist Alice Miller has written about "poisonous pedagogy ... a tradition of child-rearing that attempts to suppress all vitality, creativity, and feeling in the child and maintain the autocratic, godlike position of the parents."[25] This *Schwarze Pedagogik*, or black pedagogy, was a soul-killing ideology, and it ended up taking over German society. It taught that children needed to be harshly disciplined, their wills broken, and their "obstinacy" and "exuberan[ce]" forcibly suppressed.[26] A certain J. Sulzer wrote a book admonishing parents to "drive out willfulness from the very beginning by means of scolding and the rod."[27] The parenting manuals called for the deliberate withholding of attention and even of food from infants, "for inculcating the 'art of self-denial' into infants."[28] It is doubtful whether this ideology really helps anyone learn self-control, but it certainly does succeed in crippling children emotionally. Of course, the children who go through such a brutal experience can only develop one of the anxious forms of attachment: either ambivalent or avoidant. This is not the end of the matter; they still have a chance of developing helpful adolescent and adult relationships, although they will experience difficulties, especially if they buy into the false ideology of strictness.

Versions of this same ideology still prevail in many parts of society, East and West. How common is it, when parents beat their children,

---

25. Alice Miller, *Thou Shalt Not Be Aware: Society's Betrayal of the Child*, trans. Hildegarde and Hunter Hannum (New York: Farrar, Straus & Giroux, 1984), 18.
26. Alice Miller, *For Your Own Good: Hidden Cruelty in Child-Rearing and the Roots of Violence*, trans. Hildegarde Hannum and Hunter Hannum (New York: Farrar, Straus & Giroux, 1983), 10.
27. Ibid., 11.
28. Alice Miller, *Paths of Life: Seven Scenarios* (New York: Vintage, 1998), 166.

to tell them that it is for their own good?[29] It is a falsehood, but one that the parents (themselves the victims of childhood violence) have come to believe. Usually what the child really learns is not obedience or self-control, but lack of empathy, even for themselves. They learn to suppress their feelings, "for to reveal their true feelings risked the loss of their mother's love."[30] We are taught to cultivate toughness, which is really a cold denial of feeling. "Lack of empathy for the suffering of one's own childhood can result in an astonishing lack of sensitivity to other children's suffering. When what was done to me was done for my own good, then I am expected to accept this treatment as an essential part of life and not question it."[31]

The children are taught to suppress their natural reactions to beatings and cruelty, and they learn to cooperate with their abusers. "Victims of child abuse would prefer *not* to know about their own victimization [out of] the desire to spare the parents, the desire to salvage a usable childhood, and the fact that the abuse itself has generated lasting negative feelings toward the child they once were."[32]

So there seem to be four main steps involved in swallowing the poisonous pedagogy: (1) being punished and mistreated; (2) having to suppress one's feelings about the mistreatment; (3) believing the treatment to be for one's own good; and (4) handing on this kind of parenting to the next generation of defenseless children. As people grow, however, they can halt this process at some point, although it takes the very difficult step of recognizing how damaged one is and repudiating the falsehood that accompanies the abuse. To a large extent, this means undoing step 2, being able to *speak* about one's pain and say that the mistreatment was wrong. This makes it easier, then, to reject steps 3 and 4.

Parents who cannot fully articulate how they were hurt, and have not recognized how wrong that treatment was, will mistreat their own

---

29. Miller, *For Your Own Good*, 16.
30. Donald Capps, *The Child's Song: The Religious Abuse of Children* (Louisville: Westminster John Knox, 1995), 5.
31. Miller, *For Your Own Good*, 115.
32. Capps, *Child's Song*, 18.

children, partly "out of an inner compulsion to repeat their own history,"[33] and partly out of a kind of twisted revenge. Of course, Hitler represents this phenomenon in its extreme stage. He parrots the *Schwarze Pedagogik* when he proclaims, "Whatever is weak must be hammered away.... Violent, masterful, unafraid, cruel youth is what I want."[34] He wanted to kill in others what had been killed in him. His politics arose out of his damaged selfhood. "The persecution of the Jews permitted [Hitler] to *persecute* the weak child in his own self that was now projected onto the victims. In this way he would not have to experience grief over his past pain."[35] Scapegoating begins at home: "The exploitation of this mechanism for political purposes would be impossible without this kind of upbringing."[36]

It seems that all of us, in differing degrees, have been under the spell of a poisonous doctrine about "discipline" and "control," and have cultivated our own tough exteriors to protect ourselves against a violent world. We all seem, to one degree or another, to be damaged by this false and cold-hearted teaching. Those who were most overwhelmed by this treatment are those who developed avoidant attachment. Those who developed ambivalent attachment are more capable of breaking out of this prison of false teaching.

A compassionate therapist can help trauma survivors learn to feel again, to realize that what was done to them was wrong. Even though this will awaken dormant anger, it will allow this emotion to *move*, to be processed, and the person can have normal feelings again. "Consciously experiencing one's own victimization instead of trying to ward it off provides a protection against sadism; i.e., the compulsion to torment others."[37] We really are not helpless victims, although we can *feel* helpless for a certain period of time.

Later in this book, I will make a connection between this matter of abusive "discipline" and one of the New Testament authors whom I

---

33. Miller, *For Your Own Good*, 116.
34. Miller, *Paths of Life*, 165.
35. Miller, *For Your Own Good*, 191.
36. Ibid., 90.
37. Ibid., 197.

will be considering. Next I want to develop my own theory about the psychological construct that underlies atonement.

Ideologies of Payment through Suffering

I draw on aspects of a number of authors and theories, but my own original theory is that at the basis of atonement theology is a pattern of *payment through suffering*, a strategy that children learn as a means of coping with parental inconsistency, rejecting, and bullying. This ideology is learned through experience; it is not innate, and it does not reflect the truth about God's attitude. Ideologies of payment through suffering arise out of the experience of children having to appease moody or violent parents by suffering punishments.

A theology that teaches that the wrath of God was averted by the sacrificial death of Jesus replicates the conditioned behavior of averting parental wrath by being seen to "take your punishment" (or have somebody take it *for* us). Punishments in such families often take a ritualized form. Children have to suffer a certain amount or for a certain period to "pay for" their infractions (or imagined infractions).

Children with ambivalent or avoidant attachment have learned mistrust. The idea that salvation required a sacrificial death is based on mistrust. It proceeds on the assumption that survival requires that someone be paid off. There is no other way to get by if "our God is a consuming fire" (Heb. 12:29). The children of tyrannical parents end up believing in atonement through suffering. The soterio-logic of atonement reflects this background in appeasing harsh parents.

I am building on what Sandor Rado found, but going further. The child is not just trying to win back the parent's affection, but has been taught that he must be *seen* to suffer in order to satisfy the parent. Children who experience punishment will yet seek to bond with the parent; in fact, "punishments" can "activate the attachment system."[38] People with ambivalent or avoidant attachment histories will find that certain atonement theories ring true, or sound strangely familiar.

---

38. Kirkpatrick, *Attachment, Evolution, and the Psychology*, 83.

One can even speak of an *ideology* of compensatory suffering, which develops in an environment of parental mistreatment and which becomes intellectualized in the doctrine of salvation from a wrathful God through a sacrificial death. The psychological ideology precedes and underlies the religious ideology. The religious ideology then reinforces the psychological pattern and transmits the ideology to the next generation through parental instruction and "discipline."

The religious ideology is destructive. The belief that divine violence was averted by a sacrificial payoff to God degrades one's moral sense and undermines the concept of divine justice. In this system, God is a hypocrite, demanding love and forgiveness but not practicing it, instead practicing retribution, and offering release only upon receipt of a payment in blood.

The biggest threat to Christianity is not any hostile external ideology or power, but the internal threat posed by a manipulative psychology of sacrifice, which turns God into a payment-demanding tyrant, a corrupt judge, or a temperamental spirit. Such materialistic thinking drags Christianity back to primitive religion (not to Judaism).

Christianity is in danger of losing its grip on monotheism whenever it assumes that a stern Father could extend salvation only after he had seen the ritual sacrificing of his gentle Son. Such a theology takes brutality for granted, revealing an underlying psychology of traumatic adjustment; the abusive parent is appeased through the suffering of a substitute (really a scapegoat). Often one of the children is singled out for particular punishment. Eric Bermann writes of families "routinely victimizing at least one of its weakest members—namely a child."[39] Such a "child is the logical, even ideal, repository for the accumulated frustrations, projections, and displacements of the parents"[40] who cannot—or *will* not—take responsibility for their own aggressiveness. I think such children learn how to endure suffering so as to satisfy the parents.

---

39. Eric Bermann, *Scapegoat: The Impact of Death-Fear on an American Family* (Ann Arbor: University of Michigan Press, 1973), 278.
40. Ibid., 281.

Not Your Fault

The emotional high point of the film *Good Will Hunting* is when cocky young Will and his unconventional psychiatrist, Sean, share some stories about how they were beaten by their fathers or foster fathers. Both are from South Boston, and have learned to be tough. Sean has said how he could tell from his father's approach that it was going to be a bad night, and he would provoke him to draw attention, "so that he wouldn't go after my mom or sister." Will offhandedly tops this story with his own story of being beaten with a wrench.

Will mentions his file, which Sean is holding, and asks, "What's it say in there? 'Will has an attachment disorder.' All that stuff? 'Inability to form relationships.'" Sean looks sad, and then says, "I don't know a lot, but you see this folder? All this shit? It's not your fault." Will says, "I know." Sean repeats it. Will says, "I know." Sean says, "No you don't. It's not your fault," and he goes on saying it, with real feeling. Will keeps saying "I know," and starts to back away. Sean won't stop saying it. Will shoves him, and says, "Don't fuck with me, Sean, not you." But Sean won't stop. Now Will's tough exterior breaks, and tears are coming down his face, then he explodes into crying. Sean hugs him, and says, "It's not your fault," one last time. After a while, he says, "Fuck them anyway."

Indeed, the deepest and most painful damage that most of us have suffered was not self-inflicted but was imposed by others in our environment, and it is not our fault. This is an insight that Christianity should have been able to utter but was not able to. Psychiatry was able to utter it, and some streams within Christianity are now catching up on that point. We need to be able to say that some people's deepest problem is not that they are sinful but that they have been *sinned against*, abused. There *are* people who need to be reminded that they are sinful, who are egotistical or judgmental, although they, too, might have been mistreated when young. Many people were damaged—really, *assaulted*—at an early age, and need to be told "Everything that's in your early childhood—it's not your fault!"

Certain people may need to be able to say, "I am sinful and I need God's grace or I will have no way of escaping my selfishness." These people find the sin-and-forgiveness doctrine helpful. For others, being told that they are sinners just perpetuates the abuse they have suffered. Jesus reaches out to both kinds of people in Matthew 9, both the sick and the sinner: "Those who are well have no need of a physician, but those who are sick.... For I have come to call not the righteous but sinners" (Matt. 9:12–13). For some people, the appropriate image is that they are *sick*. For others, *sinner* is what hits home. In either case, people can turn to the Great Physician. In both cases, people need to be aware of being in a condition of spiritual neediness. But one size does not fit all when it comes to spiritual psychology.

Shame-inducing theology is not appropriate for that large percentage of humankind who need recognition of the fact that people sinned against *them*. They do not need to be told that they are sinners, but rather that Jesus knows what they have endured, and what they are still going through. They need to have a sense of being "loved and valued."[41] *That* would be the gospel for *these* people! And they may need help with learning how to forgive themselves; although victimized, they may have learned to take the blame and to hate themselves.[42]

We must recognize the need of *individual people* when preaching the gospel. Jesus tailored his message to the individual people he met. He knew that the tax collector Zacchaeus needed to be shown some respect, some friendliness, and it changed that little man's life. But he needed *both* messages, since he was apparently sinning against people by overtaxing them. He said he would restore any excessive taxes that he had collected, with a penalty payment on top of that (Luke 19:8). But the first problem that Jesus addressed was that Zacchaeus was disrespected in his town, and Jesus changed his life by showing him respect and understanding.

---

41. Stephen Pattison, "Shame and the Unwanted Self," in *The Shame Factor: How Shame Shapes Society*, ed. Robert Jewett, with Wayne L. Alloway Jr. and John G. Lacey (Eugene, OR: Cascade, 2011), 25.
42. David M. Rhoads and Sandra Roberts Rhoads, "Justification by Grace: Shame and Acceptance in a County Jail," in Jewett, with Alloway and Lacey, *Shame Factor*, 90–91.

Jesus knew that the woman with an issue of blood had also been disrespected, had been treated as invisible. He called her forward, for everyone to see; "she came trembling," and Jesus said, "Daughter, your faith has made you well" (Luke 8:47–48; or, in the NAB, "has saved you"[43]), giving *her* the credit for her healing. *Her* faith had made her well. She may now "go in peace" (Luke 8:48). Healed and *visible*, not loathed and having to lurk around the edges of society, she can finally know some peace. These are examples of Jesus healing someone's shame, which is a much deeper problem than guilt. Shamed people feel damaged; they come *trembling*, but they leave in peace, restored, *seen*, and loved.

Our religious ideas are often shaped by what we learned in childhood, colored by our experience with our parents. Sometimes we adopt our parents' attitudes, and sometimes we reject them, fighting for our own individually held values. God is there, and Jesus' Spirit is there, to help us "fight the good fight of faith" (1 Tim. 6:12). This is the meaning of "work out your own salvation with fear and trembling" (Phil. 2:12)—it means do your best, follow your best judgment, knowing "God who is at work in you" (2:13). My point is that sometimes a person needs someone to recognize how difficult the road to maturity has been. People need some pastoral care. But how compassionate can our pastoral care be if our concept of salvation is full of threats and punishment?

A Case of Ambivalent Attachment

Of course, the more crude and ugly formulations of atonement are not in the Bible. But we would be whitewashing if we pretended that there is no linkage whatsoever. Ideas that occur in the Bible are later taken literally and turned into the grotesque doctrines that I have mentioned only briefly here. My area is biblical studies, and I would now return to that by looking first at Paul and then at Hebrews, the two main

---

43. "Saved" is actually more accurate, since the word is σέσωχεν, *sesōken*, the perfect tense of σώζω, *sōzō*, the verb for "save," which can also refer to becoming healthy, so "made well" is not completely off base.

sources of atonement teachings in the New Testament. In the following chapters, I will occasionally refer back to the theories mentioned here, but the theories can remain in the back of our minds as we look at the writings. The reader can use his or her own judgment and imagination to recall the theory while encountering the theology.

At this point, I will only add that I think Paul experienced ambivalent attachment as a child, and that it persisted into adulthood. Obviously, ambivalent attachment does not make one unfit for human society, incapable of brilliant thinking, or disabled from tender-hearted ministry. It only makes the road to maturity more tumultuous and some of life's transitions more drastic. It can lead to an intense separation from each stage as one moves on to the next stage. One "dies" to the previous life and is reborn to a new life (Rom. 6:4–8; 7:4); the old life seems like death "at work in our members" (Rom. 7:5). Whatever advantages one had before one now considers to be "loss" and "rubbish" (Phil. 3:7–8). Actually, I think it possible that most people in both Jewish and gentile cultures at that time grew up with ambivalent attachment, although most people did not experience such a profound life-transformation as Paul did. Further, the psychological literature suggests that the person with an ambivalent attachment pattern is "most likely to turn to God to meet attachment needs," while the person with secure adult relationships does not have a burning need for God, and the avoidant person has little desire for a close relationship.[44]

Evidence for the allegation of ambivalent attachment is found in anxiety of conscience. It is not just Paul who felt deceived by sin (Rom. 7:11), incapable of doing right (Rom. 7:18, 23), and condemned by the law (Rom. 3:7)—at least until Christ delivered him "from the law of sin and death" (Rom. 8:2).

I will revisit Paul's psychology only at the end of the following chapter; first it is necessary to engage in some basic exegesis, especially of Paul's use of sacrificial and other cultic metaphors.

---

44. Kirkpatrick, *Attachment, Evolution, and the Psychology*, 139–40. Quote is on 140.

4

Rescue and Disgust in Paul

I begin by showing how "sacrifice" has been redefined over time. The original setting in ritual slaughter and blood-sprinkling is undetectable in today's usage of "sacrifice."

The Abstraction of Sacrifice in Paul's Theology

The modern concept of "sacrifice" is the product of a long evolution in the direction of continued abstraction and moralizing, so that "sacrifice" is now very far removed from its original cultic setting. Now we say that soldiers sacrifice their lives, parents sacrifice their time for their children, and athletes sacrifice comfort in order to train diligently. "Sacrifice" now signifies effortful self-giving involving some loss or pain.[1] Gift exchange and purification are no longer discernible in the way the term is used.

The element of self-giving was already being stressed by Greek playwrights and Jewish Maccabean authors who used sacrificial imagery to illustrate the acts of martyrs. The connection with

---

1. "Sacrifice is thus a symbolic action signifying self-donation" (Robin Stockitt, *Restoring the Shamed: Towards a Theology of Shame* [Eugene, OR: Cascade, 2012], 112).

SACRIFICE AND ATONEMENT

martyrology was heightened by Paul: "one has died for all" (2 Cor. 5:14); "weak believers for whom Christ died" (1 Cor. 8:11); "died for us" (Rom. 5:8; 1 Thess. 5:10). Beyond the heroic self-giving for the benefit of others, there is eternal soteriological (saving) meaning ascribed to Jesus' death. The "sacrifice" of Jesus is pictured as more meaningful than the death of any previous martyr, and more far-reaching than the animal sacrifices with their temporary and local results.

When Christians today read the words of Paul, that God put Christ forward as the new place of atonement "in his blood" (Rom. 3:25), they hear this metaphor differently than the people of Paul's time heard it. Paul's audience would have understood him to be picturing Christ as the new mercy seat (see "The Cultic Moment at the New Mercy Seat," below), or (in Rom. 8:3) a more perfect purification offering than those presented in the Jewish cult. They would have understood Christ as accomplishing the purification and reconciliation that the cult was believed to accomplish. The literal cult was superseded, but the cultic *idea* was perpetuated.

Due to a strong current resistance to the word *supersession*, it is necessary to make the important distinction between *ideational* supersession and *ethnic* supersession. I do not see Paul or Hebrews teaching ethnic supersession: they did not say that the gentiles had replaced the Jews. But they *do* repeatedly present *ideational* supersession—certain realities (the Messiah as mercy seat, the Christian community as a new "temple," 1 Cor. 3:16) are superseding other realities (the literal mercy seat and the Second Temple). The sacrificial image implies that Christ's death accomplished either purification from sin or compensation for human sinning.

When Paul speaks of Jesus dying as a sin offering or a Passover offering (Rom. 8:3; 1 Cor. 5:7), he is preserving the *logic* of cult, even the suggestion of *magical effectiveness* that cult implies, but the concept of sacrifice has been transformed, and is taken metaphorically (of course, the Hebrew system did not allow human sacrifice). Cultic thinking is not transcended but abstracted, spiritualized; it is an apotheosis of cult. Salvation comes through the new, *abstract* significance, which will include some old and some new concepts. We have to look closely at each passage and at the surrounding material to see what is being communicated.

It is important to remember that the cult of Judah (like that of other cultures) was *national*, and to remember how radical the change suggested by Paul was, to have a cultic idea that was universal, not national. Of course, universalistic thinking was already emerging as a (strong) minority position within Judaism, most vividly expressed in Second and Third Isaiah. Paul is affirming the universal when he asks, "Is God the God of Jews only? Is he not the God of Gentiles also?" (Rom. 3:29), just as Jesus had when he said, "In no one in Israel have I found such faith" as he found in a certain Roman (Matt. 8:10). Paul preaches God's open offer of salvation to Jews and gentiles alike; the offer is "to everyone" (Rom. 1:16; cf. 3:22). Part of what a purity system does is codify a feeling of disgust for foreigners. It would have been impossible to promote the universal availability of salvation while maintaining the national cult.[2] The metaphorical "sacrifice" of Christ has universal, not national, significance.

When Paul uses the images of the Jewish cult, he is using the logic of *superseded* cult. But the logic is still cultic, and it is accompanied by a new, literal cult (Eucharist and baptism). It is not just the death of Christ that is pictured in cultic terms. Paul also can speak of "the Christian life as a λογικὴ λατρεία,"[3] *logikē latreia*, which is the "spiritual worship" of Rom. 12:1, or more literally, "logical service."[4] Paul is speaking of enlightened worship with a term that is encountered in both Jewish and gentile religious thought.[5]

---

2. Walter Houston, *Purity and Monotheism: Clean and Unclean Animals in Biblical Law*, JSOTSup 140 (Sheffield: Sheffield Academic, 1993), 279.
3. W. D. Davies, *Paul and Rabbinic Judaism: Some Rabbinic Elements in Pauline Theology*, rev. ed. (New York: Harper, 1948), 239.
4. Colin Gunton, "The Sacrifice and the Sacrifices: From Metaphor to Transcendental?," in *Trinity, Incarnation, and Atonement: Philosophical and Theological Essays*, ed. Ronald J. Feenstra and Cornelius Plantinga Jr. (Notre Dame: University of Notre Dame Press, 1989), 222.
5. Gentile: *Corpus Hermeticum* 13.19 ("rational sacrifice," Everett Ferguson, "Spiritual Sacrifice in Early Christianity and Its Environment," in *ANRW* 23.2:1154); Jewish: Testament of Levi 3.6 ("a rational and bloodless oblation"; *OTP* 1:789).

Conflation with Martyrdom

As seen in the chapter 1 section "Atonement Ideas in the Hebrew System," forgiveness is part of what the sacrificial cult was thought to achieve; otherwise sacrifice would have no power as a metaphor of salvation. When the notion of martyrdom (or "noble death") is added to cultic imagery, it activates a range of religious emotions. The solemn emotions associated with holiness are joined with the moral and tragic emotions aroused by the heroic death of a martyr.

Noble death was a main theme in Greek literature, and it was expressed through cultic metaphors in the plays of Sophocles and Euripides. In one of the latter's plays, Iphigenia says that she is dying for Greece: "Sacrifice me, sack Troy. That will be my monument for long ages. . . . Lead me to the altar to sacrifice."[6] Plato pictures Socrates as a martyr for Law, refusing to be broken out of jail because that would be a betrayal of the laws of Athens.[7]

We see a linkage of martyrology and *Jewish* sacrificial metaphor in 2 and 4 Maccabees. There, martyrs give speeches expressing the vicarious saving effect their deaths will have in ways that seem to anticipate Pauline thought: "Be merciful [ἵλεως γενοῦ, *hileōs genou*] to your people, and let our punishment suffice for them. Make my blood their purification, and take my life in exchange for theirs" (4 Macc. 6:28–29). The courageous self-giving of the martyrs saves the nation: "Because of them our enemies did not rule over our nation, the tyrant was punished, and the homeland purified—they having become, as it were, a ransom for the sin of our nation. And through the blood of those devout ones and their death as an expiation [ἱλαστήριον, *hilastērion*], divine Providence preserved Israel that previously had been afflicted" (4 Macc. 17:20–22). The vicarious saving power of martyrs' deaths is expressed through the language of sacrifice, with an emphasis on payment (ransom) and substitution (my life for theirs).

---

6. Euripides, *Iphigenia at Aulis* 1398–99, 1555; from Moses Hadas and John McLean, *Ten Plays by Euripides* (New York: Bantam, 1960), 348, 352.
7. Plato, *Crito* 50A–52E. See Barbara E. Reid, *Taking up the Cross: New Testament Interpretations through Latina and Feminist Eyes* (Minneapolis: Fortress Press, 2007), 27.

Sacrifice and martyrdom are conflated, and understood to be substitutionary.[8] Similarities between the atoning deaths in 4 Maccabees and Romans 3 are intriguing, but, since 4 Maccabees may have been written a few decades later than Romans, no compelling argument can be made for a literary influence in either direction.[9]

I see the Maccabean martyr stories as exotic fantasies based on the underlying psychology of manipulative atonement; I recall the observations of Sandor Rado: "Self-punishment takes place in the hope of absolution."[10] "He is reprimanded, must make a confession, take his punishment, promise never to do it again and ask for forgiveness."[11] Only, for the martyr there is no "again," no second chance. The forgiveness that he gains is for others. It is a perfect fantasy: projecting one's fear of punishment onto a literary hero, imagining the hero suffering a terrible punishment but not having to suffer it oneself, instead gaining the atonement that his suffering brings.

Cultic Concepts and Salvation

Paul draws on some of the same emotions and concepts as the Maccabean literature, but has crucial new themes, the most obvious being Christology, forgiving love, and (potentially) universal salvation.

The real significance of the sacrificial cult for Paul is its role as *promise*, a prefiguration of salvation. As a *type*, it is important; as a rite—not so much. The implication is that the sacrificial system was not fully effective, though Paul never actually says that. But one could say that he makes the cultic metaphor *more real* than the cultic practice. Of course, Christianity also generates a new cult (primarily the Eucharist) that is given sacrificial meaning and even has *literal spiritual* force. People in Corinth who observed it without sufficient seriousness or

---

8. Jarvis J. Williams, *Christ Died for Our Sins: Representation and Substitution in Romans and Their Jewish Martyrological Background* (Eugene, OR: Pickwick, 2015), 86–95, 135.
9. Douglas A. Campbell, *The Deliverance of God: An Apocalyptic Rereading of Justification in Paul* (Grand Rapids: Eerdmans, 2009), 648–49.
10. Sandor Rado, "The Problem of Melancolia," in *Psychoanalysis of Behavior: The Collected Papers of Sandor Rado*, vol. 1, *1922–1956* (New York: Grune & Stratton, 1956), 51.
11. Sandor Rado, "Rage, Violence, and Conscience," in *Psychoanalysis of Behavior: The Collected Papers of Sandor Rado*, vol. 2, *1956–1961* (New York: Grune & Stratton, 1962), 148.

worthiness got ill and even died (1 Cor. 11:27–30). This takes the power of the Eucharist literally, but not as literally as Ignatius of Antioch, writing about fifty years later, who will call the Eucharist "the medicine of immortality, and the sovereign remedy by which we escape death," and will warn, "There is judgment in store even for the hosts of heaven . . . if they have no faith in the blood of Christ."[12] Threat and literal-mindedness seem to go together.

Paul is content to let the cultic symbol be powerful and suggestive without drawing allegorical meanings from numerous material aspects of the cult (as Hebrews does) or pushing it into a literalizing reading (as Ignatius does). Even Paul's reading in 1 Corinthians 11 is mainly ethical: do not come to the Lord's supper drunk, or show off your wealth (11:21). Paul suggests that Christ died as a sacrificial martyr, with a cleansing/forgiving overflow that benefits others. He feels no need to explain the cultic logic. A combined martyrdom-sacrifice concept was already widespread enough that he could use it, and people would understand.

Paul's teachings are directed toward moral and spiritual progress, and the formation of a spiritual and ethical community. Yet when it comes to describing the soteriological moment, he usually chooses either judicial or cultic imagery, or both. The term "blood" certainly signals a death, probably a sacrificial one (Rom. 3:25; 5:9; 1 Cor. 10:16; 11:25–27). However, the crucifixion is not all-sufficient; the resurrection is also a necessary part of the salvation formula (Rom. 4:25; 5:10; 1 Cor. 6:14; 15:4).[13]

It is never made clear which aspect of sacrifice, purification or compensation, Paul has in mind. There is plenty of space for the reader's own interpretation.

---

12. Ignatius, *Eph.* 20.2; *Smyrn.* 6.1. From Maxwell Staniforth, ed. and trans., *Early Christian Writings*, rev. Andrew Louth (London: Penguin, 1987), 66, 102.
13. Elliott argues that Paul considered the expiatory death "by itself to be inadequate and potentially misleading" (Neil Elliott, *Liberating Paul: The Justice of God and the Politics of the Apostle* [Maryknoll, NY: Orbis, 1994], 128).

The Cultic Moment at the New Mercy Seat

Sacrificial metaphors occur at key moments in Paul's soteriological passages. None is more important than the extended metaphorical passage in Romans 3, where he refers to Jesus as ἱλαστήριον, *hilastērion*. Paul is here forming a metaphor out of the Day of Atonement ritual. Let us begin with the NRSV rendering of these verses, even though it will be necessary to correct a serious translation mistake found there: "All have sinned and fall short of the glory of God; they are now justified by his grace as a gift, through the redemption that is in Christ Jesus, whom God put forward as a sacrifice of atonement by his blood, effective through faith" (Rom. 3:23–25a).

Daniel Bailey has successfully shown that the NRSV and NIV mistranslate ἱλαστήριον when they render it "sacrifice of atonement," a translation driven more by doctrine than by good lexical work. In ancient Jewish or gentile Greek literature, "ἱλαστήριον never denotes an animal victim in any known source."[14] As explained in chapter 1, in the Septuagint the ἱλαστήριον (or כַּפֹּרֶת, *kappōret* in Hebrew) is the mercy seat[15]—the gold lid or top piece of the ark of the covenant, housed in a forbidden room, the Most Holy Place, in the wilderness tabernacle (probably standing for the Jerusalem temple). The ark (or *box*) of the covenant is said to contain the tablets of the law (Exod. 25:21; Deut. 10:5). The ark of the covenant was taken by the conquering Chaldeans when the temple was destroyed in 586 bce, but even when it was physically present in the Most Holy Place, it was only seen by the high priest. There was no ark physically present during the Second Temple period, but that hardly matters since most Israelites only heard about it or read about it but never saw it; it either was present—or was *no longer* present—in a forbidden room.

The purification ceremony on Yom Kippur (Day of Atonement) is the

---

14. Daniel P. Bailey, "Jesus as the Mercy Seat: The Semantics and Theology of Paul's Use of *Hilasterion* in Romans 3:25," *TynBul* 51 (2000): 156.
15. As noted in chapter 1, "mercy seat" has become a recognized technical term for the *kappōret*; the English term was coined by William Tyndale, who translated it from Luther's *Gnadenstuhl* (Daniel P. Bailey, "Jesus as the Mercy Seat: The Semantics and Theology of Paul's Use of *Hilasterion* in Romans 3:25" (PhD diss., Cambridge University, 1999, 6 §7, 174–75).

most important ritual activity of the year. The high priest would enter the Most Holy Place on Yom Kippur to sprinkle sacrificial blood on the *hilastērion*, to cleanse the temple from the worst of the impurity that had accumulated during the year. Thus Paul's metaphor does fit within the sacrificial arena, since the *hilastērion* is the geographic center of the sacrificial cult. But to translate it "sacrifice of atonement" (NRSV, NIV) is to follow popular atonement thinking rather than to accurately translate the word.

In Rom. 3:25, Paul follows *hilastērion* with two prepositional phrases: διὰ [τῆς] πίστεως, *dia [tēs] pisteōs*, "through faith," and ἐν τῷ αὐτοῦ αἵματι, *en tō autou haimati*, which could mean "in his blood" (NASB) or "by his blood" (NRSV). Thus we have the difficult construction ὃν προέθετο ὁ θεὸς ἱλαστήριον διὰ [τῆς] πίστεως ἐν τῷ αὐτοῦ αἵματι. If we connect the two prepositional phrases, we get the implausible and unparalleled phrase "faith in his blood." It is more likely that διὰ πίστεως should be linked with ἱλαστήριον, yielding a noun phrase like "a mercy seat of faith." Bailey suggests that "the ἱλαστήριον of the age of faith or the ἱλαστήριον accessed by faith,"[16] while the blood phrase "reads better with the verb."[17]

Why an "age" of faith? Paul frequently implies a sharp divide between the old age and the new age, as when he condemns "the present evil age" (Gal. 1:4) or says "now that faith has come" (Gal 3:25), or speaks of a "new covenant . . . of spirit. . . . The greater glory" (2 Cor. 3:6, 10). Thus, as he frequently does, Paul is contrasting the new, spiritual way with the old, fleshly way.

I offer my own correction to the NRSV of Rom. 3:24–25a, with my words in brackets: "They are now justified by his grace as a gift, through the redemption that is in Christ Jesus, whom God put forward as a [mercy seat of] faith, [by means of] his blood." Frank Matera suggests: "whom God publicly displayed as a mercy seat—appropriated through faith—by his blood (3:25a)."[18]

---

16. Ibid., 7 §1, 177.
17. Ibid., 7 §2.8, 203.
18. Frank J. Matera, *Romans*, Paideia (Grand Rapids: Baker Academic, 2010), 98.

We should take a look at the cognates of ἱλαστήριον, even if we prefer (as I do) a concrete translation of ἱλαστήριον in Rom. 3:25. Semantic range is always relevant. The ἱλασ- word group suggests a situation where someone is made ἵλεως, "propitious" or "appeased." God is supplicated to "be merciful" (ἵλεως γενοῦ) in LXX Exod. 32:12; Amos 7:2; Deut. 21:8 (cf. ἱλάσθητι, *hilastheti*, in Luke 18:13). The plea for propitiation or mercy seems to be inherent in the base meaning of ἱλασ- words. The meaning of the verb ἱλάσκομαι, *hilaskomai*, and its compound ἐξιλάσκομαι, *exilaskomai*, is "appease" or "propitiate," although in Levitical passages where the word translates כפר, the best translation is "purge."[19] And so a general meaning for ἱλαστήριον, based on etymology, is "place of atonement" or "place of propitiation." T. W. Manson makes a plausible case that the (concrete) "mercy seat" image is used in Rom. 3:25 to assert that Christ is the new (abstract) place of atonement.[20] Gordon Fee argues that the word refers both to "the 'place' of atonement" and to the "mercy-seat."[21]

Bailey emphasizes that ἱλαστήριον is not reducible to an active verb; it is a place noun specially coined by Jews to refer to the mercy seat, just like θυσιαστήριον, *thysiasterion*, was unquestionably coined by Jews (and not borrowed by pagans) to refer to an Israelite altar as a "place of sacrifice."[22] Hence, the biblical ἱλαστήριον does not expiate, but is the *place* where expiation occurs, just as a θυσιαστήριον does not sacrifice, but is a place where sacrificing occurs, and as an auditorium does not hear, but is a place where hearing occurs.

Bailey argues that the usage of ἱλαστήριον in Greco-Roman sources arose independently from its specific use in the Septuagint; in standard Greek usage, ἱλαστήριον means "durable votive offerings to the pagan deities"[23] or "propitiatory gift or offering."[24] The occurrence in 4 Macc.

---

19. Dirk Büchner, "Ἐξιλάσασθαι: Appeasing God in the Septuagint Pentateuch," *JBL* 129 (2010): 237–38.
20. T. W. Manson, "'ILACTHRION," *JTS* 46 o.s. (1945): 4.
21. Gordon D. Fee, "Paul and the Metaphors for Salvation: Some Reflections on Pauline Soteriology," in *The Redemption: An Interdisciplinary Symposium*, ed. Stephen T. Davis, Daniel Kendall, and Gerald O'Collins (Oxford: Oxford University Press, 2004), 58.
22. Daniel Bailey has directed my attention here to J. A. L. Lee, *A Lexical Study of the Septuagint Version of the Pentateuch*, SBLSCS 14 (Chico, CA: Scholars Press, 1983), 52.
23. Bailey, "Jesus as the Mercy Seat," *TynBul*, 156. (The article has the exact same title as the dissertation, so the article must be signified by showing the journal name.)

17:22 ("their death as a propitiatory offering," ESV) is an example of standard Greek usage: a votive offering or memorial; another Jewish writer following this sense is Josephus, *Antiquities of the Jews* 16.182, where Herod, out of the fear of God, erects a marble monument as a ἱλαστήριον. While I accept Bailey's lexicographic judgment that the concrete "mercy seat" (a place, not an instrument) is Paul's meaning, I think that semantic range and etymology are still relevant. There is a propitiatory background to the Pauline and Septuagint usage of ἱλαστήριον. There is a reason the Septuagint translators chose to use a term that, etymologically, signifies "place of propitiation": God is made propitious at the mercy seat. Propitiation is in the shared semantic background of both Septuagint and pagan occurrences of ἱλαστήριον.

Let us look closely at what Paul is saying about salvation in 3:24–25. Is there anything in the *sequence* of terms that reveals anything? Justification happens "through the redemption that is in Christ Jesus," which seems to say that justification follows redemption. Redemption seems to be synonymous with Christ's being put forward as a mercy seat of faith, and justification then follows. "Justified" means literally "made to be just," but in actual usage it means "acquitted" or "pardoned" in a court of law. Scholars have sometimes spoken of acquittal, but since that could imply actual innocence, it is more accurate to say that Paul is speaking of a pardon,[25] or perhaps not having to face any charges at all, since a powerful patron shields us: since Christ "intercedes for us," no one would dare to "bring a charge against" us (Rom. 8:33–34).

Paul is linking several metaphors when he says people are justified through the redemption payment that is Christ's death as the new mercy seat. The cultic death has a judicial (pardon) and economic (redemption) effect. *How* is the mercy seat effective? Through his

---

24. Bailey, "Jesus as the Mercy Seat," *TynBul*, 157–58. Bailey credits this definition to LSJ, s.v. ἱλαστήριος, "II. ἱλαστήριον ... 2. *propitiatory gift* or *offering*." For recent debates, see Alexander Weiss, "Christus Jesus als Weihegeschenk oder Sühnemal? Anmerkungen zu einer neueren Deutung von *hilasterion* (Röm 3,25) samt einer Liste der epigraphischen Belege," *ZNW* 105 (2014): 294–302 (citing Bailey as disagreeing with the votive offering interpretation, 296n6), and the response by Stefan Schreiber, "Weitergedacht: Das versöhnende Weihegeschenk Gottes in Röm 3,25," *ZNW* 106 (2015): 201–15.
25. Fee, "Paul and the Metaphors for Salvation," 66.

blood, through his redemption payment, or through our faith? *Yes.* All are correct. Christ's death is a sacrifice, a redemption payment, something that grants pardon, and it must be grasped by our faith.[26] The sacrificial death (a cultic idea) has a redemptive and pardoning result. Several realms are brought together, but it does seem that the cultic image (ἱλαστήριον) is the center of gravity. Salvation takes place at the (metaphorical) cultic location.

Paul is showing both some continuity and some discontinuity with the Jewish cult. He is distancing himself from the *literal* cultic practice, but retains the cultic *concept*. The blood sprinkling at the new ἱλαστήριον leads to either purification or propitiation, so we have "obtained access to this grace" and had "the wrath of God" averted (Rom. 5:2, 9). The death is effective in *cultic, judicial,* and *personal* ways.

The great mid-twentieth-century scholar C. H. Dodd argued that the sacrificial metaphor stood for expiation (cleansing), not propitiation (appeasement). God himself "set forth a means of expiation," so "the sacrifice of Christ" is not "a means of soothing an angry Deity."[27] However, Paul elsewhere says if we "obey not the truth ... there will be wrath and fury" (Rom. 2:8). Jesus "rescues us from the wrath that is coming" (1 Thess. 1:10); we are "saved through him from the wrath of God" (Rom. 5:9). Being rescued from wrath certainly implies conciliation or appeasement.

Although Paul does not really think that God was made propitious (Rom. 5:6–8 shows God *not* being persuaded, but taking the initiative), that is exactly the implication of the cultic metaphors he uses. Every metaphor has an afterlife, independent of the author's intention. The primitive undertones of a cultic metaphor can override the high-minded theology of the person who formed the metaphor.

---

26. The faith of believers is frequently emphasized by Paul. I am not convinced by those (such as Richard Hays and Douglas Campbell) who insist that *pisteōs Iēsou Christou* in Rom. 3:22 must refer to the "faithfulness of Christ"—to Jesus' own faith. Rather, "The reiteration of the inclusive social scope of 'all who have faith' in 3:22 suggests that Paul is focusing on the faith of believers rather than the faithfulness of Christ" (Robert Jewett, *Romans: A Commentary*, Hermeneia [Minneapolis: Fortress Press, 2007], 278). Aside from saying that Christ was "obedient to the point of death" (Phil. 2:8), Paul never discusses Christ's faith or inner attitudes.
27. C. H. Dodd, *The Meaning of Paul for Today* (London: Fontana, 1920, 1958), 109.

Kinds of Substitution

What kind of substitution does Paul envision? Clearly there are substitutionary ideas in Paul, but it is important to distinguish *penal* substitution from cultic substitution and economic substitution. Rohintan Mody claims "that penal substitution is clearly present in 3:25b–26 and is implied in the idea of redemption,"[28] but really it is *cultic* substitution that is clear from ἱλαστήριον, and *economic* substitution that is clear from ἀπολύτρωσις, *apolytrōsis*, not *penal* substitution in either case. One could possibly base a "penal" argument on Christ being "handed over to death for our trespasses [παραπτώματα, *paraptōmata*]" (Rom. 4:25), or on "who is to condemn?" and other judicial terms in Rom. 8:33–34, or perhaps on "becoming a curse for us" in Gal. 3:13. It is far from clear, even in those verses, whether Christ is suffering someone else's penalty, while in Romans 3 penal substitution is not at all indicated. God's righteousness is definitely present (3:21–22, 25b), as is believers' being rectified (3:24, 26), but this happens "apart from the law" (3:21). It is not law, but "the law of faith" (or "the principle of faith," NAB) that is operative (3:27). Jew and gentile are justified "through that same faith" (3:30). Paul says nothing about penal substitution here. Even the reference to "condemned [κατακρίνω, *katakrinō*] sin in the flesh" in Rom. 8:3 is not overtly substitutionary. Romans 8:1–4 is about God and Christ accomplishing what the law was powerless to do, not only condemning sin but also empowering us to fulfill "the just requirement [δικαίωμα, *dikaiōma*] of the law" (8:4). The emphasis is not on penalty, but on our being able to accomplish the "good thing" (another possible translation of δικαίωμα) of the law, now that the power of sin is broken. Christ suffers in 8:3, but the thrust of the passage is about God and Christ doing what the law was unable to.

In chapter 7, I will look at the historical development of the penal substitution theory of atonement. Here I only briefly summarize it. It

---

28. Rohintan K. Mody, "Penal Substitutionary Atonement in Paul: An Exegetical Study of Romans 3:25–26," in *The Atonement Debate: Papers from the London Symposium on the Theology of Atonement*, ed. Derek Tidball, David Hilborn, and Justin Thacker (Grand Rapids: Zondervan, 2008), 125.

begins with the idea that everyone is thoroughly sinful. As John Stott says, "It is no use giving us rules about how to behave; we cannot keep them."[29] Consequently, everyone deserves hell (although why people should *deserve* hell if they cannot *help* breaking the law is never really answered). Advocates of this theory insist that God could not just forgive sin but that there *must* be punishment. "God had to satisfy his own holiness in dealing with the problem of human sin."[30] God is angry. I quote Stott again: "If evil did *not* provoke him to anger he would forfeit our respect."[31] Humans are totally unable pay the penalty for sin, but the Son of God agreed to pay the sin debt by dying on the cross: "The fully justified curse that rests on those who break God's law was transferred to Jesus on the cross."[32]

Most scholars know that this is not an accurate summary of Paul's theology. Some claim it has nothing in common with Paul. I and most scholars think that it does contain parts of Paul's thinking, but exaggerates and distorts them, while neglecting other important elements. Some aspects of penal substitution are present in Paul, but not the whole theory, and not in every atonement passage. The kind of substitution that is front and center in Romans 3 is *sacrificial* substitution, which is cultic, not penal. It *does* involve matters of life and death, favor or disfavor from God, but that does not mean that a sentence was transferred from some persons to another person. It is just too easy to assume (due to the theology that has been pounded into our heads from the time of Augustine to the present day) that penal substitution is present any time the death of Christ is mentioned. We should question the assumptions that popular opinion pushes.

Morna Hooker has effectively argued that Paul is picturing "interchange" with his atonement metaphors: Christ takes on our sinful and helpless condition so that we might take on his

---

29. John Stott, *Basic Christianity* (1958; repr., Downers Grove, IL: InterVarsity Press, 2008), 103.
30. I. Howard Marshall, "The Theology of Atonement," Society of Evangelical Arminians, posted March 29, 2013, evangelicalarminians.org/wp-content/uploads/2013/03/Marshall.-The-Theology- of-the-Atonement.pdf. There are no pages given, but this remark occurs in the text between footnotes 44 and 45.
31. John Stott, *The Cross of Christ* (Downers Grove, IL: InterVarsity Press, 1986), 124.
32. Stott, *Basic Christianity*, 128.

righteousness and abundant life. "Christ shared our humanity, our estrangement from God, in order that we might share his sonship."[33] She (rightly) argues that "the idea of substitution is inadequate" to describe Paul's soteriology, for substitution would not entail such an exchange; nor can substitution explain participation: "the necessity for our dying *with* Jesus."[34] It is not a matter of Christ taking the believer's place, but of the believer sharing Christ's place: "Christ's death for us involves us in dying with him."[35]

We should notice ways in which Christ is a *representative* rather than a substitute. The terms are similar, but not identical. Christ as model or even trailblazer is a *representative* concept. As Paul says, "Those who receive the abundance of grace and the free gift of righteousness exercise dominion in life through the one man, Jesus Christ....One man's act of righteousness leads to justification and life for all" (Rom 5:17–18). This is not what a substitute is expected to do. Christ as representative blazes a trail, and we follow. Christ opens up the way and shows what transformation is like, which substitutes generally do not do.

Nevertheless, we can hardly avoid the notion of substitution when we look at passages such as "Christ died for our sins" (1 Cor. 15:3) or "one has died for all" (2 Cor. 5:14). Simon Gathercole helpfully argues that the death is definitely substitutionary (Christ enduring something so that others need not endure it), but he does not argue that it must be *penal* substitution; one must distinguish substitution from penalty, representation, expiation, and propitiation; there can be substitution that is not "penal."[36] It ends up being harder to argue that there is no hint of substitution in Paul, as David Brondos seems to be doing,[37] than to recognize that substitution is *part* of the Pauline mix, but one that must not be allowed to dominate, or to push out nonsubstitutionary

---

33. Morna D. Hooker, *Not Ashamed of the Gospel: New Testament Interpretations of the Death of Christ* (Grand Rapids: Eerdmans, 1994), 34.
34. Ibid., 29.
35. Ibid., 30.
36. Simon Gathercole, *Defending Substitution: An Essay on Atonement in Paul* (Grand Rapids: Baker Academic, 2015), 17–19.
37. David A. Brondos, *Paul on the Cross: Reconstructing the Apostle's Story of Redemption* (Minneapolis: Fortress Press, 2006), 108–23, 133, 138.

ideas like Christ conquering the *appeal* of sin, and believers being transferred to the realm of grace, being spiritually transformed and able to discern the will of God, living *in* Christ and *with* Christ perpetually.

One problem with those, like Mody, who argue so vehemently for penal substitution in Paul is that they want to make it all-controlling, throttling Paul until he confesses only one doctrine and one metaphor. But Paul is not that simple. He is suggesting that Christ's death has a solemn and holy value (like a sacrifice), a rescuing value (like a redemption payment), and a heroic self-giving value (like a scapegoat-martyr). If Jesus' death were simply and solely a penal substitution, that would not deliver anyone from the *power* or appeal of sin, but Paul teaches deliverance from the realm of sin into the realm of grace (Rom. 5:21; 6:14), and an end to the appeal of sin (we are "no longer . . . enslaved" but are "freed from sin," Rom. 6:6, 22). Furthermore, forcing a penal interpretation on Paul cuts off the life force of his teaching. Paul is not *just* talking about the cross, but also about transformation, new life, and sharing in the resurrection.

Steve Chalke suggests that penal substitution is "violent . . . thinking" in which God is "first and foremost concerned with retribution for sin."[38] But if everything centers on Jesus' death, what was the use of his whole life *before* his death, or of his resurrection and ascension afterward? Chalke asks, if the gospel is all about "Jesus' death, what was the good news he told his followers to preach (Luke 9:6) before the crucifixion? And if God needed a sacrifice to placate his anger, how could Jesus forgive sins before his sacrifice had been made?"[39] Penal substitution treats the death of Christ as the only thing that matters, but there are other themes that are crucial in Romans: God is also God of the gentiles, salvation is by faith (chaps. 3–4), Christ saves us from enslavement to the realm of death (chaps. 5–7), the Spirit brings life and deliverance (8:10–24), believers are transformed and able to discern the will of God (8:29; 12:2), they are humble and

---

38. Steve Chalke, "The Redemption of the Cross," in Tidball, Hilborn, and Thacker, *Atonement Debate*, 35, 39.
39. Ibid., 39.

fulfill the law by loving (12:3–13:10). Still, the atoning death of Christ is central: "We were reconciled to God through the death of his Son" (5:10); "[God] who did not withhold his own Son, but gave him up for us all" (8:32).

But the sacrificial metaphor is not the only one. "Atonement" or exchange also occurs with the redemption and scapegoat metaphors.

Other Atonement Images in Paul

Atonement through Christ's sacrificial death does occur in Paul, but he is also careful to bring in scapegoat and redemption models for the death of Christ, which he mixes with the sacrificial metaphor so that no single image becomes dogmatic—although that is exactly what happened in later theology.

Expulsion Rituals: Sin Transported

Another one of the central purification rites performed at Yom Kippur is the scapegoat ritual. The metaphysics of scapegoat is very primitive. Scapegoat belongs to the category of expulsion rituals, those rites in which sin, curse, or disease are dumped onto a *body*, which is thought to literally carry away the undesirable thing. The term "expulsion ritual" is used to denote this ritual and similar ones in neighboring cultures, which are *not* sacrifices, although they are frequently lumped with sacrifice in academic works.

The scapegoat is a sin porter. The priest "shall lay both his hands on the head of the live goat, and confess over it all the iniquities of the people of Israel . . . putting them on the head of the goat, and sending it away into the wilderness" (Lev. 16:21). Similarly, the Hittites would drive out a ram and a female slave, bearing a curse into the enemy camp; the Greeks would periodically expel a *pharmakos* ("a medicinal"), a human victim who was selected, ritually abused, and driven out of the city, transporting a disease or impurity.[40] In Athens, there was an annual rite of driving a man (or a man and a woman) out of the

---

40. Gustav Stählin, "Περίψημα," in *TDNT* 6:84–87.

city "with a fixed rite of humiliation to secure the purification of the country.... Their being led round the city was usually coupled with a curse," and, by some accounts, with stoning.[41]

In many ways, the metaphysics of expulsion ritual is the opposite of what happens in sacrificial offering. The sacrificial animal is pure and remains pure, while the scapegoat begins in a pure state but is physically loaded with impurity. The sacrificial animal is treated with care and even respect, while "the scapegoat is mistreated."[42] The scapegoat is pinched, spat on, cursed, and struck.[43] The sacrificial animal is offered to the Lord at the central ritual shrine, while the expulsion victim is not an offering at all, but is driven "into the wilderness to Azazel" (probably a demon) (Lev. 16:10).

It seems obvious that this is a very primitive ritual. Sins are literally transferred to the goat, who exports them out of the community. Both the quasi-physical quality and the demonic element "seem to show that behind the moralized form of the ritual there lies an earlier, nonmoral, stage."[44] Sin or curse projection was a common enough ritual pattern that it would be recognizable when used as a metaphor. Even in cities where such rituals were no longer practiced, people would know about them through their traditions.

There is something about expulsion imagery that is particularly vivid for Paul. It pictures not only the saving effect of Jesus' death but also what happens in the lives of believers, and especially of apostles. Paul applies a scapegoat image to himself and other apostles in 1 Cor. 4:13. Here we read, "We have become like the rubbish [περικαθάρματα, perikatharmata] of the world, the dregs [περίψημα, peripsēma] of all things, to this very day," using two terms that were sometimes applied

---

41. Martin Hengel, *The Atonement: The Origins of the Doctrine in the New Testament* (London: SCM, 1981), 24–25; see also Walter Burkert, *Greek Religion: Archaic and Classical*, trans. John Raffan (Oxford: Blackwell, 1985), 82–83.
42. Daniel Stökl Ben Ezra, "Fasting with Jews, Thinking with Scapegoats: Some Remarks on Yom Kippur in Early Judaism and Christianity, in Particular 4Q541, *Barnabas* 7, Matthew 27 and Acts 27," in *The Day of Atonement: Its Interpretations in Early Jewish and Christian Traditions*, ed. Thomas Hieke and Tobias Nicklas (Leiden: Brill, 2012), 175.
43. Mishnah, Yoma 6.4; Barnabas 7.6–8; Tertullian, *Adversus Marcionem* 3.7.7; Daniel Stökl Ben Ezra, *The Impact of Yom Kippur on Early Christianity: The Day of Atonement from Second Temple Judaism to the Fifth Century*, WUNT 163 (Tübingen: Mohr Siebeck, 2003), 31, 88, 152, 157, 159.
44. S. H. Hooke, "The Theory and Practice of Substitution," *VT* 2 (1952): 9.

to the Greek *pharmakoi*,[45] the human "scapegoats" of whom his readers would have known. Paul has come to accept that apostles will be treated like scum, victimized, made "a spectacle to the world" (1 Cor. 4:9), even while they bring a message of life and hope. Paul uses these humbling facts as part of his rebuke to some proud and well-to-do Corinthians.

The scapegoat image has rich implications for Paul's theology. It can be changed from its original meaning of banishing something impure, into the notion of a representative victim dying for the community. If Christ was banished for us, and opened up new possibilities for us, then heroic meaning is added to the scapegoat image. Christ's death becomes representative and exemplary. Christ's body bears away sin, but he also serves as our model for breaking the hold of sin over our *own* bodies: believers "have crucified the flesh with its passions and desires" (Gal. 5:24). Christ's death is sacrificial: God sent Christ "as a sin offering" (NRSV marginal reading), through which God "condemned sin in the flesh" (Rom. 8:3). I think Paul is combining the sacrificial and scapegoat images here. He uses the Septuagint term for the sin offering (περὶ ἁμαρτίας, *peri hamartias*),[46] but it is the scapegoat, not the sacrificial offering, that bears condemnation *in its flesh*. So the death is representative and also, crucially, *exemplary* (so that "sin will have no dominion over you," Rom. 6:14).

By identifying with Christ's death, the believer takes on Christ's ability to destroy sin: "Our old self was crucified with him so that the body of sin might be destroyed, and we might no longer be enslaved to sin" (6:6). It is the *believer's* body of sin that is destroyed. Unless we combine the representative and exemplary meanings, and fuse them in an understanding of *participation in Christ*, we cannot understand Paul's logic here. Christ conquered sin for us, but he also enables us to do it in our own bodies: "So you also must consider yourselves dead to sin and alive to God in Christ Jesus" (Rom. 6:11); this pictures Christ as

---

45. Stählin, "Περίψημα," 6:84–85.
46. Williams, *Christ Died for Our Sins*, 162; Hastings Rashdall, *The Idea of the Atonement in Christian Theology* (London: Macmillan, 1919), 93; James D. G. Dunn, *Romans 1–8*, WBC 38A (Dallas: Word, 1988), 422.

representative, or model. By being "obedient ... to the ... teaching," we are "set free from sin" (Rom. 6:17-18; see also 8:10). With Christ, you can make sure that sin does not "exercise dominion in your mortal bodies" (6:12). Asceticism is certainly implied: "By the Spirit you put to death the deeds of the body" (Rom. 8:13). The scapegoat image is also useful for picturing sinfulness being driven out of one's body (see the section "Disgust," below).

This conquest of sinful passions is enabled first by the Savior's power over sin and death, and then by the believer's power to make a faith-connection to the Savior. Believers are saved by the Savior *and* by their faith (by the rope thrown to us, and by our *grabbing* the rope). But the Savior's power comes first and last. "If we have died with Christ, we believe that we will also live with him" (Rom. 6:8). The believer participates in Christ, replicates his conquests, his suffering, even his death (at least symbolically), and finally his resurrection. Christ's was an actual death; the believer's is a symbolic one: "If we have been united with him in a death like his, we will certainly be united with him in a resurrection like his" (6:5). "The cup of blessing that we bless, is it not a sharing in the blood of Christ?" (1 Cor. 10:16). This is what Pauline scholars call "participationist" theology: the believer becomes actually connected with the Messiah, with both his death and his life-giving power. One learns to live *in* Christ. God "will give life to your mortal bodies," and he will do so "if, in fact, we suffer with him so that we may also be glorified with him" (Rom. 8:11, 17). For Paul, Christ is the great transporter and transmitter. He transports sin and death out of our lives, and transmits life and goodness into them: "giving us his Spirit in our hearts" (2 Cor. 1:22).

This complex teaching was soon lost to Christian theology; it is not found in the Pastoral Epistles. The theologies that follow Paul emphasize the ransoming death of Christ, toning down Paul's message about Christ as transmitter of divine qualities to us: "that in him we might become the righteousness of God" (2 Cor. 5:21); "made righteous" (Rom. 5:19). This exchange of divine for human, and of incorruptibility for decay, came to be called *theōsis*, or "deification."[47]

It is a kind of spiritual irony or divine reversal of our condition. Philosopher Eric Voegelin refers to the life of transformation: "In the letters of Paul, the central issue is not a doctrine but the assurance of immortalizing transfiguration through the vision of the Resurrected."[48]

"Scapegoating" has become an increasingly common term denoting the psychological and political phenomena of social groups projecting unwanted characteristics onto other social groups or individuals, and then repudiating and persecuting those chosen targets. Many authors over a period of several centuries contributed to this extension the meaning of the term "scapegoat."[49] René Girard developed a theory that scapegoating was practiced by all societies, that religion and mythology covered it up and lied about it, but that biblical religion (especially the gospel) exposed and repudiated this pattern of violence. "Just like the Hebrew Bible, the Gospels defend the victims wrongly accused and expose their persecutors."[50] It is an interesting theory, with its advocates and critics.[51]

Redemption

The notion of Christ's having made a costly payment for our salvation

---

47. The technical term *theōsis* was not coined until the late fourth century, by Gregory of Nazianzus, but the idea of believers taking on divine qualities is present in Jesus' teaching (see Stephen Finlan, "Deification in Jesus' Teachings," in *Theōsis: Deification in Christian Theology*, ed. Vladimir Kharlamov, PTMS 156 [Eugene, OR: Wipf & Stock, 2011]: 2:21–41), and was prominent in the teachings of Paul, Irenaeus, Athanasius, Gregory of Nyssa, Maximus the Confessor, and others (see the first volume: *Theōsis: Deification in Christian Theology*, ed. Stephen Finlan and Vladimir Kharlamov, PTMS 52 [Eugene: Wipf & Stock, 2006], and also Stephen Finlan, "Can We Speak of Theōsis in Paul?," in *Partakers of the Divine Nature: The History and Development of Deification in the Christian Traditions*, ed. Michael J. Christensen and Jeffery A. Wittung [Grand Rapids: Baker Academic, 2007]).
48. Eric Voegelin, *Order and History*, vol. 4, *The Ecumenic Age* (Baton Rouge: Louisiana State University Press, 1974), 256.
49. Just some of the people who contributed to the extension of the meaning of the term "scapegoat" are Calvin, early Calvinists, Boston Puritans, British Protestants, James Frazer, and René Girard (David Dawson, *Flesh Becomes Word: A Lexicography of the Scapegoat or, the History of an Idea* [East Lansing: Michigan State University Press, 2013], 45–134).
50. René Girard, *I See Satan Fall Like Lightning*, trans. James G. Williams (Maryknoll, NY: Orbis, 2001), 122.
51. To list just one of each; an advocate: S. Mark Heim, *Saved from Sacrifice: A Theology of the Cross* (Grand Rapids: Eerdmans, 2006); a critic: Hans Boersma, *Violence, Hospitality, and the Cross: Reappropriating the Atonement Tradition* (Grand Rapids: Baker Academic, 2004).

is a central belief for many Christians; in fact, for many, "redemption" is synonymous with "salvation." In the Hebrew and then Greco-Roman worlds, however, it had a secular meaning. It did not originate in the cultic realm but in economic dealings.

In Rom. 3:24, Paul writes, "They are now justified by his grace as a gift, through the redemption [ἀπολυτρώσεως, *apolytrōseōs*, genitive form] that is in Christ Jesus." Ἀπολύτρωσις, *apolytrōsis* (nominative form), is commonly used throughout Greek literature for the ransoming of hostages[52] or for the freeing of a slave by making a manumission payment.[53] It can also refer to the ransoming of property.[54] Ransom payments are in mind when Plutarch speaks of pirates flaunting "their ransomings [ἀπολυτρώσεις, *apolytrōseis*] of captured cities."[55] Some scholars wish to look more at the λυτρ- group of words than at ἀπολύτρωσις itself. Benjamin Ribbens writes: "Such a sense of payment is evident in some LXX texts [Exod. 21:8; Lev. 25:24], but in the LXX λυτρ- terms are used predominantly to refer to Israel's liberation from Egypt and liberation from exile.... Deut 7:8 ... Isa 43:1."[56] But Ribbens does admit that Paul and his readers "knew that ἀπολύτρωσις included a sense of payment."[57] In the New Testament Epistles, words of this group can describe the saving death of Christ,[58] while in the Gospels, λυτρο- words can signify the salvation that Jesus brings, with (Matt. 20:28; Mark 10:45) or without a logical linkage to his death (Luke 1:68; 21:28; 24:21).

Ἀπολύτρωσις would be a powerful image for the slaves in Paul's audience, who would have yearned to be able to purchase their freedom, or to have someone purchase it for them. This same image of slave manumission is contained in Paul's twice-uttered remark "you

---

52. Dunn, *Romans 1–8*, 169. Polybius used it to signify the ransoming of captives in *Histories* 2.6.6.
53. David Hill, *Greek Words and Hebrew Meanings: Studies in the Semantics of Soteriological Terms* (Cambridge: Cambridge University Press, 1967), 76; Hooker, *Not Ashamed of the Gospel*, 26.
54. Williams, *Christ Died for Our Sins*, 118.
55. Plutarch, *Pompey* 24.4; *Plutarch's Lives*, vol. 5, *Pompey*, trans. Bernadotte Perrin, LCL (Cambridge: Harvard University Press, 1917), 179.
56. Benjamin J. Ribbens, "Forensic-Retributive Justification in Romans 3:21–26: Paul's Doctrine of Justification in Dialogue with Hebrews," *CBQ* 74 (2012): 557.
57. Ibid., 558.
58. Rom. 3:24; 1 Cor. 1:30; Col. 1:14; Eph. 1:7, 14; 4:30; Tit. 2:14; Heb. 9:12, 15.

were bought [ἠγοράσθητε, ēgorasthēte, from ἀγοράζω, agorazō] with a price" (1 Cor. 6:20; 7:23), and again in the use of a cognate verb to speak of being freed from the slavery of the law: "Christ redeemed [ἐχηγόρασεν, exēgorasen, from ἐξαγοράζω, exagorazō] us from the curse of the law by becoming a curse for us" (Gal. 3:13). The term *agorazō* ("buy") can be used for ordinary purchases in the marketplace or for ransoming hostages or manumitting slaves;[59] or the outright purchase of slaves,[60] while *exagorazō* ("buy back") is frequently used to refer specifically to the manumission of slaves.[61] In the New Testament, it signifies buying a linen shroud (Mark 15:46), food (Luke 9:13), a field, or a great pearl (Matt. 13:44, 46).

What is most important to notice, now that Paul's main atonement metaphors have been listed, is how he repeatedly and vividly mixes them, in a way that stimulates reflection. Paul and his successors link social/economic redemption language (ἀπολύτρωσις, ἐξαγοράζω, ἀγοραζω, λυτρόομαι [apolytrōsis, exagorazō, agorazō, lytroomai,]) with cultic terminology (αἵμα, καθαρίζω, ἄμωμος [haima, katharizō, amōmos]) (Rom. 3:24-25; Gal. 3:13; Tit. 2:14; 1 Pet. 1:18-19; Rev. 5:9). This mixing can produce confusion or argument if people insist on trying to narrow his soteriology down to one simple concept, or to get him to produce a rigidly logical account of exactly how atonement takes place. Rather, Paul offers a suggestive *range* of images, in ways that work well as preaching tools, but do *not* work well for philosophic exactness or rigidly logical doctrine. In Gal. 3:13, Paul has a legal curse ("curse of the law") paid for ("redeemed") through a ritual exchange ("by becoming a curse for us"). He has Christ's death combining many kinds of exchange. What matters for Paul is that, through this transaction, Jesus wins freedom for the slaves of sin.

The image of sacrifice suggests sacred time and space, holy

---

59. Gordon D. Fee, *The First Epistle to the Corinthians*, NICNT (Grand Rapids: Eerdmans, 1987), 264-65. BAG, 12, lists P.Oxy. 1149, 5 and Dittenberger's *Sylloge Inscriptionum* 844, 9, as examples of its usage for manumission of slaves.
60. Dale Martin, *Slavery as Salvation: The Metaphor of Slavery in Pauline Christianity* (New Haven: Yale University Press, 1990), 63.
61. J. B. Lightfoot, *St. Paul's Epistle to the Galatians: A Revised Text with Introduction, Notes, and Dissertations* (London: Macmillan, 1869), 138; M. Eugene Boring, Klaus Berger, and Carsten Colpe, *Hellenistic Commentary to the New Testament* (Nashville: Abingdon, 1995), 463-64.

procedure, and a solemn moment of contact with divinity. Paul blends the powerful ritual images with other metaphors for the transactional moment: the death amounted to a ransom or manumission payment (Rom. 3:24), or to a pardon in the final judgment (Rom. 8:33). In Rom. 8:3, a judicial notion ("condemned sin") is blended with both a scapegoat image ("sinful flesh") and a sacrificial metaphor ("a sin offering," NIV). In Gal. 3:13, the redemption payment takes on both a sacred and a legal character. Of supreme importance for Paul is that believers recognize that Christ's death had a saving effect. The exact mechanics of the saving action are less important, and in fact are deliberately kept ambiguous through the combining of metaphors.

Paul insists on joining two or three metaphors almost every time he speaks of the efficacy of the Messiah's death, allowing the various metaphors to interpret each other. The judicial condemnation of sin takes on a suggestion of ritual, either the solemnity of sacrifice or the violence of scapegoat. Some images that could be confusing are made sensible by recognizing this blending of metaphors: "You have died to the law through the body of Christ" (Rom. 7:4) blends a scapegoat image (a *body* taking on sin) with rescue from the tyranny of the law.

Paul's legacy was assured, his influence guaranteed, by both the emotional power and the explanatory power of his preaching on sin and salvation, slavery and rescue, the Messiah's obedience and heroic martyrdom. But his mixed metaphors yield some mixed results. His cultic metaphors give meanings to salvation that are simultaneously spiritualizing, moralizing, and magical, making it inevitable that Christianity would manifest both more advanced moral insights *and* more retrogressive superstitious ideas than are usually found in Judaism. The special value attaching to the Savior's "blood" or his "sacrifice" draws primitive and magical ideas into the picture, to be blended with spiritual and ethical meanings, many of which come from the teachings of Jesus himself.

But there are problems here. The redemption metaphor *itself* indicates that salvation was not free—a price was paid. "You were bought with a price" (1 Cor. 6:20; 7:23) perpetuates the notion of God granting salvation after being paid off, although Paul is making a bigger point in both of those passages. The point in 1 Cor. 7:23 is that, when believers are saved, they come under the domain of a new Lord, and they will no longer seek to measure up to the world's opinion. The point in 1 Cor. 6:20 is that, even in their bodies, believers are "members of Christ," and they are showing infidelity if they join with prostitutes (6:15). In both cases, the purchase slogan is meant to show that the Lord is the real master. I respect this *main* point of Paul's, but I think it gets swamped under the notion of a literal blood purchase, which forms the basis of many people's idea of salvation. This perpetuates the harsh notion of divine vengeance offset by the persuasive power—the *purchasing* power—of suffering. This is manipulation through suffering, and it is corrosive of mature ethics and philosophy.

If sin had to be paid for through the death of the Son, then sins were not actually forgiven. Real forgiveness is never purchased. If salvation is *bought*, it is not *free*. The concept of purchased salvation undermines the unity of purpose of Father and Son. Stanislas Lyonnet may be correct to say that the New Testament redemption metaphor intends to picture the goodness of God and the painful or "onerous character of redemption," not a *literal* price paid to the devil nor to the Father.[62] But the afterlife of this metaphor (its interpretation by generations of believers) is exactly that. The problem is inherent in the metaphor itself, which suggests either that God is not all-powerful (if God had to pay the devil) or not all good (if God was bribed). These distortions were not intended by Paul, but the seeds of potential misinterpretation were planted by him.

And Paul's successors flatten out his complex vision and take his metaphors literally. Paul's language is simplified into slogans in the deutero-Pauline letters. "Redeem" is identified with "purify," and "ransom" is welded to "blood": "He it is who gave himself for us that he might redeem us from all iniquity and purify for himself a people of his own" (Tit. 2:14); "You were ransomed . . . with the precious

---

62. Stanislas Lyonnet, "The Terminology of Redemption," in *Sin, Redemption and Sacrifice: A Biblical and Patristic Study*, AnBib 48 (Rome: Biblical Institute, 1970), 118.

blood of Christ" (1 Pet. 1:18–19). Paul's inheritors heighten redemption, understanding sacrifice as a kind of redemption. Paul's multiform and flexible teaching is simplified and taken literally, turning the salvation event into a crude purchase through sacrificial blood. It gets worse as time goes on, and the metaphors are hardened into doctrines expressed by Augustine, Gregory the Great, Luther, and Calvin. Then atonement becomes a nightmarish scenario of God being appeased by a ritual murder, a holy atrocity. Of course, this does not give us a true picture of God as taught by either Jesus or Paul, but Paul's metaphors did open the door to this recrudescence of primitive ideas. Paul may have overestimated his readers' ability to recognize his metaphors *as* metaphors. Many Christians forget that these are meant to picture what *sort* of saving result Jesus' death had, rather than to be descriptions of a *literal* cultic or redemption transaction carried out over Christ's dead body. They seem to be unaware of how far this materialistic image is from the heavenly Father as taught by Jesus, but rather more resembling a primitive concept of Zeus!

The Trouble with Images

Since Christian atonement has so many troubling undercurrents, it is not surprising that most preachers do not actually delve very deeply into the logic of atonement. Atonement is frequently preached, but rarely explained. This is because atonement relies on beliefs that have been repressed or forgotten. Attempts to argue that Christian atonement ideas are the *literal* fulfillment of the Old Testament cult are always awkward and inconsistent, since we no longer believe that sacrificial blood *literally* cleanses impurity from holy places, or that a scapegoat *actually* carries away sin from a community.

Most Christians today are largely unconscious of the ancient cultic logic of impurity removal that underlies their notions of atonement and would not, if pressed, defend the effectiveness of blood as an impurity cleanser, or of the scapegoat as a sin porter. Atonement metaphors are based on a forgotten metaphysics. Atonement doctrine is therefore symbolic and suggestive, and thrives largely on rationalizations that have been created by theologians and preachers down through the ages. Most atonement preaching emphasizes the heroic Messiah who came to "die for our sins" (1 Cor. 15:3) and to fulfill the old covenant. Many preachers and theologians will attribute new and spiritual meaning to sacrifice and "blood." Very few will admit that the metaphysics of sacrifice is essentially *magical* (a symbolic action that results in a real cleansing). Christian atonement theology is constantly having to find new rationalizations, and to suppress the underlying matrix of fear, violence, and magical beliefs.

Paul's cultic images were compelling at the time of their utterance since people knew those cultic practices well, but the images have lost much of their poignancy for those who have never seen animals offered as a sacrifice or driven out as a scapegoat, or known anyone who was released through the payment of a ransom. Still, even as purely abstract images, sacrifice and redemption carry power for many people who never experienced the literal ritual practice. But the images that Jesus chose—forgiving an errant son, showing kindness to an injured stranger, showing mercy to underlings as one has been shown mercy by a boss—are more accessible. They resonate with people in any time or place. The images chosen by Jesus are less subject to obsolescence than those tied to sacrifice and scapegoat. The Jesus imagery of growth, fairness, diligence, wedding feasts, demanding bosses, humble widows, grumpy brothers, and forgiving fathers retains a vividness and relevance in any society.

The image of sacrifice was vivid in its own day, but it has obscured the message of Jesus for people of subsequent ages, who need to hear about salvation disentangled from sacrifice, scapegoat, and the manipulative concept of martyrdom. Paul's great achievement was to disentangle the gospel from national and purity boundaries, but he then reentangled it with spiritualized cultic concepts. Although we have abandoned the ritual systems, the mentality that undergirded those systems is still unconsciously present: a mentality of appeasing God with sacrificial offerings, and so manipulating the Deity into viewing us with favor. This was not Paul's intention; in fact, he argued *against* manipulation when he stressed that God was setting out to rescue us and reconcile us (Rom. 5:5-8; 2 Cor. 5:18-20), but the sacrificial *images* that he uses are essentially manipulative, even against his best intentions. Even those passages about God's initiative that I just mentioned end with cultic images of Jesus' blood saving us "from the wrath of God" (Rom. 5:9), and God "ma[king] him to be sin" for us (2 Cor. 5:21). In the minds of most of those who receive the teachings, the underlying cultic logic overwhelms the more enlightened teaching. The problem is inherent in the cultic metaphors themselves.

Despite attempts to spiritualize sacrifice and scapegoat, they are manipulative rituals. With sacrifice, either God is manipulated through a food bribe, or impurity is manipulated (cleansed) by blood magic. With scapegoat, impurity or sin are manipulated onto a victim who is then brutally expelled. Paul saw *humans* as the ones who practice political scapegoating, but he involves God in the scapegoating of Jesus if God made Christ to be sin (2 Cor. 5:21), and if salvation could not be achieved any other way.

To rationalize sacrificial and scapegoat images and join them to the teaching about the love of God is to allow contradictory motives to be imputed to God. We must ask why God could not open up the way of salvation without utilizing the way of blood sacrifice or victim banishing? Sacrifice and scapegoat evoke instincts about the universe as dangerous and unpredictable. It is not God but *people* who are bound by these ancient anthropomorphic and transactional religious ideas. The grace and forgiveness of God is undermined by being linked to sacrificial death, which implies payment. True forgiveness involves no payment. Forgiveness is not present if payment is demanded. If salvation was "bought with a price" (1 Cor. 6:20), it was *not* the result of free forgiveness. There can be forgiveness, or there can be purchase, but not both at the same time.

Some authors seek to "transform" or redefine atonement.[63] But without understanding the psychology of atonement, the attempt is

---

63. Theodore W. Jennings Jr., *Transforming Atonement: A Political Theology of the Cross* (Minneapolis: Fortress Press, 2009); Scot McKnight, *A Community Called Atonement*, Living Theology (Nashville: Abingdon, 2007).

doomed. Trying to leap over the errors of the last two thousand years and recover the liberating gospel will not go very far unless one can explain the unhealthy thinking that permeates Christianity, the manipulative psychology of sacrifice and atonement that distorts the religion of Jesus. It is not social categories (rich or poor, left or right) that threaten to make Christianity irrelevant, but a psychology of salvation through sacrificial payoff. This repulsive idea will continue to generate hypocritical leaders, unhealthy followers, and angry rejecters. Paul does not seem to have anticipated what a crude and cynical doctrine would be derived from his teaching, although maybe he should have: the potential was there in his cultic metaphors.

Can biblical studies recover Paul's emphasis on spiritual renewal and Christlike transformation while confronting the troubling transactional ideas carried in his cultic metaphors? Can we recover the transformative trust in God by which Jesus himself lived?

Paul's Psychology

Paul was very much a man of his time, a Jew with a strong moral code and belief that God would someday judge the just and the unjust, but Paul was also very much a Hellenistic person, able to utilize Hellenistic rhetorical forms and to make Stoic-sounding statements (1 Thess. 2:9–12;[64] Rom. 1:19; 5:3–5[65]). His strong asceticism was not particularly unusual for his time, but it has some interesting psychological underpinning. It is part of his intense battle with sin.

Disgust

Scapegoat imagery has a particular psychological appeal for Paul, since he has an intense personal need to expel the "sinful passions . . . at work in our members," in which "nothing good dwells" (Rom. 7:5, 18). He has a deep emotional need to get rid of bad qualities and take on good ones, to be transformed, to *become* someone else, better than he is.

---

64. Abraham J. Malherbe, *Paul and the Thessalonians: The Philosophical Tradition of Pastoral Care* (Philadelphia: Fortress Press, 1987), 48.
65. Dunn, *Romans 1–8*, 250.

RESCUE AND DISGUST IN PAUL

He has a sharp consciousness of the need for the old self to be removed and replaced, "so that ... we too might walk in newness of life.... Our old self was crucified with him so that the body of sin might be destroyed, and we might no longer be enslaved to sin" (Rom. 6:4, 6). He is deeply ashamed of "the body of sin." His passion is very real when he cries, "Who will rescue me from this body of death?" (Rom. 7:24). His asceticism is clearly seen: "Put on the Lord Jesus Christ, and make no provision for the flesh, to gratify its desires" (Rom. 13:14).

Paul describes captivity to sin and a need for dramatic rescue from it. This rescue comes when the Messiah's body stands in for our condemnable bodies, carrying away the sin: "You have died to the law through the body of Christ" (Rom. 7:4); "There is therefore now no condemnation for those who are in Christ Jesus" (Rom. 8:1). There may be a substitutionary element here, but Paul wants to emphasize liberation and transformation. Believers must replicate Christ's death to sin, which means both the repudiation of sinful sensuality and willingness to suffer mistreatment while living in a sinful world (Rom. 6:6–8; 8:5–9, 17).

Paul has a strong sense of disgust with something alien inside, directing his behavior. Sin was able to "exercise dominion in your mortal bodies" (Rom. 6:12). Something *inside* is wicked: "It is no longer I that do it, but sin that dwells within me," which is "making me captive to the law of sin that dwells in my members" (7:17, 23). He is disgusted with his slavery to the flesh: "I know that nothing good dwells within me, that is, in my flesh" (7:18). There needs to be outside intervention by a power stronger than sin: "If Christ is in you, though the body is dead because of sin, the Spirit is life because of righteousness" (8:10).

He also is disgusted with improper behavior in the churches, an inappropriate mixing of holiness and impurity: "What agreement has the temple of God with idols? For we are the temple of the living God.... Separate from them, says the Lord, and touch nothing unclean" (2 Cor. 6:16–17). This probably refers to keeping separate from gentile religions, in particular the mystery cults that were quite popular in the cities. So Paul shares the common Jewish disgust with gentile mystery religions, but he is not disgusted with gentiles themselves. His ability to create, organize, and nurture churches with a largely gentile population seems to reflect an ability to genuinely love gentiles.

I must touch lightly on the lengthy debate about the "I" in Romans 7. Some scholars have been overly narrow. Following Werner G. Kümmel, they insist that the "I" in Romans 7 is purely rhetorical or fictive, with no shred of autobiography, no relevance to Paul's own psychology.[66] This is a rigid position. *Of course* there is a hypothetical or rhetorical aspect to the fictive conversation that we see in Rom. 7:7–25, but that does not mean that there is none of Paul's personal experience in it. In fact, Romans 7 describes a state of mind that both author and reader can understand all too well, since it is always possible to fall back into fleshly thinking.[67] "With the flesh I am a slave to the law of sin" (Rom. 7:25). And sin is still a (potentially) present reality for Paul and for the believer. It would make no sense to spend so much time on the power of sin (Romans 5–8) if it were completely irrelevant for the believer.

Gerd Theissen astutely comments that the psychological insights found in Romans 7–8 could only come in retrospect, *after* salvation and deliverance from "the law of sin and death" (Rom. 8:2). One takes on a new identity and can approach God without anxiety: "Only the reappropriated identity illumines the preceding conflict. Only from Christ is light shed on Adam's hopelessness."[68] And so, Romans 7 is a hypothetical conversation, but it looks at *real* helplessness in the face of sin and flesh, at the mind's guilty anxiety in the face of law, and at the reality of a transforming power that can deliver one from helplessness and anxiety. (Anxiety is the chief feature of those who experienced ambivalent attachment to their primary caregiver.)

Once again, we need to notice that Paul sees a permanent conflict

---

66. Stanley Stowers supports Kümmel's view ("it does not include Paul," *A Rereading of Romans: Justice, Jews, and Gentiles* [New Haven: Yale University Press, 1994], 264), but Gerd Theissen refutes that view (*Psychological Aspects of Pauline Theology*, trans. John P. Galvin [Philadelphia: Fortress Press, 1987], 177–78, 191).
67. James D. G. Dunn, *The Theology of Paul the Apostle* (Grand Rapids: Eerdmans, 1998), 474–76. Underlying the applicability of this passage to all readers is the likelihood that "the 'I' is an existential self-identification with Adam, *adam*, 'Everyman'" (ibid., 99).
68. Theissen, *Psychological Aspects of Pauline Theology*, 265.

between Spirit and flesh; "those who are in the flesh cannot please God.... If by the Spirit you put to death the deeds of the body, you will live" (8:8, 13). All will turn out well through "the help of the Spirit of Jesus Christ" (Phil. 1:19). The "Spirit of Christ" or "the Spirit of God dwells in you" (Rom. 8:9). (In Paul's writings, there is no difference between "the Spirit," "the Holy Spirit," "the Spirit of Christ," and "the Spirit of God.")

Jesus did not have Paul's fundamentally conflictual view; he saw nature herself testifying of truth (the birds of the air, the lilies of the field, fruit-bearing trees, Matt. 6:26–30; 7:17). Jesus, having a healthy-minded religion, did not put conflict at the center, as Paul did: "The body is dead because of sin" (Rom. 8:10).

Paul stressed the necessity of sacrificing one's selfishness, which can be considered a kind of dying: "Present your bodies as a living sacrifice, holy and acceptable to God, which is your spiritual worship" (Rom. 12:1). There needs to be deep personal *change*: "Be transformed by the renewing of your minds" (12:2). It is like being created anew, without sin corrupting everything: "If anyone is in Christ, there is a new creation" (2 Cor. 5:17).

Paul's disgust is not the same as the food disgust we mentioned in connection with purity systems in chapter 1, although it does bear a resemblance to manifestations of disgust in connection with "the sense of justice."[69] He shows a common Jewish disgust for gentile carryings-on: "Fornicators, idolaters, adulterers, male prostitutes, sodomites, thieves, the greedy, drunkards, revilers, robbers—none of these will inherit the kingdom of God" (1 Cor. 6:9–10). But he can also appeal to gentile customs at times. When disgusted with the person who broke a sexual law (1 Cor. 5:9), he claims the support of universal law, not of Torah specifically: this particular "sexual immorality [πορνεία, *porneia*]" is "of a kind that is not found even among pagans [ἔθνεσιν, *ethnesin*: the nations]" (1 Cor. 5:1).

Sexual immorality is a particular concern in 1 Corinthians. Paul

---

69. Disgust, fear, and the sense of justice are emotions connected to impurity, according to Thomas Kazen, *Issues of Impurity in Early Judaism*, ConBNT 45 (Winona Lake, IN: Eisenbrauns, 2010), 13.

cautions, "The fornicator sins against the body itself" (1 Cor. 6:18). There may be a link between disgust and compensation, since this is followed by "you were bought with a price; therefore glorify God in your body" (6:20). I have said that atonement as compensation is manipulative: seeking to persuade God to be favorable. Atonement as the cleansing of a disgusting condition is manipulative in a different way: seeking to cleanse the self, to remove impurity.

We saw in chapter 1 that disgust is one of the motivating factors of purity systems. Paul is not making an appeal to the Jewish purity system, but he retains a personal echo of this system in his disgust over the selfish sensuality that he sees as dominating human behavior. "Whatever does not proceed from faith is sin" (Rom. 14:23). Jewish cult and morals helped to shape Paul's mind to some degree. He has a particular concern about sexual impropriety, selfishness, and cruelty.

Shame

Paul knows something about the *inner* experience of the scapegoated person, about *shame*, which differs from guilt. Guilt is the consciousness of having done wrong; shame is the feeling of *being* wrong, of being exposed to hostile attention. The nature of the exposure can vary; it can be the feeling of being exposed as ridiculous or despised or helpless. Shame is the experience of feeling "flawed at the center of one's being. It is about self.... 'I am a bad person.'"[70] I would say, though, that it is not always about badness; shame comes when one feels helplessly abused, weak, victimized. Jill McNish says that shame comes with feelings of "our unlovability," arising from being abandoned, isolated.[71]

And yet, shame is originally a protective and healthy emotion; it was not placed there just to torment us. Carl Schneider tells us, "The function of shame is to preserve wholeness and integrity."[72] Just as a

---

70. Jill L. McNish, "The Bible and the Psychology of Shame," in *Psychology and the Bible: A New Way to Read the Scriptures*, vol. 3, *From Gospel to Gnostics*, ed. J. Harold Ellens and Wayne G. Rollins (Westport, CT: Praeger, 2004), 241–42.
71. Ibid., 254.
72. Carl D. Schneider, *Shame, Exposure and Privacy* (Boston: Beacon, 1977), 49.

growing plant needs its roots to be concealed from the light, so there is a part of our "psychic life" that has "roots which function" away from the light.[73] Shame alerts us against premature participation in sex: "When shame fails, disgust ensues. Shame inhibits the sexual impulse until the self as a whole responds to the other person in his or her wholeness."[74] But the chronic experience of shame is crippling. It can lead to "a condition of lasting alienation, toxic unwantedness."[75] It can "induce a sense of persistent inferiority, worthlessness, abandonment . . . violation, defilement."[76] Others experience shame only periodically and in certain circumstances, but it is painful enough to make them go to almost any length to avoid a repetition of the experience.

McNish theorizes that "what the Christian story did was to constellate the human shame archetype—the inborn human shame propensity—around events in the life and ministry of Jesus of Nazareth. . . . A person who transformed and was transformed in shame [who] refused to deploy the defenses to shame that the rest of us humans often deploy: rage, acting out . . . withdrawal, contempt, blaming."[77] She argues that people are able to confront and process their own feelings of shame by reflecting on Jesus' experience—and transcendence—of shame. The goal is a healthy recovery of identity and freedom.[78] "To the extent that we were honestly . . . to confront our own shame . . . we would not be tempted to treat others as outcasts."[79]

Indeed, one can see Paul frequently confronting the experience of shame, transcending it, and coming out the other side. He had a deep experience of the fact that "power is made perfect in weakness" (2 Cor. 12:9). Scholars often speak of the theme of reversal in Paul ("whenever I am weak, then I am strong," 2 Cor. 12:10), or the theme of *kenosis*, being emptied. Related to this is the determination to overcome arrogance and to recognize the futility of boasting (Rom. 3:27; 1 Cor.

---

73. Ibid., 37.
74. Ibid., 61.
75. Stephen Pattison, "Shame and the Unwanted Self," in *The Shame Factor: How Shame Shapes Society*, ed. Robert Jewett, with Wayne L. Alloway Jr. and John G. Lacey (Eugene, OR: Cascade, 2011), 13.
76. Ibid., 16.
77. McNish, "The Bible and the Psychology of Shame," 252.
78. Ibid., 248.
79. Ibid., 257.

4:7, 18; 13:4). This experience of reversal and transcendence is simultaneously spiritual and psychological. Although the experience is intense and life-changing, it may take some time to really heal the emotional scars left by any prolonged experience of being shamed. But there is no limit on the intensity of personal feeling and meaningfulness that can develop in one's relationship with God: "I will boast all the more gladly of my weaknesses, so that the power of Christ may dwell in me. Therefore I am content with weaknesses, insults, hardships" (2 Cor. 12:9–10). Paul seems to score highly in the ability to experience shame without pathological reaction, without withdrawal, hatred, or despair. He has really experienced God's love.

The antidote to shame is unfortunately disguised in the NRSV's translation of Rom. 5:5 ("hope does not disappoint us"). Some other translations get it right: "Hope does not put us to shame [καταισχύνει, *kataischynei*], because God's love has been poured out into our hearts through the Holy Spirit" (Rom. 5:5 NIV, ESV). I would recommend an even simpler translation of the first half: "Hope does not shame us." And so love is the antidote to shame.

In summary, what are my main psychological points about Paul? I have said that he had experienced an inner conflict between sin and a desire to obey God; that he is disgusted with the "sinful passions" (Rom. 7:5) that seek to drive him; that he intensely desires a scapegoat-like expulsion of sin from his body; that he has a strong mystical attachment to the life, death, and resurrection of Christ as it enables him to see himself "crucified with him so that the body of sin might be destroyed" (Rom. 6:6). All of this seems to reflect an adult mind that grew up from an ambivalent attachment experience. His experience of Christ gave him secure and mature attachment, enabling him to overcome "confidence in the flesh" (Phil. 3:4), to gain the upper hand over anxiety, not to "fall back into fear" (Rom. 8:15), and to face shame and be unafraid of it, even to understand the nature of Christlike service to be the enduring of shame for the sake of others. To some degree, Paul took on the heroic and loving character of his Savior, and he teaches us that we can do the same. He sought to empower people to be liberated from their own ambivalent attachment habits ("all who are led by the Spirit of God are children of God," Rom. 8:14; "we are always confident . . . for we walk by faith, not by sight," 2 Cor. 5:6–7).

However, I do think that Paul's atonement ideas are fundamentally manipulative. They are not just a product of Paul's psychology, but they cater to a widespread psychological "need" to manipulate parents whose love is inconsistent and ambivalent. The atonement image and the "bought with a price" metaphor (1 Cor. 6:20; 7:23) allow people to retain manipulative concepts, reflecting ambivalent attachment to God. Anxiety remained even in Paul's triumphant spiritual experience; he was never comfortable in his body, and he said believers "groan inwardly while we wait for adoption, the redemption of our bodies" (Rom. 8:23). He still had anxiety about moral pollution: "Let us cleanse ourselves from every defilement of body and of spirit, making holiness perfect in the fear of God" (2 Cor. 7:1). Further, the image of the Savior's "blood" having special value is linked to ancient and now obsolete concepts of ritual purification.

Paul's atonement images were eventually turned into simple slogans and then into inflexible dogmas by his successors. Yet withal, I think Paul had a far greater mind and soul than any of his successors. Paul is the first great Christian philosopher. It just so happens that we need to use some of his truths and insights to distance ourselves from those of his images that were so effective when he first preached them but which now are socially obsolete and psychologically harmful.

The Problem with Atonement

The fundamental problem with atonement theology is not what it says about Jesus but what it says about God, a Deity who either did not *want* to forgive or *could* not forgive until there was a sacrifice or a payment for sins. Common sense (*spiritual* sense) militates against such a view. After all, "Would it not be strange, if a tolerably good father can forgive and forget, and God can not?"[80]

---

80. Horace Bushnell, *Christ and His Salvation: In Sermons Variously Related Thereto* (New York: Charles Scribner, 1864), 296.

That comes from the great nineteenth-century pastor and writer Horace Bushnell. He concentrated on Christian sacrifice in another book, affirming the self-giving of Christ, while repudiating the complicated legal fictions and "schemes of satisfaction, made up for God."[81] Bushnell accepts the term *vicarious*. He understands "vicarious sacrifice" only to be what love *always* is, for "love is a principle essentially vicarious in its own nature."[82] Christ bore our sickness "in the sense that He took them on His feeling, had His heart burdened by the sense of them."[83] But it does not mean, as Calvin insisted, that he became guilty or bore God's wrath, even for a moment. "It does not mean that He took their ill desert upon Him by some mysterious act of imputation, or had their punishment transferred to His person.... For that kind of penal suffering would satisfy nothing but the very worst injustice."[84] The aim of the sacrificial love of God and Jesus is what true love's aim always is: the health and restoration of the loved ones. "God Himself takes our sinning enmity upon His heart, painfully burdened by our broken state, and travailing, in all the deepest feeling of His nature, to recover us to Himself."[85]

Self-giving and tender care such as Christ and God show for us are "nothing strange.... There is a Gethsemane hid in all love."[86] When theologians construct legal schemes and sacrificial payments, Bushnell writes, they have put a "dry stubble of reason"[87] in place of God's dynamic love. Legal concepts obscure the transformation that divine love brings. One can base "the whole significance of His incarnate mission upon the power to be exerted in character"[88]—exerted in *our* character.

Bushnell's healthy-minded theology and love-saturated philosophy inspire me to try to find a way to state my insights without offending

---

81. Horace Bushnell, *The Vicarious Sacrifice Grounded in Principles of Universal Obligation* (New York: Charles Scribner, 1871), 14.
82. Ibid., 7.
83. Ibid., 9.
84. Ibid., 10–11.
85. Ibid., 12.
86. Ibid., 12.
87. Ibid., 13.
88. Ibid., 30; and see 109.

the spirituality of honest believers. I would try to find out where the religious instincts of the honest believer are correct, and respect those, while attacking only the misteachings and distortions that have become attached to the teaching. It may be that "atonement," for some believers, means no more than the saving outreach of God, the self-giving of Jesus, and these insights must not be offended. What must be attacked is the cancerous doctrine that God needs to be paid off, that the death of Christ was a sort of legal bribe to God. Unfortunately, it is exactly this concept that has become the primary understanding of many Christians. As such, it can hardly be simply ignored, but must be critiqued, and so, my approach is more confrontational than Bushnell's.

5

Answers to Atonement

I will discuss three scholars who, in different ways, react against atonement, particularly the penal substitutionary theory, which has become such a dominant interpretation. The first scholar downplays atonement altogether, and suggests Paul's focus lies elsewhere. The second denies that any hint of propitiatory thinking is present in Paul. The third mostly avoids the issue by redefining atonement to mean new covenant, community, and transformative living. While I admire the motives of each of these scholars, I must respond that certain atonement ideas really are central for Paul, and that Paul's teachings did form the ancestry of the more troubling atonement theories that we face today.

Paul Is "Participationist"

The first scholar to be considered is E. P. Sanders, who argues that even when Paul uses sacrificial imagery, the emphasis is not cultic but participationist. For instance, in 2 Cor. 5:14, where "one has died for all; therefore all have died," the result clause speaks of participation in his death, not of expiation.[1] Paul's bigger point has to do with ethics and community (as in the next verse, 5:15, where people no longer live for themselves). The cultic image is there because "Paul inherited the view that Christ died for trespasses."[2] Citing such passages as Phil. 3:10–11 and Rom. 8:17, Sanders says, "The prime significance which the death of Christ has for Paul is not that it provides atonement . . . but that, by *sharing* in Christ's death, one dies to the *power* of sin . . . with the result that one *belongs to God*. . . . The transfer takes place by *participation* in Christ's death."[3] Present and future transformation are what matter; the past reconciliation (atonement) is of secondary importance: "Reconciliation is only preparatory to being given new life. By itself, it is not a term which is capable of showing how one obtains life."[4]

But this does not do justice to the views of one who called his life mission "the ministry of reconciliation" (2 Cor. 5:18). Besides, reconciliation and life are bound together. One sentence earlier, Paul had said, "If anyone is in Christ, there is a new creation . . . everything has become new!" (2 Cor. 5:17). And these sentences are followed by that summing-up statement, where atonement and transformation are linked: "For our sake he made him to be sin who knew no sin, so that in him we might become the righteousness of God" (2 Cor. 5:21). It is twisted exegesis to say that, for Paul, an *unimportant* atonement is followed by an *important* participation and transformation. Sanders creates a false dichotomy between atonement and participation in Christ. Atonement opens the door for participation and transformation to happen. If atonement were of minor significance, it would not form the culminating point in some of Paul's most impassioned discourses (Romans 3; Romans 4; 5:1-11; 1 Cor. 5:1-8, 2 Corinthians 5; Galatians 2).

Sanders is right to draw our attention to the importance of participation, as in Rom. 8:17 ("joint heirs with Christ . . . we suffer with him so that we may also be glorified with him"). And it is helpful to establish that Paul uses cultic imagery to make a soteriological point,

---

1. E. P. Sanders, *Paul and Palestinian Judaism* (Philadelphia: Fortress Press, 1977), 464–65.
2. Ibid., 463.
3. Ibid., 467–68.
4. Ibid., 470.

but then moves beyond the cultic to the ethical and communal level. In Romans 12, believers are a "living sacrifice" (12:1), but no metaphorical temple is mentioned; the setting is believers' *lives*: minds experience "renewing," and are able to "discern what is the will of God" (Rom. 12:2).

Participationism raises the subject of the intensification of the sacrificial idea through abstraction and internalization. Suffering itself is given new meaning, but it is a mixed blessing. An unintended aftereffect of the sacrificial metaphor is to give rise to a grandiose kind of asceticism, opening the door for saintly and moralistic bullies who exalt the value of suffering as a spiritual practice, which will happen in subsequent centuries of the early church.

Paul Is "Restorative"

Another thinker, Ted Grimsrud, is eager to affirm a positive message of healing rather than any kind of "mechanism" of salvation: "The revelation of God's justice in Jesus has to do with God's healing and restorative work. So, God 'put forward Jesus' [Rom. 3:25] out of love in order to heal—not out of mechanistic holiness that requires a violent sacrifice in order to satisfy God's honor or turn away God's anger."[5]

It is God's own compassion that saves, Grimsrud insists, and that is true throughout the Bible: "Paul makes clear, in full continuity with the Bible's salvation story, that the salvation he describes comes to humanity due to God's initiative. As Paul presents God here, God has no need for appeasement or satisfaction."[6]

It sounds beautiful, but does it adequately describe Paul's angle? Are not *both* God's initiative and satisfaction theology present, for example, in Rom. 5:5–11? It is "God's love" that is demonstrated through the Christ dying (5:5, 8), but Christ "died for the ungodly" thus saving us "from the wrath of God" (5:6, 9), and we were reconciled to God "through the death" (5:10), so the death did somehow change our

---

5. Ted Grimsrud, *Instead of Atonement: The Bible's Salvation Story and Our Hope for Wholeness* (Eugene, OR: Cascade, 2013), 202.
6. Ibid., 205.

relationship to God. Paul the preacher will draw on different concepts and weave them together, but he does seem to picture a sacrificial transaction taking place. The weakness in Grimsrud's argument becomes clear when he says that not only Paul but the whole Bible reflects Jesus' view of salvation: "The dynamics of justice that undergird salvation in the Bible are best understood as restorative and not retributive.... In Jesus, as in the Old Testament, God responds to brokenness not with punitive violence but with unconditional mercy."[7] Further, the Old Testament sacrificial cult had nothing to do with appeasement: "The Hebrews express their gratitude by giving offerings to God.... These are not ways to appease God's righteous anger so much as concrete expressions of remorse."[8]

I wish Grimsrud were right, and that there were no violent theology in the Bible, no appeasement, nothing we need to outgrow, but this is wishful thinking. It simply is not accurate, at least as regards Paul's belief, to say that "Jesus's death provides no new content in relation to the essence of salvation."[9] This is correct as regards Jesus' *own* teachings, but for Paul, for 1 Peter, for Hebrews, the death *did* produce new content. In their understanding, it made salvation possible. We cannot wish this away, but we do need to address how it differs from what Jesus himself taught.

Finally, on page 236, Grimsrud does admit that there are some violent and retributive passages in the Bible, but he insists that retribution is secondary, and "mercy is central."[10] He wants the whole Bible to say, "Nothing needs to happen to change God's disposition toward human beings.... God does not need some sort of sacrificial violence in order to satisfy God's honor or appease God's wrath."[11]

This is certainly true, but it is not what every part of the Bible says. Rather than trying to make the whole Bible speak with one voice, it is better to acknowledge that the truth value of the texts varies,

---

7. Ibid., 226, 230.
8. Ibid., 228–29.
9. Ibid., 233.
10. Ibid., 236.
11. Ibid., 87.

and to admit that we are choosing the Jesus viewpoint, reading with the "Jesus lens," as Sharon Baker says. She writes: "We need to make his life and teachings the lens through which we interpret the Bible, imagine God, and construct our theology."[12] Perhaps Baker should call it the "Jesus standard" rather than "lens," since she is not talking about wearing rose-tinted glasses, but recognizing where Jesus' view differs from some Bible texts.[13]

Paul Is "New Covenantal"

Michael Gorman has written a masterful book that argues that atonement theories have tended to be "atomistic ... separated from ethics, spirituality, ecclesiology,"[14] and often overlooking "the larger purpose of God in the Messiah's suffering and death; the larger purpose is to create a new people who will ... bear universal witness to the new covenant."[15] Citing the eucharistic reference to a "new covenant" (1 Cor. 11:25), Gorman says that, for Paul, "Jesus himself interpreted his own death as the inauguration of the new covenant."[16]

Therefore Gorman finds it odd that theories of atonement, both the classic ones and the new ones generated by scholars, are strangely indifferent to the new covenant theme, and disconnected from the gospel's focus on spiritual transformation and community renewal. Looking at the many places where Paul emphasizes "hospitality or service," Gorman argues, "There is no cleansing without discipleship, no vertical relationship without horizontal relationships, no atonement without ethics.... Ethics is atonement in action."[17] He further (and correctly) notes the scarcity of theological study of the "gospel of peace" (Eph. 6:15; see also Luke 7:50; Rom. 8:6; 14:17; 16:20; 1 Thess. 5:23, which draw on "covenant of peace" in Isa. 54:10, and

---

12. Sharon L. Baker, *Executing God: Rethinking Everything You've Been Taught about Salvation and the Cross* (Louisville: Westminster John Knox, 2013), 87.
13. Ibid., 86–88.
14. Michael J. Gorman, *The Death of the Messiah and the Birth of the New Covenant: A (Not-So) New Model of the Atonement* (Eugene, OR: Wipf & Stock, 2014), 20.
15. Ibid., 39.
16. Ibid., 53.
17. Ibid., 46, 55.

peace eschatology in Isaiah 2, 9, and 32).[18] The main exception to this neglect is Willard Swartley.[19]

An important point that Gorman makes is that "the New Testament writers are far less interested in the *mechanics* of atonement than they are in the *results* of atonement."[20] Gorman would like Christians to move forward spiritually, to enact the ethics and spirituality that Jesus revealed. That is why I can say his book is very helpful, even while I criticize his harmonizing efforts. He seems to think that distorted atonement theologies will fade away if Christians make real spiritual progress. That may be correct, but I think he underrates the problems created by those who cling to retributive theology and substitutionary atonement: the damage they do to their children and to the church.

Gorman looks at Grimsrud's "non-atonement model," commending several aspects of it, but says we cannot "conclude that Jesus' death is first and foremost the consequence of evil Powers to which Jesus appropriately responds. Rather, the death of Jesus is first and foremost the work of God and God's Son."[21] But this creates a worse problem: thinking that God would not extend forgiveness until the death of his son as a sacrifice. To say that the death of Jesus was God's work is to leave in place the biggest theological error and the worst psychological trap. Further, "to explain Jesus' death as a redemptive act of God is to shift responsibility for human treachery onto God."[22]

I wish to stress this point, giving it its own section.

The Son Was Not Intended to Be Killed

We need to reject the very idea that the Father *required* the death of the Son. Especially in Matthew, Mark, and Luke, I find evidence that Jesus himself said otherwise. Jesus' parable of the tenant farmers shows that God did not intend his son to be killed: the vineyard owner sent his

---

18. Ibid., 133, 143–58.
19. Willard M. Swartley, *Covenant of Peace: The Missing Peace in New Testament Theology and Ethics* (Grand Rapids: Eerdmans, 2006).
20. Gorman, *Death of the Messiah*, 210.
21. Ibid., 18.
22. Donald Capps, *The Child's Song: The Religious Abuse of Children* (Louisville: Westminster John Knox, 1995), 118.

servants to the tenants "to collect his produce" (Matt. 21:34; cf. Mark 12:2), and when they beat and drove away his servants, he sent his son "to them, saying, 'They will respect my son'" (Matt. 21:37; Mark 12:6). The owner sent his son to be *respected*, not to be killed; to collect some produce (which stands for spiritual growth), not to be ambushed, which displeased the owner. Jesus, by this time, expects to be killed, but he makes it clear that *this is not God's will*.

The next passage in Matthew is a parable in which a king calls people to join "a wedding banquet for his son" (22:2). It is meant to be a joyous feast. But again the king's messengers are mistreated, and the king is "enraged" (22:6-7). This is because the coming of the Son of God was meant to be celebrated—but not in a nationalistic way: people should stop thinking of the Messiah as the son of David: "If David thus calls him Lord, how can he be his son?" (Matt. 22:45; cf. Mark 12:37). Jesus is not a militant "son of David," but a humble king, "mounted on a donkey" (Matt. 21:5; cf. John 12:15; referring to the peace king in Zech. 9:9).

Jesus wept over Jerusalem: "if you ... had only recognized on this day the things that make for peace! ... You did not recognize the time of your visitation from God" (Luke 19:42, 44). He genuinely wished they had accepted the Messiah. He did not come in order to be rejected! In Luke, this story is soon followed by the parable of the wicked tenants, and again, the servants and the son are sent to receive "his share of the produce of the vineyard" (20:10)—to receive some sign of spiritual progress, and to exercise his normal rights as the owner's son, not to be mistreated.

Scholars have examined at great length the three warnings of his coming death that each of the Synoptic Gospels has Jesus issuing to his disciples. Occasionally, the scholars notice that there is *no* atonement teaching in these warnings (Mark 8:31-33; 9:30-32; 10:32-34; and parallels). They are wholly of a *warning* nature, meant to prepare his disciples for disappointment and sorrow, even for the crushing of their pride and ambition—a kind of ego death. Not once does Jesus say he will die as a sacrifice, or that forgiveness of sins is dependent on his death, or that anything in the relationship with God will be changed. These are not *interpretations* of his death at all, but concrete warnings about arrest, mistreatment, execution—but also of resurrection to follow. The point is to train his apostles for disappointment, and also for the surprise of the resurrection, so they will not be crushed and then elated—although that is exactly what happened. As with many of Jesus' lessons, this one didn't sink in, apparently.

There *was* a lesson that the disciples understood, I think. It is when Jesus indicts the religious leaders for valuing the symbol (temple, altar) more than the reality symbolized (Matt. 23:16–22), and valuing religious minutiae more than the "weightier matters of the law: justice and mercy and faith" (23:23). But later Christians slid back into the practice of valuing the symbol over the reality, when they exalted the cross and theories about the cross more highly than Christ's own teaching, valuing atonement *concepts* over the reality of God's love (which the ideas were meant to communicate). Jesus' going to the cross was an example of God's love in action, but salvation was not magically dependent on that tragic event any more than it was dependent on his family's regrettable misunderstanding of him, or his disciples' grasping for power in the kingdom, or any of the other examples of foolish incomprehension that Jesus faced.

God will accept anyone who wants to repent and be reconciled to God, but God did not require a ritual killing in order to make that reconciliation possible. The notion that a ritual killing was necessary is what I call "crazy-making theology." It is unhealthy thinking, it does not fit with the picture of the Father that Jesus painted, and it has harmful effects within families, communities, and individual minds, teaching that love has to be purchased through suffering.

I do think Paul opened the door to difficulties by teaching that the death of Christ was the necessary precondition for reconciliation, and in order to teach us unselfishness: "He died for all, so that those who live might live no longer for themselves, but for him who died and was raised for them" (2 Cor. 5:15). Faced with the shame and horror of the Messiah being killed, Paul assigns soteriological meaning to it, picturing it as necessary. Faced with a lemon (the Messiah's crucifixion), Paul make lemonade out of it, but this lemonade created new theological problems: calling an atrocity inevitable and even God-willed. The atrocity was humanly imposed; it was *not* God's will. None of the atrocities that humans commit are God-willed. We need to grow up morally, take responsibility for our own actions, repudiate *all* brutality, and stop blaming God for it.

In Gorman's system, I would fit in with those who offer a "non-atonement model," but I do not use Grimsrud's strategy of denying that propitiation is present in the Bible at all. Gorman admits that it is present, but insists it is a minor theme, not a problem.[23] Both Grimsrud and Gorman say there is no real problem with the Bible, and they try to make it speak with one voice. I think we need to admit that there really *are* some problematic concepts in the Bible, some passages that do not reflect the attitude and spirit of Jesus, that would fail the test of reading with the Jesus lens.

Gorman makes a very good case, but he simply dodges the problems with atonement, allowing atonement to disappear within a larger discussion of new covenant and community. By "atonement" he really means the whole range of salvation and spiritual living, so he can always direct attention away from any problems with atonement. I agree that new covenant ought to be explored more thoroughly, and that it needs to be connected with the *person* of Jesus, with his *lived* revelation of God, but we should reject the primitive idea that the new covenant required his death, and stop thinking of his death as a payment.

Gorman smoothes over and harmonizes important differences in the New Testament record. He rightly says, "Jesus' entire ministry was one of inaugurating the reign and the peace of God," but the immediately preceding sentence says that Acts 10 "reinforces the way in which Luke sees Jesus' death as God's act of peacemaking."[24] This is *not* what Acts 10 says; it does not make the death the key moment. In that passage, Peter

---

23. Gorman, *Death of the Messiah*, 226.
24. Ibid., 184.

shows Jesus bringing about peace and salvation through his life and resurrection: God drew people from "every nation . . . preaching peace by Jesus Christ—he is Lord of all" (Acts 10:35–36). "He went about doing good and healing all who were oppressed by the devil" (10:38). He was put to death, "but God raised him on the third day," he appeared to believers afterward; he is "ordained by God," and "everyone who believes in him receives forgiveness through his name" (10:39–43). Peace is made *not* through the death, but *through him* and his whole ministry, his "doing good," "healing," appearing to believers after the resurrection, and offering forgiveness through his *name* (his power and divinity). This leads to a very important point that merits its own section.

Luke-Acts Is Not Cross-Centered

Luke-Acts is indeed peace-centered, Jesus-centered, and salvation-centered, but it is not cross-centered. Jesus' death is part of the narrative, but it is not the place where peace is made. Acts 10:36 links peace with the *person* and preaching of Jesus. Jesus saves because of *who he is* ("Lord of all"), not because of what happened to him. The passage establishes that Jesus' whole ministry brought life and forgiveness; everything is *not* made dependent on the death. Yet Gorman turns it into atonement theology, assimilating Luke to Paul: "We have now explored the basis of peace in Paul and Luke: the death of Jesus as the critical moment in God's peacemaking."[25] But it is simply inaccurate to say that Paul and Luke both make the crucifixion the key moment of salvation, that they invest Jesus' death with the same meaning. This forcible harmonizing simply allows Paul to gobble up Luke. A focus on the death as soteriological and central is true of Paul, Hebrews, 1 Peter, 1 John, and probably Revelation; but only *somewhat* true of Mark, Matthew, and John. We should not think of any of these Gospels as a passion story with an extended introduction. These three Gospels attach some soteriological meaning to Jesus' death, but they spend

---

25. Ibid., 185.

more time on the teaching and healing activities of Jesus, which are at least as central in bringing salvation as is the death of Jesus. The messages of the Gospels suffer serious distortion if we reduce them to extended narratives based on a Pauline formula. Rather, some Pauline ideas have had significant influence on John's Gospel, and limited influence on Mark's and Matthew's.

There are three New Testament books that simply do not fit the death-as-the-saving-moment agenda. The Epistle of James never mentions the death of Jesus; for James, there is saving significance to "the implanted word," "works," "wisdom from above," "draw[ing] near to God," and "the prayer of faith" (1:21; 2:24–26; 3:17–18; 4:8–10; 5:15–16). Of course, Luke and Acts do not fit into the death soteriology. For Luke (author of both of these works), it is the *whole* life of Jesus, and especially the resurrection, that bring salvation. Since Luke is the author of more material in the New Testament than anyone else, and is the one who is most aware of the need to consult multiple "eyewitnesses" and to be "investigating everything carefully" (Luke 1:2–3), he is probably the most important biographer of Jesus—and he does *not* make atonement the basis of his understanding. Luke, of course, contains many of the same stories and even wording as Mark and Matthew, but we need to notice the differences. There is a lesson in all three Gospels about unselfish service of others, which Mark and Matthew finish with the unusual and quite out-of-place[26] saying, "The Son of Man came not to be served but to serve, and to give his life a ransom for many" (Mark 10:45; Matt. 20:28). Luke, although he has the same story and the same message about serving others (22:24–27), does not contain the ransom saying. It is no accident that Luke does not have this atonement passage.

In Jesus' warnings of the passion as they occur in Luke, there is a certain fatalism about his coming death: "The Son of Man must undergo great suffering"; "Let these words sink into your ears: The Son of Man is going to be betrayed into human hands"; "Everything that is

---

26. Alexander J. M. Wedderburn, *The Death of Jesus: Some Reflections on Jesus-Traditions and Paul*, WUNT 299 (Tübingen: Mohr Siebeck, 2013), 64–65.

written about the Son of Man by the prophets will be accomplished"; "They will kill him" (Luke 9:22, 44; 18:31, 33), but Luke sees this as the fate of almost any prophet: "It is impossible for a prophet to be killed outside of Jerusalem. Jerusalem, Jerusalem, the city that kills the prophets" (13:33–34). "The Wisdom of God said, 'I will send them prophets and apostles, some of whom they will kill and persecute'" (11:49). In Luke's understanding, Jesus is not killed in order to bring salvation, but because he is a prophet (and more than a prophet). As Stephen asks: "Which of the prophets did your ancestors not persecute?" (Acts 7:52).

In fact, there is only one undoubted atonement passage in all of Luke's extant writings, and even here "Luke appears to be repeating ancient terminology without making its theology his own."[27] The passage is in Acts, where he allows Paul to say, "Shepherd the church of God that he obtained with the blood of his own Son" (Acts 20:28).

In order to back up my assertion that this is actually *the only* atonement passage in Luke-Acts, I must look closely at the Lukan Eucharist. In Luke 22:17–18, Jesus raises the cup and speaks about not drinking again until the kingdom of God comes; the cup then awkwardly reappears in 22:20 accompanied by an atonement saying ("the new covenant in my blood"). In the opinion of many New Testament scholars (including me), the atonement-colored material in 22:19b–20 was inserted early in the manuscript tradition, probably to make Luke fit with the liturgical wording that was becoming standard in the churches. The one and a half verses that speak of atonement were not present in the oldest Western manuscript nor in the oldest translations (Latin, Syriac, and Boharic) of Luke, nor in the lectionaries, and are considered an interpolation (insertion) by the important text critics B. F. Westcott and F. J. A. Hort.[28] They call it a "Western non-

---

27. Joel B. Green, "Death of Jesus," in *Dictionary of Jesus and the Gospels: A Compendium of Contemporary Biblical Scholarship*, ed. Joel B. Green, Scot McKnight, and I. Howard Marshall (Downers Grove, IL: InterVarsity Press, 1992), 160.
28. B. F. Westcott and F. J. A. Hort, *Introduction to the New Testament in the Original Greek with Notes on Selected Readings* (1882; repr., Peabody, MA: Hendrickson, 1988), appendix, 63–64. The originality and scope of Westcott and Hort's work is discussed in Bart D. Ehrman, *Misquoting Jesus: The Story behind Who Changed the Bible and Why* (San Francisco: HarperSanFrancisco, 2005), 121–25.

interpolation," which means it was *not* interpolated into the oldest Western manuscript (D), but *was* interpolated into the manuscript tradition early on, and is found in most Greek manuscripts. Most of the Western noninterpolations were located "in the last three chapters of Luke."[29] The saving power of "blood" is not found anywhere else in Luke, and in only one verse in Acts. Even when the "blood" wording is present, it occurs in different locations in the Eucharist in different manuscripts, which suggests scribal insertion in a period preceding standardization of the text.

Without the blood wording, Jesus' words at the Eucharist in Luke involve eagerness to share with the disciples, sadness about leaving, and a promise to share again in the eschatological banquet in the kingdom of God, culminating in the simple statement "this is my body" (22:19a), which probably means "let this symbolize the life I have shared with you here." It is an intimate moment of final sharing, and a commemoration of his life with the apostles; it is not a Pauline theology of his death as a sacrifice. We cannot force that onto Luke, although Christians have been doing exactly that ever since the additions to the Lukan Eucharist were made.

In a speech in 1997, Professor Joel Green said that Luke does not *reject* atonement (he says Acts 20:28 shows that), but the cross is definitely not the basis of salvation for Luke; Jesus' Sonship, resurrection, ascension, and the outpoured Holy Spirit provide the basis for salvation (Acts 2:33; 5:30; 10:43).[30]

We have become so used to "this is my blood" (and the atonement ideas that come with it) that we find it hard to think of a Eucharist without blood wording, but the likely original version of Luke is not the only first-century Eucharist without blood. The Didache, a church order and catechetical document as old as parts of the New Testament, has a detailed eucharistic text with no blood wording. The wine

---

29. Alexander Souter, *The Text and Canon of the New Testament* (New York: Charles Scribner's Sons, 1913), 139–40. Strengthening the case that a disputed text is an interpolation is when, in the scholars' judgment, it is much harder to believe that such a passage was *removed* by a scribe than to believe it was *inserted* by a scribe. Scribes tend to heighten, not to reduce, Christology.
30. My paraphrase of Joel Green's remarks given at Pacific School of Religion, March 24, 1997. I am *not* claiming that Joel Green supports all my views on atonement.

SACRIFICE AND ATONEMENT

symbolizes "the holy vine of David, your child, which you have revealed through Jesus, your child" (9.2).[31] The word translated "child" (παιδός, *paidos*) could also be translated "servant," and it almost certainly echoes the Servant of the Lord passages in Isa. 42:1 and 43:10. So the wine is interpreted messianically. The Messiah stands for Israel, and the vine is a very old symbol for Israel, as seen in Ps. 80:8 ("you brought a vine out of Egypt"); Hos. 10:1 ("Israel is a luxuriant vine"); and Num. 13:23 (the discovery of an enormous vine by Israelite spies). But in the Didache, the prayer is for "your church" (10.5), not Israel. The bread, the grain of which was gathered from "the hills and then was brought together and made one," stands for "your Church ... brought together from the ends of the earth" (9.4). The eucharistic prayer is addressed to "our Father" (9.2–3), not to the God of Israel. Thus the messianism is internationalized, as in the New Testament. But the Eucharist is bloodless, as is the likely original version of Luke. What matters about Jesus in this ritual is not his death, but his revelation of God: "The life and knowledge which you revealed through Jesus, your child" (9.3); "the knowledge and faith and immortality which you revealed through Jesus, your child" (10.2). Jesus brings salvation and knowledge of God (an important Old Testament concept: Prov. 2:5; Isa. 11:9; Jer. 9:24; Hos. 4:1, 6; 6:6), but his death is mentioned nowhere in the Didache! What matters is Jesus as Messiah and revealer. He is not pictured as sacrificial victim.

To study the historical Jesus, we have to use all the ancient sources, and not forcibly harmonize them. We need to allow the New Testament's most prolific author to retain his resistance to atonement, and notice the testimony of that New Testament–era text the Didache, which has a nonbloody and nonatoning Eucharist. I do not think that Jesus imparted any atonement meaning to his coming death or to his teachings about salvation, but the idea emerged early within Christianity, and it came to influence the manuscript tradition, bringing Luke into conformity with other eucharistic passages,

---

31. From Cyril C. Richardson, ed. and trans., *Early Christian Fathers* (New York: Touchstone, 1996), 175.

particularly the Pauline wording, "the new covenant in my blood" (1 Cor. 11:25).

Paul's Eucharist is the earliest with blood wording (not surprisingly), and then Mark's (14:22–25), written in approximately 44 and 69 CE respectively. Matthew simply draws on his source Mark. Luke dates from the late 80s, and the Didache from some time in the first century CE. The Didache may even be earlier than 80 CE, if the Gospel of Matthew drew on it, as some think.[32] We have been under the spell of atonement theology for so long that it comes as a shock to learn that the original Eucharist might have had no atonement message at all. It was a simple ceremony of remembrance and promise, where Jesus recalled his time with the apostles and looked ahead to the future kingdom, when he would commune with them again.

---

32. Affirming this view is John J. Clabeaux, "The Ritual Meal in Didache 9–10: Progress in Understanding," in *The Didache: A Missing Piece of the Puzzle in Early Christianity*, ed. Jonathan A. Draper and Clayton N. Jefford, SBLECL 14 (Atlanta: SBL, 2015), 222. Mentioning this view along with different views is Jonathan A. Draper, "Conclusion: Missing Pieces in the Puzzle or Wild Goose Chase? A Retrospect and Prospect," in Draper and Jefford, *Didache*, 534. Asserting a mid-first-century date is Aaron Milavec, "When, Why, and for Whom Was the *Didache* Created? Insights into the Social and Historical Setting of the *Didache* Communities," in *Matthew and the Didache: Two Documents from the Same Jewish-Christian Milieu?*, ed. Huub van de Sandt (Minneapolis: Fortress Press, 2005), 63.

6

Fear and Loathing in the Epistle to the Hebrews

Hebrews' Dilemma about Sacrifice

Hebrews has a major problem that he seems unable to solve.[1] Hebrews considers the Jewish sacrificial cult to be a prefiguration of the self-offering of Christ, but also criticizes the cult for being superficial and material. Hebrews creates a problem for himself when he insists that this ineffective ritual prefigured the atonement that Christ would bring. But sacrifice is more than just a model or a metaphor for Hebrews; he takes the purifying and saving power of Christ's sacrifice quite literally. Sacrifice and priesthood are not just "images"; they "operate . . . as . . . divinely-revealed explanatory systems," explaining salvation as a *cleansing*,[2] a καθαρισμός, *katharismos* (1:3).

For Hebrews, forgiveness was made available because of Christ's sacrificial death, despite the strange passage where the antisacrificial

---

1. I refer to the unknown author of Hebrews as "Hebrews," and treat the author as male.
2. Stephen R. Holmes, "Death in the Afternoon: Hebrews, Sacrifice, and Soteriology," in *The Epistle to the Hebrews and Christian Theology*, ed. Richard Bauckham et al. (Grand Rapids: Eerdmans, 2009), 248, 255.

129

words of Psalm 40 are attributed to Jesus: "When Christ came into the world, he said, 'Sacrifices and offerings you have not desired'" (Heb. 10:5). This *could* imply the rejection of sacrifice, but Hebrews undoes that possibility by saying that Jesus "made purification for sins"; that the earthly temple was a "shadow of the heavenly one"; and that "in these sacrifices there is a reminder of sin" (Heb. 1:3; 8:5; 10:3). I. Howard Marshall is correct to note that this "suggests some limited efficacy to the sacrifices."[3] Hebrews has more continuity than discontinuity with cultic *thinking*. In fact, Hebrews actually raises the status of sacrifice by making it soteriological.

And yet, the sacrificial cult is criticized as having the following weaknesses:

- The cult had only a temporary effect: cleansing had to be constantly repeated, in contrast with Christ's "once for all" cleansing (7:27; 10:12).
- The old way is now superseded: "the law has only a shadow of the good things to come" (10:1).
- The old was superficial: it was only "for the body . . . . their flesh" (9:10, 13); it could "never take away sins" (10:11).

Hebrews builds on both the cult's *inadequacy* and its (limited) *usefulness*. The cult can be pictured as partially effective ("flesh is purified," 9:13) or criticized as ineffective ("that cannot perfect the conscience," 9:9). Either point can be used christologically. When Hebrews says the cult was ineffective, he is using the logic of *replacement*: Christ's atonement was *effective*, which the cult's was not (not fully, anyway). When he says that the cult was partially effective, he is using the logic of *fulfillment*: by "the blood of goats and bulls . . . their flesh is purified; how much more will the blood of Christ . . . purify our conscience" (9:13-14). What happened in the old way now occurs in a *new* way, but "how much more." There is a new priest, a greater tent, a better sacrifice. "Through

---

3. I. Howard Marshall, "Soteriology in Hebrews," in Bauckham et al., *Epistle to the Hebrews and Christian Theology*, 267.

the greater and perfect tent ... he entered once for all into the Holy Place ... with his own blood, thus obtaining eternal redemption" (9:11–12).

We are not telling the whole story if we cite only Hebrews' cult-critical passages or only the fulfillment passages. Both treatments occur, and Hebrews has great difficulty trying to unify these two approaches. The tension in Hebrews' attitude(s) toward sacrifice creates a problem for Christian theology. Critiquing the cult as inadequate while insisting that it was a prefiguration of the self-offering of Christ means that Christ's atonement was based on a practice that was ineffective, superficial, and (until Christ came) incoherent. This is the dilemma that Hebrews never really solves, although he labors at it.

Paul never has this problem, since he never criticizes the cult and does not seek to find symbolic meanings in all its details. Hebrews is strongly dependent on the sacrificial metaphor. Paul has more inventiveness and freedom, using sacrificial metaphors but switching easily to other images, even preferring to mix the metaphors, and never allegorizing on the sacrificial ritual. Hebrews allegorizes many details of the cult: veil, sanctuary, priest, transporting and sprinkling of blood. Hebrews is determined to find levels and nuances of meaning in the sacrificial ritual and apply them to Christ. Hebrews may have the longest antisacrificial passage in the New Testament (10:1–11), but he does not go very deep; he never quotes any of the more intensely antisacrificial passages that favor something else over sacrifice (as Hos. 6:6, "I desire mercy, not sacrifice" [NIV], quoted by Jesus in Matt. 9:13; 12:7), or that openly mock sacrifice.

> Will the Lord be pleased ...
>   with ten thousands of rivers of oil?
> Shall I give my firstborn for my transgression? (Mic. 6:7)

Hebrews *needs* the sacrificial model to a much greater degree than Paul does; without it, he could not communicate his concept of salvation. We get a much better understanding of Hebrews' attitude through his dozens of sacrificial images than in his single antisacrificial passage. Hebrews has no need for a continuation of the Levitical priesthood (Heb. 7:11), but he has *every* need for sacrificial concepts.

Hebrews is hampered by his inability to conceive of salvation in any noncultic way, which leaves him unable to solve the difficulty of how it is that God created an ineffectual sacrificial system. Nevertheless, he affirms continuity between God's prior revelation and the current one. It may be that his critique of the old covenant is *socially* motivated, "a polemic against a competing theology of atonement,"[4] motivated by a desire to wean Jewish Christians from Jewish practices.

Hebrews is so attached to atonement that he imposes it on Old Testament texts where it is not present. Hebrews 9:19–20 recalls the initial covenant sacrifice. In Exod. 24:8, Moses sprinkles "the blood of the covenant" on the congregation, sealing them to the promise to obey the covenant. It is not an atoning rite but a promise sealed by a potential self-curse. It is equivalent to saying, "If we break this agreement, let our blood be upon us [let us be killed]." Hebrews alludes to this event in 9:19–20, and then immediately imposes atonement on it, conflating it with the blood of the purification offering in 9:21–22, thus adding "purification and atonement, a connection that is entirely absent from the Exodus account."[5] Everything is drawn into the orbit of atonement. He "misrepresents the Levitical cult as a system exclusively concerned with communal atonement" for *sins*, leaving out the purgation of *ritual* impurity, as when he connects the daily *tamid* rite with sin in Heb. 7:27.[6]

Typology and Obsolescence

Both the hermeneutic of replacement and the hermeneutic of fulfillment are kinds of typology: the sacrificial system was a type (τύπος, *typos*, an image, the impress of a seal) of the better thing—the "how much more," the "better sacrifices," "the good things to come"

---

4. Susan Haber, *"They Shall Purify Themselves": Essays on Purity in Early Judaism*, ed. Adele Reinhartz, EJL 24 (Atlanta: SBL, 2008), 156.
5. Ibid., 146.
6. Ibid., 154, including n52.

(9:14, 23; 10:1). The animal sacrifices were "not the true form of these realities"; they could not "take away sins" (10:1, 4). There needed to be "a change in the law" (7:12). Christ brings "a better covenant" (8:6); "he abolishes [ἀναιρέω, anaireō] the first in order to establish the second" (10:9). He came "to remove sin by the sacrifice [θυσία, thysia] of himself" (9:26). Now that Christ has brought "forgiveness ... there is no longer any offering for sin" (10:18). Thus is the sacrificial system made obsolete: "In speaking of 'a new covenant,' he has made the first one obsolete [πεπαλαίωκεν, pepalaiōken]. And what is obsolete and growing old [γηράσκον, gēraskon] will soon disappear" (8:13). (Cognate with those Greek words are our English words *Paleolithic* and *geriatric*.)

Of course, this is not a blanket condemnation of Judaism, nor is it anti-Jewish at all. In fact, Hebrews clearly states that Jesus came for "the descendants of Abraham" (2:16). Nor is there any indication that the blessing has passed from the Jews into the hands of other people.[7] So this is not "supersessionist" in an ethnic sense, but it is certainly a kind of *conceptual* or *ideational* supersession. Certain ideas and symbols supersede older beliefs and symbols: there is "another priest arising ... the abrogation of an earlier commandment because it was weak and ineffectual ... the introduction of a better hope" (7:11, 18–19).

Mary Schmitt is not correct in arguing that Hebrews applies obsolescence only to the cultic regulations, not to the Torah itself, and that only the priestly commandments on sacrifice have been set aside.[8] Schmitt's statement that νόμος, nomos (law) occurs only in "arguments about explicitly cultic matters" in chapters 7–10[9] is misleading, since it overlooks the fact that Hebrews is considering the law as a whole, not just its cultic measures. "When there is a change in the priesthood, there is necessarily a change in the law as well" (7:12). "Jesus has now obtained a more excellent ministry, and to that degree he is the mediator of a better covenant," and "better promises" (8:6). "Law,"

---

7. Correctly, Richard B. Hays, "'Here We Have No Lasting City': New Covenantalism in Hebrews," in Bauckham et al., *Epistle to the Hebrews and Christian Theology*, 152, 154, 161.
8. Mary Schmitt, "Restructuring Views on Law in Hebrews 7:12," *JBL* 128 (2009): 196.
9. Ibid., 198n27.

"ministry," "covenant," and "promises" are not restricted to cultic meanings.

What about Morna Hooker's suggestion that Christ's death "fulfilled the purpose of the cult, but has at one and the same time done away with the whole system"[10]? It seems obvious that the literal sacrificial system is no longer necessary (for Hebrews), but what about the cultic idea, the metaphorical sacrifice? That is not done away with, but is repeated numerous times throughout the epistle.

Perhaps Hebrews uses the sacrificial image like a ladder for ascending to a height, then pulls up the ladder—rejects the image—once he has reached that height. This is the question (and the suggestion) of Oskar Skarsaune, whether "the cultic institution of the Old Covenant was a self-consuming artifact? A ladder the author discards after having climbed it."[11] Skarsaune is picking up on a theme from Richard Hays in the same collection, who suggests that Hebrews uses concepts that readers will understand, but then "unsettles ... the readers and destabilizes their interpretative categories" in order to "lead the reader beyond its own rhetoric."[12] Skarsaune goes further, suggesting that Hebrews uses, and then discards, the image of sacrifice. The ladder image is vivid, but the argument is unconvincing (although the *reader* may go beyond Hebrews, taking the logical step of rejecting sacrifice altogether, which Hebrews was unable to do).

Some of what has been interpreted as antisacrificial would more accurately be called *antiearthly*, or rather: stressing the superiority of the heavenly to the earthly. This is where Hebrews is interweaving Platonic (actually, Middle Platonic) ontology with Jewish eschatology. The earthly temple is just "a sketch and shadow of the heavenly one" (8:5), and it clumsily copies the heavenly. "The *sketches* of the heavenly things," that is, the earthly temple, had "to be purified with these rites, but the heavenly things themselves need better sacrifices than these"

---

10. Morna D. Hooker, "Christ, the 'End' of the Cult," in Bauckham et al., *Epistle to the Hebrews and Christian Theology*, 205.
11. Oskar Skarsaune, "Does the Letter to the Hebrews Articulate a Supersessionist Theology? A Response to Richard Hays," in Bauckham et al., *Epistle to the Hebrews and Christian Theology*, 182.
12. Hays, "Here We Have No Lasting City," 169–70.

(9:23). As above, so below, but imperfectly. The "true form [εἰκόνα, *eikona*]" (10:1) is not found in things visible.

In Platonic thinking, singularity is superior to multiplicity; unity is characteristic of the divine. Hebrews uses this principle when he compares Jesus' one-time sacrifice to the repeated Levitical sacrifices.[13] Sacrifice would no longer have been needed if it had successfully cleansed the conscience. The limitedness of earthly sacrifices is shown by their repetition; the divinity of Christ's sacrifice is shown by its singularity: Christ "offered for all time a single sacrifice for sins" (10:12).

Some scholars wish to deny that there is any Platonic viewpoint in Hebrews; they insist that only a wholly Jewish eschatology is present, but these categories are not mutually exclusive. Jewish works such as the Wisdom of Solomon and the Testaments of the Twelve Patriarchs incorporate the Middle Platonic belief in the superiority of heavenly to earthly, and of singularity to multiplicity, without ceasing to be thoroughly Jewish. A number of early Christian writers blend Jewish eschatology with Platonic ontology, both intellectualizing authors (Origen, Clement of Alexandria) and popularizing ones (Epistle of Barnabas, *Shepherd* of Hermas). Jewish concepts of covenant, redemption, and purification are obviously central for Hebrews, but popularized versions of Platonic principles are also present. He is drawn to the Platonic idea of the earthly as a (poor) copy of the heavenly.

Unfortunately Hebrews seems unable to imagine the heavenly level except in terms of the earthly, and without much transformation. The heavenly is cleansed by a blood ritual, just as is the earthly. We "enter the sanctuary by the blood of Jesus" (10:19).

It is the heavenly sanctuary that is meant. David Moffitt has convincingly argued that Hebrews follows the Levitical concept in having atonement take place, not at the moment of death, but when the blood is brought into the sanctuary—the *heavenly* sanctuary: "It is

---

13. Luke Timothy Johnson, *Hebrews: A Commentary*, NTL (Louisville: Westminster John Knox, 2006), 244.

not the death/slaughter of Jesus that atones, but the presentation of his life before God in the heavenly holy of holies."[14] In Heb. 9:11, 24, the author has "Jesus entering and moving through a structure that actually exists in heaven.... Jesus is doing in heaven what the high priests do annually on earth," except that he presents "his atoning offering to God *in heaven*."[15] Moffitt points out that Jesus could not perform this priestly function while still on earth ("Now if he were on earth, he would not be a priest at all," 8:4); "Jesus can only serve as a high priest in heaven,"[16] so the crucifixion is not the actual moment of atonement for Hebrews, but his presentation of himself and his blood in the heavenly sanctuary. Some verses that show this emphasis on entrance to the heavenly sanctuary, or on sitting down next to God in heaven, are 8:5; 9:11–12, 23–25; 10:20.

Of course, it is not just the death that matters; the whole sacrificial process is important.[17] What Moffitt emphasizes is that the carrying of the blood into the holy of holies is the climactic moment. Still, we find Hebrews repeatedly returning to Jesus' "suffering of death," "ma[de] ... perfect through sufferings," "a death has occurred that redeems them," "to remove sin by the sacrifice of himself" (2:9–10; 9:15, 26).

New Covenant, Old Logic

Hebrews tries to develop the logic of "a new covenant ... not like the [old] covenant" (8:8–9), but as soon as he starts to discuss it, he notes that "even the first covenant had regulations for worship" (9:1). He describes the sacrificial furnishings in 9:2–8, and sums up with "This is a symbol of the present time" (9:9), but they deal only with bodily things, while Christ's offering deals with the eternal (9:10–14). But everything in the new replicates something in the old: there are "tent," "blood," "sprinkling," being "offered," to "purify," "a death,"

---

14. David M. Moffitt, "Blood, Life, and Atonement: Reassessing Hebrews' Christological Appropriation of Yom Kippur," in *The Day of Atonement: Its Interpretations in Early Jewish and Christian Traditions*, ed. Thomas Hieke and Tobias Nicklas (Leiden: Brill, 2012), 221.
15. David M. Moffitt, *Atonement and the Logic of Resurrection in the Epistle to the Hebrews*, NovTSup 141 (Leiden: Brill, 2011), 225–27.
16. Moffitt, "Blood, Life, and Atonement," 211–12.
17. Ibid., 221.

and "redeem[ing]" (9:11–15). Bloodshed in the *old* is given as the reason ("thus") for bloodshed in the *new*: "Under the law almost everything is purified with blood, and without the shedding of blood there is no forgiveness of sins. Thus [οὖν, *oun*] it was necessary for the sketches of the heavenly things to be purified with these rites" (9:22–23). "There had to be life for life or blood for blood."[18]

Hebrews retains the priestly concept rather than developing the noncultic "new covenant" concept of Jeremiah. The new covenant in Jeremiah involved a deep inward transformation without any priestly involvement; God says, "I will put my law within them, and I will write it on their hearts" (Jer. 31:33). Hebrews quotes this passage twice (8:10; 10:16), but still has atonement being accomplished vicariously by the "high priest" or "great priest" (2:17; 10:21), unlike Jeremiah's God-wrought change. In Jeremiah's vision, people know God for themselves ("They shall all know me," Jer. 31:34).

Where forgiveness was direct and unmediated for Jeremiah, it has to be mediated through "the offering of the body of Jesus Christ" for Hebrews (10:10). The great prophets were ready to leave sacrificial thinking behind, but the New Testament Epistles resuscitate it (none more vigorously than Hebrews), and attach it to the more advanced ideas they get from Jesus' own teaching. New Testament theology is an amalgam of profound revelation with retrogressive sacrificial teachings.

Just as Jeremiah's radical vision was partly domesticated and altered by a Deuteronomistic editor who introduced standard temple-centered theology, so is Jeremiah's new covenant idea domesticated and altered by the sacrificial thinking in Hebrews. The logic of salvation is based on what "even the first covenant" did, "under the law" (Heb. 9:1, 22). Thus it is blood that brings redemption (9:12). Priestly categories drown out the radical change of heart that Jeremiah envisioned.

Sacrificial soteriology also obscures Jesus' teaching that the way to God is already open, without any reference to his coming death, but affirming, "Your faith has saved you; go in peace" (Luke 7:50); "do not

---

18. John Stott, *The Cross of Christ* (Downers Grove, IL: InterVarsity Press, 1986), 138.

fear, only believe" (8:50); "the kingdom of God is within you" (Luke 17:21 NIV, TEV, NRSV margin). Without any priestly intermediary, people can "do the will of God" (Mark 3:35; John 7:17; cf. Matt. 12:50), can "hear the word of God and do it" (Luke 8:21), can be "faithful" (Luke 16:10), can have "good treasure of the heart" (Luke 6:45; cf. Matt. 12:35), can be "pure in heart" (Matt. 5:8). Extreme pessimism about the human ability to love and obey God may find some biblical support, but not in the viewpoint of Jesus.

Unfortunately, popular Christian theology follows Hebrews' notion that Christ accomplished an atonement *like* the atonement brought about by the sacrificial system, only more effective. There is no sign of Paul's multimetaphoric picturization of Christ's death resembling several different kinds of deliverance. And Jesus' idea of salvation as freely offered, like a father's love, without cultic magic, is absent, although it is found in the biographies (the Gospels).

Is Hebrews Free of Selfish Reciprocity?

Now I glance at the theory of Jason Whitlark, which denies the presence of any give-to-get reciprocity in Hebrews. Whitlark spells out how reciprocity works in Greek sacrifice. The Greek gods expected to be shown "honor in the form of sacrifice and votive gifts for divine benefits."[19] A key feature of reciprocity-motivated worship is "indebted gratitude ... the return of gratitude to benefactors."[20] What is not convincing is Whitlark's argument that "the cooperative mutual dependence characteristic of reciprocity finds no place in ... Hebrews."[21] He claims it is not present because eschatology and pessimistic anthropology *are* present: people are not trustworthy clients who are repaying the patron's benefits, but are sinners who are

---

19. Jason A. Whitlark, *Enabling Fidelity to God: Perseverance in Hebrews in Light of the Reciprocity Systems of the Ancient Mediterranean World* (Milton Keynes, UK: Paternoster, 2008), 45. Whitlark carefully documents these attitudes in "pagan" religions, but wants to defend the Bible against the allegation that it also reflects this attitude. My point is that *some* biblical books and characters accept the selfish reciprocity system (Exodus, Proverbs), some reject it (Hosea, Micah, Jesus, James), and others adopt some aspects of reciprocity while critiquing others (Hebrews, Paul).
20. Ibid., 19, 41.
21. Ibid., 166.

powerless and require "divine enabling."[22] Whitlark's major goal is to refute David deSilva's assertion that Hebrews *does* think in terms of patronage and reciprocity, that "fidelity to God in Hebrews ... arises out of ... a debt of gratitude" as seen in Heb. 1:1–3; 12:2, 28; 13:16; and elsewhere.[23]

But the "gratitude" and "feeling of indebtedness"[24] that are key features of reciprocity-motivated worship are found in Hebrews as well. Whitlark admits that Hebrews uses "the language of indebtedness, owing, repaying," but only in *one* place, 12:28 ("let us give thanks, by which we offer to God an acceptable worship with reverence and awe").[25] He says Hebrews rises above reciprocity thinking, because it is "motivated by faith in a promised future," and not "indebted gratitude that arises out of past benefits."[26] He allows that Hebrews sets out "to shape and transform the cultural values and language,"[27] but this is really a concession that Hebrews *does* use reciprocity values and language. As deSilva points out, one of Hebrews' main terms, "'grace' (*charis*) was the keyword within the ancient social systems of friendship, patronage, and benefaction."[28] Hebrews uses the standard patronage terms "grace" and "help" numerous times (just a few are 2:9, 16–18; 4:16; 13:9), along with warnings of the danger of ingratitude, "neglect," or "spurn[ing]" (2:3; 6:4–6; 10:26–29; 12:25–29).[29] It may be that deSilva overdoes his argument for God as patron in Hebrews (to the detriment of God as Father, an important concept in the epistle [2:10–11; 12:7–9]), but his findings cannot be dismissed as easily as Whitlark would like.

Whitlark concedes that "though the prophecy in Jeremiah or its surrounding context does not mention the cult or sacrifice, Hebrews

---

22. Ibid., 124–25, 130–31, 144–46, 151, 155. "Divine enabling" is on 146.
23. Ibid., 141; re: David A. deSilva, *Perseverance in Gratitude: A Socio-Political Commentary on the Epistle to the Hebrews* (Grand Rapids: Eerdmans, 2000), 87, 474–76, 433.
24. Whitlark, *Enabling Fidelity to God*, 41–47, 76–79, 89, 129.
25. Ibid., 142.
26. Ibid., 143; Heb. 11:1 shows this future promise (144).
27. Ibid., 142–43.
28. David A. deSilva, *The Letter to the Hebrews in Social-Scientific Perspective* (Eugene, OR: Cascade, 2012), 103–4.
29. See deSilva, *Letter to the Hebrews*, 101–3, 117–18, 123.

filters its interpretation of the new covenant through the cult of the old covenant."[30] Indeed! But that cultic "filter" severely distorts the prophetic idea. The Major Prophets (Isaiah, Jeremiah, and Ezekiel) speak of being clean after conversing with God, of a cleansed people walking on a highway called the Holy Way, of a new covenant and law written on the heart, of being sprinkled clean and having a new spirit within (Isa. 1:18; 35:5-8; Jer. 33:8; 31:31-34; 32:38-41; Ezek. 36:25-27), but this cleanness is metaphorical and spiritual, not cultic. God makes the people loyal "in their hearts" (Jer. 32:40). There is nothing of sacrifice there; in fact, there is no priestly imagery at all in Jeremiah 31–32, but images of family, farming, festival, discipline, return from exile, love and honesty ("heart").

Innocent Blood and a Fury of Fire

When Hebrews speaks of "a fearful prospect of judgment, and a fury of fire that will consume the adversaries" (10:27), he is matching the most threatening messages of the Old Testament: "In the fire of his passion the whole earth shall be consumed" (Zeph. 1:18). Nor is this any kind of "corrective" punishment; Luke Timothy Johnson rightly sees the fiery prospect in Hebrews 10 as "vengeance."[31] Hebrews is disgusted with backsliding Christians who "spurned [καταπατήσας, katapatēsas] the Son of God" (10:29); God "will repay [ἀνταποδώσω, antapodōsō]" (10:30), using the verb the Septuagint uses for God repaying apostates and enemies (Lev. 18:25; Deut. 32:41).[32]

As if this focus on blood and violence were not enough to suggest psychological disturbance, there is a chilling focus on the unique power of *innocent* blood. Innocence is the key factor in his reasoning about the effectiveness of the blood of Christ. Jesus' is "sprinkled blood that speaks a better word than the blood of Abel" (12:24). Jesus "offered himself without blemish to God" (9:14).

Blood is a constant theme in the second half of Hebrews. The

---

30. Whitlark, *Enabling Fidelity to God*, 152; cf. 163.
31. Johnson, *Hebrews*, 264.
32. Ibid., 266.

repeated reference to attaining safety through the blood of the innocent one (9:7–14, 18; 10:19–22; 11:28; 12:24; 13:12–21), and the linkage of parental punishment of children to God's punishment of sin, has suggested to some interpreters that the author's childhood was marred by parental violence.[33] My years of studying atonement lead me to conclude that one of the unconscious foundations of atonement thinking is an ideology of *payment through suffering*. I see this in the notion that Jesus is "now crowned with glory and honor because of the suffering of death," and that God saw fit to "make the pioneer of their salvation perfect through sufferings" (2:9–10).

Hebrews tells believers not to "lose heart when you are punished by" God (12:5). Suffering is corrective in his view. *Because* the Lord "addresses you as children," you must endure the Lord's discipline (12:5). Enduring harsh discipline is what good children *must do*. "We had human parents to discipline us, and we respected them.... They disciplined us for a short time as seemed best to them, but he disciplines us for our good" (Heb. 12:9–10). It seems that Hebrews identifies with his abusers and is trapped in the system of abuse, repeating the ideology that punishment is good for us: "Now, discipline always seems painful rather than pleasant at the time, but later it yields the peaceful fruit of righteousness to those who have been trained by it" (12:11). Jesus is offered as our model: "bear the abuse he endured" (13:13). Hebrews even uses punishment as proof of God's love (12:6–7); if you do not receive such "discipline ... then you are illegitimate and not his children" (12:8).

For anyone with psychological knowledge, all this exaltation of "discipline," "punishment," and "enduring abuse" is a red flag indicating a background in abusive treatment. Unfortunately, an abused child can "come to believe that the punishment is an expression of the parent's love."[34] Further, I think there is a link between the abuse-habituated mentality and the inclination toward ritual categories.

---

33. Donald Capps, *The Child's Song: The Religious Abuse of Children* (Louisville: Westminster John Knox, 1995), 68–75.
34. Ibid., 7.

SACRIFICE AND ATONEMENT

Again and again does Hebrews express salvation in ritual categories: Jesus "made purification for sins" (1:3); believers are "sprinkled clean" by "the blood of the covenant" (10:22, 29). Blood is everywhere, and the normal reaction to seeing human blood (horror) is suspended. Instead, there is an abstract glorification of blood. Finally, in verse 24 there is a mention of love, but it is linked with the threat that, if we sin, "there no longer remains a sacrifice for sins, but a fearful prospect of judgment, and a fury of fire" (10:26–27). The law of Moses had prescribed punishment for lawbreakers; now, Hebrews threatens, "How much worse punishment do you think will be deserved by those who have spurned the Son of God, profaned the blood of the covenant by which they were sanctified, and outraged the Spirit of grace? . . . Vengeance is mine, I will repay" (10:29–30).

The worries about sin, profanation, and punishment bespeak a pattern of extreme distress. It seems likely that Hebrews had a strict religious upbringing with hypercritical parents, contributing to a nervous perfectionism. Hebrews fastidiously distinguishes the "sacrifices . . . that cannot perfect the conscience" from "the blood of Christ," whose sacrifice will "purify our conscience" (Heb. 9:9, 14). The obsession with perfection (2:10; 5:9; 6:1; 7:11, 19, 28; 9:9, 11; 10:1, 14; 11:40; 12:2, 23) may be a response to having been harshly judged as a child, creating a perfectionist and judgmental cast to his adult form of religion.

Fear-filled ideas of God are linked with the childhood strategy of coping with parental rage by means of payment through suffering. Even Christ "learned obedience through what he suffered; and having been made perfect, he became the source of eternal salvation for all who obey him" (5:8–9). No other New Testament author explicitly speaks of Jesus being perfected by suffering, and certainly not that it taught him obedience, the way an authoritarian father might "teach" his son a lesson. This seems to arise out of Hebrews' own painful experience of always needing to appease an angry parent.

Hebrews' very harsh views of God probably reveal an avoidant attachment pattern as a child. Paul seems to have experienced ambivalent attachment, but Hebrews had a more severe and painful childhood, with parents who were abusive, at least in their religious teaching.

Donald Capps sees "paranoia as one of the main psychological consequences of child abuse ... the sense that the body, the will, and the self are at risk."[35] Capps sees paranoia in Hebrews' citation of Old Testament texts that arouse "his pervasive sense of being endangered," as in the story of how God was provoked by Israel, speaking of those "whose bodies fell in the wilderness," because they were "disobedient" (Heb. 3:17–18).[36] It is the sin of "disobedience" (4:3, 6, 11) that summons up the "word of God ... sharper than any two-edged sword ... able to judge the thoughts and intentions of the heart" (4:12). This intruding and judgmental gaze of God "strikes the greatest terror in the heart of the child."[37]

Making disobedience the all-consuming sin, one that carries the death penalty, reveals a background in authoritarian (and insecure) parenting. Children who are severely punished learn to expect punishment, to consider it normal.

Hebrews says things that sound like they come straight out of the pedagogy manuals of which Alice Miller wrote: "We had human parents to discipline us, and we respected them. Should we not be even more willing to be subject to the Father of spirits and live?" (Heb. 2:9). "Discipline ... yields the peaceful fruit of righteousness" (Heb. 2:11). This rings very false to me, not because I think Hebrews is lying, but because I think he is under the spell of poisonous teaching.

Miller sees the punishing God as part of the poisonous pedagogy which teaches that children must be shamed to make them obedient. Children who were treated harshly learn to articulate an ideology of "just deserts" when they become adults. Western religion has played into the hands of poisonous pedagogy. "God the Father is easily offended, jealous, and basically insecure; He therefore demands

---

35. Ibid., 46; he is citing Philip Greven, *Spare the Child: The Religious Roots of Punishment and the Psychological Impact of Physical Abuse* (New York: Knopf, 1991), 168–69.
36. Capps, *Child's Song*, 70–71.
37. Ibid., 71.

obedience and conformity."[38] Miller is not a theologian, but her goals correlate well with the gospel: both involve cultivating healthy-minded and respectful relationships. If "the truth will make you free" (John 8:32), then we will break the spell of poisonous ideologies, will cease the cycle of abusive behaviors.

Religious ideology can be the source of healing, or of terrible injury. And people tend to pass on the ideology of punishment if that is what they experienced as children. Parents can heed Jesus' warning that to "put a stumbling block before one of these little ones" is worse than "if a great millstone were fastened around your neck," can obey his command "that you do not despise one of these little ones" (Matt. 18:6, 10), and can follow his exhortation to welcome "one such child" as though welcoming him (18:5), or parents can follow the ancient advice to not "spare the rod," but to impose "the rod of discipline" (Prov. 13:24; 22:15). Religious values can inflict serious injury, or values can be enlightened by revelation and can help to heal these wounds. Many children hear a religious message that commingles love with threat. In Hebrews, every promise is accompanied by a threat: "How can we escape if we neglect so great a salvation?" (Heb. 2:3). "Having received the knowledge of the truth. . . . It is a fearful thing to fall into the hands of the living God" (10:26, 31).

Along with the ritual thinking goes the emphasis on vicariousness. Felix Cortez claims that Hebrews writes of a "deep" inward cleansing,[39] but the "depth" is all Jesus'; believers are only cleansed vicariously (9:14). This is magical thinking. It takes an aspect of Paul's teaching (believers vicariously justified) and magnifies it so as to obscure something that is equally important for Paul: believers *actually* dying to sin and being *actually* transformed and conformed to Christ by the Spirit (Rom. 6:4–11; 7:6; 8:29; 12:2; 2 Cor. 3:17–18). Hebrews turns Paul's highly participative and transformative soteriology into a secondhand

---

38. Alice Miller, *Thou Shalt Not Be Aware: Society's Betrayal of the Child*, trans. Hildegarde Hannum and Hunter Hannum (New York: Farrar, Straus & Giroux, 1984), 221.
39. Felix H. Cortez, "From the Holy to the Most Holy Place: The Period of Hebrews 9:6-10 and the Day of Atonement as a Metaphor of Transition," *JBL* 125 (2006): 546.

experience wherein one *believes* that one's inner nature has been magically transformed by Christ's ritual death.

Another Soteriology in Hebrews

I have finished each chapter with a word from the gospel. I will do that here as well, but I can actually do that by using a second model of soteriology, separate from the sacrificial one, that is found in Hebrews, one that is more consistent with the teachings of Jesus. With this completely different concept, one can use Hebrews to critique Hebrews. One can also use Hebrews' concepts of a new covenant replacing an old one, and of heavenly realities being truer than earthly, to argue that human understanding will always be limited, that further illumination will always be needed, and that we should not become too attached to our mental models, no matter how highly honored by our religious tradition. One could argue, on the basis Hebrews' own observations about sacrifice, that the latter is an inadequate model of salvation.

That *other* soteriology which Hebrews uses speaks of the saving effect of the incarnation of Christ, which is followed by our necessary imitation of him. The incarnation implies that God saves us by becoming human, by "shar[ing] flesh and blood" (2:14), understanding our sufferings, living obediently, showing us how to live, and so "bringing many children to glory" (2:10). Christ "was faithful" and inspires us "to hope" (3:6), making us "partners of Christ" (3:14), motivated to "go on toward perfection" (6:1). Jesus was perfected through prayer and obedience, and so "became the source of eternal salvation for all who obey him" (5:7–9).

I understand that Hebrews does not think he is articulating a different soteriology here. He sees the sacrificial death and the compassionate life as linked in the same salvation story. In fact, he argues that Jesus' becoming like other people is part of what qualifies him to be high priest: "He had to become like his brothers and sisters in every respect, so that he might be a merciful and faithful high priest

145

SACRIFICE AND ATONEMENT

in the service of God, to make a sacrifice of atonement for the sins of the people" (2:17).

Hebrews binds together the incarnation, the suffering, and the substitutionary death, but really he is fusing two different soteriological models together. The essential ingredients of the incarnational soteriology are that the Son of God gained direct, bodily experience of humanity by living a mortal life, one that included suffering (as all lives do), and that he remained sinless in a sinful world. There is no substitute for experience, for "walking a mile in our shoes." Jesus did this, and he gained compassion and understanding through experience, through contact with individuals of many races and backgrounds. (The heavenly Jesus undoubtedly had compassion [John 8:58; 17:4–5], but the *earthly* Jesus had to gain compassion through *experience*, as we all do.) Jesus' mortal life, loving contacts, and sinless obedience all existed before the lynching took place. To attach salvation to the murder is to add a different scheme of salvation to the incarnational one. Hebrews adds this when he says, "God . . . ma[d]e the pioneer of their salvation perfect through sufferings" (2:10), by which he means the death, which he sees as necessary to the defeat of "the one who has the power of death, that is, the devil" (2:14). But this is a different concept, separate from the idea of the Son gaining experiential wisdom, and demonstrating how to live—things that he did before he was murdered. Incarnational theology is more capable than cross soteriology of explaining how it is that Jesus was saving people (or telling them their faith had saved them) before he was killed. Substitutionary death soteriology can hardly explain how it is that Jesus saved people *before* he died.

Hebrews *starts* down the road of incarnational theology, but he detours into substitutionary atonement, about which he has more to say. Where incarnational theology *could* lead is to the realization that it was God's solidarity with humans—the divine Son's thorough sharing of human life—that opened up the way of salvation, and not a sacrifice paid either *to* or *by* God. One could then recognize that *salvation is spiritual repair, not ritual remedy*. No ritual action was required to trigger

God's love and salvation, and no death in order to conquer death. Jesus already had the power of life in him *before* he was killed, and the "power to take it up again" when it was taken away from him (John 10:18). (Admittedly, only the Gospel of John has Jesus having the power to raise himself up; Paul always speaks of *God* raising Jesus from the dead; Hebrews never actually mentions the resurrection, but it is implied in Jesus presenting himself in the heavenly temple and sitting at the right hand of God [1:3; 8:1; 10:12; 12:2].)

Sacrifice need not have become the dominant soteriological image. Hebrews has some of the themes (also present in Paul and the Gospels) that can be coordinated with the idea of salvation as spiritual growth: God's generosity, the experience of spiritual sonship, transformation, perfecting, forgiving. But sacrifice tends to overwhelm these other themes in Hebrews, and sacrifice does not coordinate well with the idea of trust and growth.

The healthy-minded religion of Jesus is quite different from the discipline- and suffering-empowered religion of Hebrews. For Hebrews, Christ had to pray "with loud cries and tears . . . and he was heard because of his reverent submission. . . . He learned obedience through what he suffered" (5:7–8). All this attention to submission and suffering, with the expectation of continued discipline at the hand of God (12:5–10), is probably related to "discipline" received as a child.

Can we recover a concept of salvation independent of atonement? I think there is sufficient basis in the Bible to do this. Numerous texts tell us that salvation depends on knowing God and knowing the Son of God: "And this is eternal life, that they may know you, the only true God, and Jesus Christ whom you have sent" (John 17:3). "Believe on the Lord Jesus, and you will be saved" (Acts 16:31; see also Rom. 10:9). "Everyone therefore who acknowledges me before others, I also will acknowledge before my Father in heaven" (Matt. 10:32). All it takes is a sincere recognition of the heart: "No one can say 'Jesus is Lord' except by the Holy Spirit" (1 Cor. 12:3). This recognition can be had independently of any mythology about Jesus' death, although it may take a conscious effort to separate this insight from concepts of atonement that are found in the same texts. Christology need not be overwhelmed by atonement.

7

Atonement Played Out

The postbiblical legacy of atonement in books, tracts, sermons, and hymns is too vast to cover in one chapter. I will only dip into the stream and follow its main movements and debates. In the middle of the chapter, I will look at an interesting psychological theory, and in the last section, I will discuss a serious, and often ignored, psychopathological development of atonement thinking.

Chronology of Theories of Atonement

The sacrificial idea took some time to become widely known and influential. If the Acts of the Apostles is any indication, the idea of the death of Jesus having a saving effect was not a widely known idea at first. It occurs in only one verse in the entire book, and then not until the twentieth chapter. I think that, in this regard, Acts is historically accurate: the death of Jesus was not at first interpreted as the crucial moment of salvation.

The early speeches of Peter in Acts repeatedly mention the unjust killing of the Messiah, but never refer to it as a saving event. The climax of Peter's speech is a call to "repent, and be baptized.... Save yourselves from this corrupt generation" (Acts 2:38, 40). The crucifixion is referred to over and over again as unjust and sinful, but not as the reason that salvation is available. God has "glorified his servant Jesus, whom you handed over and rejected" (3:13). "In this way God fulfilled what he had foretold through all the prophets, that his Messiah would suffer" (3:18). But this idea is not taken any further: the killing was foretold, and therefore it had to happen, not for atoning purposes, but because prophets are *always* persecuted, according to Acts (which *itself* is a Jewish theme: Jer. 26:15–23; Amos 7:10–13; Zech. 12:10; 13:7; Wis. 2:10–20).

Throughout Acts, people are being saved in the name of Jesus and are receiving the Holy Spirit with power and signs. In all of this, there is no indication that salvation happened *because* of the killing of the Messiah. Even when the focus is on believing in Jesus, it is not focused on his death: "By this Jesus everyone who believes is set free from all those sins from which you could not be freed by the law of Moses" (Acts 13:39). Honest repentance leads to salvation, very much in continuity with Old Testament teaching: "Repent therefore, and turn to God so that your sins may be wiped out," for "God has given even to the Gentiles the repentance that leads to life" (3:19; 11:18).

Finally, two-thirds of way through Acts, we encounter the only verse in which atonement is expressed, the sudden statement of Paul: "Keep watch over yourselves and over all the flock, of which the Holy Spirit has made you overseers, to shepherd the church of God that he obtained with the blood of his own Son" (20:28). And as suddenly as the idea appears, it is dropped. Paul talks to the elders of Ephesus about the work he has done among them, and reminds them to "support the weak" (v. 35). Technically, the "obtaining" of the church with blood is a redemptive, not a sacrificial, idea, but redemption falls within the orbit of Pauline atonement, and this statement does sound like something Paul could have said.

Paul, as early as the 40s and 50s, was using sacrificial terminology to explain why Jesus had been martyred, and we can see from the deutero-Pauline literature and the writings of Ignatius and Irenaeus that Paul's atonement ideas were echoed, adapted, and handed on, but one would hardly know this from the writings of Luke.

The idea of the sacrificial atoning death of Christ may have grown out of speculation among Jewish Christians in Antioch, where Jewish martyrology was very influential.[1] There is an "intriguing possibility that a Maccabean martyr cult existed in Antioch," with even a "grave site of the Maccabean martyrs."[2] Jewish Christians in Antioch could be the source of the idea of Jesus' death as the supreme martyr's death, although this is far from certain. It can, however, be confidently asserted that the earliest Christian message did not speak of Christ's death as atoning. As Tibor Horvath put it: "The sacrificial interpretation of Jesus' achievement is rather a late development in the theology of the early Church,"[3] taking "late" to mean a few decades. It was not part of the early teaching of the Twelve, although some of the Twelve eventually were influenced by Pauline thinking. (Pauline concepts are echoed, in varying degrees, in Mark, Matthew, John, 1 Peter, 1 John, and Revelation.)

There has never been any *standard* doctrine of atonement agreed to by the majority of churches, although an atonement conversation did develop. In recent times, it has been common to speak of "three standard theories of atonement" that arose from the second through the twelfth centuries: the ransom theory, the satisfaction theory, and the moral influence theory. There is an intriguing article by Paul Pruyser interpreting these three theories psychologically. I will look at his thesis after I have summarized the development of the main theories.

---

1. Stuhlmacher thinks that Paul's atonement ideas owe much to Antiochene Christianity, via the "Stephen circle." Peter Stuhlmacher, *Reconciliation, Law and Righteousness: Essays in Biblical Theology* (Philadelphia: Fortress Press, 1986), 67, 103–4, 175. Antioch is mentioned many times in Acts, the first time in 6:5. Paul talks about his argument with Peter in Antioch in Gal. 2:11–16.
2. Stephen Anthony Cummins, *Paul and the Crucified Christ in Antioch: Maccabean Martyrdom and Galatians 1 and 2*, SNTSMS 114 (Cambridge: Cambridge University Press, 2001), 83–84.
3. Tibor Horvath, *The Sacrificial Interpretation of Jesus' Achievement in the New Testament: Historical Development and Its Reasons* (New York: Philosophical Library, 1979), 85.

Ransom Theories

The ransom theory is really a group of theories advocated, with variations, by Irenaeus, Origen, Gregory of Nyssa, Augustine, Gregory the Great, and other church fathers in the first several centuries of the church. These theories all accept some version of the story that Adam's sin brought death to the world, and gave the devil some rights over humanity, especially the right to impose death. In all these theories, salvation is pictured as humanity's deliverance from subjugation to evil powers.

Most versions of the theory say that when the divine Word incarnated in flesh, the devil thought he had rights over *that* human as well, but he did *not* have any rights over a sinless person. So when he helped to impose death on Jesus, he overstepped his bounds and lost his rights over humanity. Some versions of this theory speak of the incarnate Word offering himself as a kind of ransom payment for the release of the human captives, hence the theory's name. Although Irenaeus cannot bring himself to say so directly, he seems to accept that a ransom was paid to the devil. But Irenaeus (like a number of other church fathers) really has more than one theory of atonement and salvation. The central and original thought in Irenaeus is "recapitulation," which has nothing to do with ransom. Recapitulation is the idea that salvation came from Christ's redeeming every stage of human life by living through it; "he passed through every age, becoming an infant for infants," and so on through all the stages of life,[4] "so as to restore [people] to God's likeness."[5] Ben Pugh observes, "Recapitulation theory takes its bearing from the incarnation rather than the death of Christ. . . . Everything Adam did, Jesus undid."[6] The rich implications of Irenaeus's incarnational thought were left largely undeveloped, except (to some degree) by Gregory of Nazianzus. Irenaeus also gives us one of the best one-line summaries of the gospel:

---

4. Quoting Irenaeus, *Adv. haer.* 2.22.4 is Mark A. McIntosh, *An Introduction to Christian Theology* (Malden, MA: Blackwell, 2008), 84.
5. David A. Brondos, *Paul on the Cross: Reconstructing the Apostle's Story of Redemption* (Minneapolis: Fortress Press, 2006), 52.
6. Ben Pugh, *Atonement Theories: A Way through the Maze* (Eugene, OR: Cascade, 2014), 26.

"Christ became what we are in order that we might become what he is."[7]

Several church fathers could not tolerate the idea of salvation coming through a ransom payment; they might have used the term, but they gave it a different explanation. Gregory of Nyssa, for instance, says that Christ acted as a "ransom in our behalf," but really it was a trick, since his divine nature "was hidden under the veil of our nature," which the devil "gulped down along with the bait of flesh, and thus, life being introduced into the house of death," death was defeated.[8] Salvation was not actually purchased, but was accomplished by Christ's sinlessness and the devil's overaggressiveness. The "ransom" was just a ruse. That is why I suggested in a previous book that we call these "rescue theories" rather than ransom theories,[9] but the latter has established itself as a recognizable term, so I am using it here. For Gregory and others, the apparent ransom actually tricked the devil into breaking the rules. This gives an oddly deceptive meaning to the incarnation: "The flesh was a veil adopted for the purpose of deceiving Satan."[10]

Some light is shed on this strange theme of trickery if we accept the idea, articulated by a number of scholars, that the ransom theory is the Christianization of an originally gnostic idea.[11] A common gnostic idea in late antiquity was that the celestial powers were hostile and held humans captive. The supreme God (who was not the creator of this world) was hidden. A lower divinity, the evil or deranged Demiurge, created and controlled the material realm in defiance of the true God, the "hidden God." The Logos, working with the hidden God, wanted to bring deliverance to humanity, so he had to sneak into the realm

---

7. Irenaeus, *Adv. haer.* 5 preface, as given in Morna D. Hooker, *Not Ashamed of the Gospel: New Testament Interpretations of the Death of Christ* (Grand Rapids: Eerdmans, 1994), 35.
8. Gregory of Nyssa, *Great Catechism* 24; quoted in David A. Brondos, *Fortress Introduction to Salvation and the Cross* (Minneapolis: Fortress Press, 2007), 70.
9. Stephen Finlan, *Problems with Atonement: The Origins of, and Controversy about, the Atonement Doctrine* (Collegeville, MN: Liturgical, 2005), 67–69.
10. L. W. Grensted, *A Short History of the Doctrine of the Atonement* (Manchester, UK: Longmans, Green, 1920), 69.
11. Ibid., 34; Hastings Rashdall, *The Idea of the Atonement in Christian Theology* (London: Macmillan, 1919), 245; Pugh, *Atonement Theories*, 3–5.

controlled by the Demiurge; he could "not reveal who he really is—like a king in disguise."[12] Of course, most of these gnostic concepts were never accepted by orthodox Christianity, but the notion of the Logos having to enter into a foreign realm fit well with the Christian idea of "the present evil age" (Gal. 1:4) being under the control of the evil "god of this world" (2 Cor. 4:4).

What about the language of sacrifice and propitiation? Origen, the influential third-century theologian and scholar, used these terms, but "he did not give them their normal sense"; in at least two passages, he completely reverses the meaning of "propitiate," so that "to convert or reform a man ... is 'to propitiate sin.'"[13] Origen sees Christ as setting out to "enable and help men to repent and become really righteous."[14] He may say that Christ's death ransomed the human race, but he seems to have typical Hellenistic martyrology in mind: he compares the result of Christ's death "with pagan stories about men dying for their country to avert plagues and other evils."[15] It was part of the great cosmic battle by which Christ triumphs over evil. Origen's focus is eschatological, hopeful, and transformative. The very reason for the incarnation was to open up the way to spiritual perfection "so that by fellowship with that which is more divine the human may become divine."[16] Christ is the life-giver and healer.

Similarly, Athanasius, in the fourth century, will use traditional language, such as "the debt owing from all" and "death on behalf of all,"[17] but he also has a teaching that centers more on the deification that Jesus made possible, saying, "He became man that we might be made God."[18] Athanasius had a synthetic concept; he will say that Christ's sacrifice is "an offering made by God to death," but his real

---

12. Pugh, *Atonement Theories*, 4.
13. Young quotes Origen, *Homilies on Leviticus* 7.2 and 5.4 in two books: Frances M. Young, *Sacrifice and the Death of Christ* (Philadelphia: Westminster, 1975), 75; and Young, *The Use of Sacrificial Ideas in Greek Christian Writers from the New Testament to John Chrysostom* (1979; repr., Eugene, OR: Wipf & Stock, 2004), 170.
14. Rashdall, *Idea of the Atonement*, 275.
15. Young, *Sacrifice and the Death of Christ*, 78–79. Grensted identifies this as Origen, *Contra Celsum* 1.1 (*Short History*, 64).
16. Quoting Origen, *Contra Celsum* 3.28 is Grensted, *Short History*, 66.
17. Grensted, *Short History*, 79–80.
18. Athanasius, *Inc.* 54; quoted by Grensted, *Short History*, 81.

emphasis seems to be on the restoration of the divine image: "The indwelling Logos restored in Man the image of God."[19]

One could question whether the ransom theory is really consistent with this focus on deification and transformation. But the only Greek father who sees the contradiction and who explicitly rejects the ransom theory is Gregory of Nazianzus, who cannot accept that God would ever need to pay anything to the devil, nor that God required any kind of payment.[20] Deification themes were already present in Irenaeus, Origen, and Athanasius, but became even more prominent in Gregory's work. Further, Gregory coined the word *theōsis*, literally translatable as "engodding," which refers to believers taking on (to a degree) the divine character. The idea became an important teaching of the Greek fathers, but it had roots in Jesus ("The kingdom of God is within you" [Luke 17:21 NIV, KJV]; "Be perfect, therefore, as your heavenly Father is perfect" [Matt. 5:48])[21] and Paul ("be conformed to the image of his Son" [Rom. 8:29]; "being transformed into the same image from one degree of glory to another" [2 Cor. 3:18]).[22]

An important current writer on atonement, J. Denny Weaver, distinguishes the ransom theory from the *Christus Victor* theory, which he prefers. Weaver is picking up on the idea of an influential book of that title written in the early twentieth century.[23] Weaver's version of *Christus Victor* drops the story line of ransom and trickery but retains the idea of a cosmic battle that Christ wins over evil.[24] Using the label *Christus Victor* enables one to partially suppress primitive or unpleasant notions about needing to deceive the devil. Weaver has a thoroughly demythologized (and therefore modern) *Christus Victor* theory.

---

19. Referring to Athanasius, *Inc.* 11–16 is Young, *Use of Sacrificial Ideas*, 193–94.
20. Gregory of Nazianzus, *Oration* 45.22; cited by Grensted, *Short History*, 81.
21. See Stephen Finlan, "Deification in Jesus' Teachings," in *Theōsis: Deification in Christian Theology*, ed. Vladimir Kharlamov, PTMS 156 (Eugene, OR: Wipf & Stock, 2011), 2:21–41.
22. See Stephen Finlan, "Can We Speak of Theōsis in Paul?" in *Partakers of the Divine Nature: The History and Development of Deification in the Christian Traditions*, ed. Michael J. Christensen and Jeffery A. Wittung (Grand Rapids: Baker Academic, 2007), 68–80.
23. Gustaf Aulén, *Christus Victor: An Historical Study of the Three Main Types of the Idea of the Atonement* (London: SPCK, 1931).
24. For instance, J. Denny Weaver, *The Nonviolent Atonement*, rev. ed. (Grand Rapids: Eerdmans, 2011), 15.

Augustine

The fifth-century author and bishop Augustine accepted some of the ransom language, but with a crucial shift: "The devil is not deceived by God, but by his own great pride"; the upshot is that "the devil . . . begins to take a subordinate place."[25] Augustine emphasized that salvation comes as the result of Christ's sacrifice: "All the Old Testament sacrifices looked forward to this sacrifice."[26] "Christ took our punishment upon Himself, destroying our guilt and putting an end to our punishment."[27] Yet Augustine stressed Christ as an example or ideal, whose "love should have the effect of inciting us to love Him in return . . . should bestir our hearts to adore the humility of God."[28] Thus does Augustine anticipate both the sacrificial themes that will become characteristic of the satisfaction theory and the exemplary themes that will characterize the moral influence theory nearly a thousand years later.

Augustine is perhaps best known for his influence on Christian anthropology: the concept of human beings. Augustine taught that humans are wholly selfish and sinful. "Radical evil was the mainspring of all human action. . . . Sin was the sphere and form of the inner life of every mortal man. . . . Sin was self-will, the proud striving of the heart . . . *lust*, never quieted, and fear revealed themselves."[29] We inherited sin from our racial parents, Adam and Eve, who transmitted it to us genetically, as it were.[30]

Augustine was a victim of abuse. He writes of being beaten by his teachers, and even begs God to deliver him from their treatment (which he actually compares with the tools of torture). And yet he excuses his tormenters, even his parents, who laughed at him when

---

25. Grensted, *Short History*, 90.
26. J. N. D. Kelly, *Early Christian Doctrines*, rev. ed. (New York: Harper & Row, 1978), 392.
27. Augustine, *Contra Faustum Manichaeum* 14.4; quoted in Kelly, *Early Christian Doctrines*, 393.
28. Kelly is citing several works (*Early Christian Doctrines*, 393).
29. Adolph Harnack, *History of Dogma*, trans. from the 3rd German ed. Neil Buchanan (1900; repr., New York: Dover, 1961), 5:65, 69–70.
30. Harnack, *History of Dogma*, 5:227; Anthony W. Bartlett, *Cross Purposes: The Violent Grammar of Christian Atonement* (Harrisburg, PA: Trinity Press International, 2001), 59; Jack Nelson-Pallmeyer, *Jesus against Christianity: Reclaiming the Missing Jesus* (Harrisburg, PA: Trinity Press International, 2001), 19.

he showed them his stripes. As with many victims of abuse, he buys into the ideology of his abusers; he ends up accepting that disobedient children deserve beatings. I have to say that authority figures who act that way are idolaters who are making false gods out of "obedience" and "discipline." Donald Capps says that when it became clear to Augustine that he had "to muffle his cries ... something died in that boy in that classroom in northern Africa,"[31] and it would later be reflected in his cold treatment of his own son.[32]

With apologies, we must speak of another Gregory. This one is Pope Gregory the Great, an influential popularizer of Augustine's teachings. He stresses the idea of sacrifice as a payment. As Gustaf Aulén summarized it, "He argues that human guilt necessitated a sacrifice; but no animal sacrifice could possibly be sufficient; a man must be offered for men.... The sacrifice must be undefiled; but there is no man without sin."[33] It is logic such as this that decides that Christ *had* to be killed or we could not have been saved. Gregory also reiterates the old ransom theory in colorful language: "Our Lord made, as it were, a kind of hook of himself for the death of the devil"; the devil bit the flesh and was caught on the hook.[34]

The Satisfaction Theory

Most atonement theories result from attempts to correct distasteful implications of earlier theories. Anselm of Canterbury, in the eleventh-century, rejects the notion that the devil has any rights over human souls, insisting that "God owed the Devil nothing."[35] Instead, Anselm argued, sin besmirched God's honor, and it was necessary that

---

31. Donald Capps, *The Child's Song: The Religious Abuse of Children* (Louisville: Westminster John Knox, 1995), 36.
32. Ibid., 29–34.
33. Aulén, *Christus Victor*, 99. The text, Gregory the Great, *Mor.* 17.46, is quoted in C. Cory and D. Landry, eds., *The Christian Theological Tradition*, ed. Catherine Cory and David Landry (Englewood Cliffs, NJ: Prentice-Hall, 2000), 193.
34. Quoting Gregory the Great, *Mor.* 33.7.14 is Richard E. Weingart, *The Logic of Divine Love: A Critical Analysis of the Soteriology of Peter Abailard* (Oxford: Clarendon, 1970), 83.
35. Rashdall, *Idea of the Atonement*, 350. See also Timothy Gorringe, *God's Just Vengeance: Crime, Violence and the Rhetoric of Salvation*, Cambridge Studies in Ideology and Religion 9 (Cambridge: Cambridge University Press, 1996), 90–91.

satisfaction be made, and honor repaid.[36] Satisfaction is not technically punishment, but is a "compensation" that "may take the place of punishment."[37] Many writers have noted how this resembles feudal society, with God as a lord who has been offended by his underlings (human beings), who then need to make *satisfaction* to the lord, showing that they *honor* the lord.[38] Picking up on an idea expressed centuries earlier by Tertullian and then by Gregory the Great,[39] Anselm teaches that Christ's innocence constitutes an abundance of *merit* that can pay off humanity's sin debt.

Satisfaction was the term for making reparation for a crime or an act of dishonoring someone. It could involve making a payment, but more often involved some kind of public suffering, something commensurate with the impropriety that was committed, and amounting to a kind of legal revenge.[40] Anselm accepts his society's notion that an offended lord *must* demand satisfaction for every act of dishonor, or the lord's authority will crumble. Thus satisfaction theory "reinforced retributive thinking," and this has been reflected in cruel judicial procedures in cultures that have this religious belief, such as medieval England.[41]

Thus, Anselm's logic of atonement is not only legalistic, it is the legalism of eleventh-century feudalism. Satisfaction seems to be quite mechanical: so much satisfaction for so much dishonor: "a quantitative equivalent for such and such quantities of sin."[42] Such computations were also the rule in the practices of penance common in the church in his day.

Timothy Gorringe says Anselm anticipated a period characterized by "a mysticism of pain which promises redemption to those who pay in

---

36. Weaver, *Nonviolent Atonement*, 16; Gorringe, *God's Just Vengeance*, 96.
37. Gorringe, *God's Just Vengeance*, 89, 94.
38. Joel B. Green and Mark D. Baker, *Recovering the Scandal of the Cross: Atonement in New Testament and Contemporary Contexts* (Downers Grove, IL: InterVarsity Press, 2000), 22; Cynthia S. W. Crysdale, *Embracing Travail: Retrieving the Cross Today* (New York: Continuum, 1999), 112; Gorringe, *God's Just Vengeance*, 93.
39. Don S. Browning, *Atonement and Psychotherapy* (Philadelphia: Westminster, 1966), 64; Pugh, *Atonement Theories*, 64.
40. Gorringe, *God's Just Vengeance*, 99–101.
41. Ibid., 7, 12.
42. Grensted, *Short History*, 143.

blood."[43] The following centuries were characterized by a focus on the sufferings of Christ, and the necessity for Christians to suffer. I see this is a religious echo of a behavior learned from strict parents: the child gets back in good graces by making a kind of payment in suffering. Without using the language of "payment," Sandor Rado writes about children engaging in self-punishment "in the hope of absolution,"[44] which could be called "the reparative procedure of expiatory behavior."[45] It is a nearly universal experience of children, this attempt to win back "the presumably offended parent."[46]

The Moral Influence Theory

Again does a new atonement theory arise as a result of an attempt to correct a distasteful aspect of the previous theory. The professor and theologian Peter Abelard, in the twelfth century, rejects Anselm's suggestion that the Father required a death to restore his honor, and that the Son's innocence provided just the price for repaying that honor. Abelard writes, "How cruel and wicked it seems that anyone should demand the blood of an innocent person as the price for anything[!]"[47] The notion is morally unworthy of God, and contributes nothing to the transformation of sinners. It is not God, but people, who need to be changed.[48] Christ's death was exemplary, designed to excite or inspire people to love.[49] This soteriology involves no *transaction*, no "deal between God and Christ," as in Anselm. "Salvation is man's ethical—in the sense of personal—response to the forgiving act of

---

43. Gorringe, *God's Just Vengeance*, 102.
44. Sandor Rado, "The Problem of Melancholia," in *Psychoanalysis of Behavior: The Collected Papers of Sandor Rado*, vol. 1, *1922-1956* (New York: Grune & Stratton, 1956), 51.
45. Sandor Rado, "Rage, Violence, and Conscience," in *Psychoanalysis of Behavior: The Collected Papers of Sandor Rado*, vol. 2, *1956-1961* (New York: Grune & Stratton, 1962), 148.
46. Sandor Rado, "The Automatic Motivating System of Depressive Behavior," in *Psychoanalysis of Behavior: The Collected Papers of Sandor Rado*, vol. 2, *1956-1961* (New York: Grune & Stratton, 1962), 171.
47. Peter Abelard, *Commentary on Romans 2*, on Rom 3:19-26; quoted in Pugh, *Atonement Theories*, 129; also quoted in Gorringe, *God's Just Vengeance*, 109.
48. Weaver, *Nonviolent Atonement*, 18.
49. Rashdall, *Idea of the Atonement*, 358.

divine love."[50] Salvation is God's revelation, and the human response. "The Son of God became man to instruct us."[51]

Abelard's great enemy, even *persecutor*, Bernard of Clairvaux (who gets to be "Saint Bernard"), attacks Abelard, and gets the clerical authorities to condemn the Paris professor. Bernard rejects the notion "that the whole reason for the appearance of God in the flesh was our education."[52] It is one of the tragedies of Christian history that Bernard does not seek some synthesis or compromise with Abelard. Both authors write about the love of God, and about human subjectivity. The vehemence with which Bernard attacks Abelard is hard to explain on doctrinal grounds alone; Abelard's remarks on atonement touched some fear in Bernard, and he lashed out without any hint of love.

Abelard's theory is appealing to many today who wish to see a recovery of the gospel's strong emphasis on the transformation and remaking of humanity. It especially seems to recover a neglected part of the apostle Paul's teachings, who said Christ died "so that in him we might become the righteousness of God" (2 Cor. 5:21), and that believers receive "righteousness from God based on faith" (Phil. 3:9). The message of transformation is essential to the gospel as Paul understood it, and Abelard recovers this principle. Some, however, cannot accept the Abelardian version of atonement because it seems to make selfless suffering a desirable experience, which bullies can use to tell people to suffer silently. Christians do need to learn how to detect narcissists, and not be manipulated by them into feeling guilty.[53] The dark underbelly of selfless suffering is that Jesus "as the obedient son, accepting violence because his father wills it," can tend to imply "that violence is supposed to happen, for the moral education of the victim or for a future reward."[54]

---

50. Paul Tillich, *A History of Christian Thought from Its Judaic and Hellenistic Origins to Existentialism* (New York: Simon & Schuster, 1967), 172.
51. Abelard, *Epitome of Theology*; quoted in Gorringe, *God's Just Vengeance*, 111.
52. Bernard of Clairvaux, *Epistle* 190.7; quoted in Grensted, *Short History*, 106. See also Pugh, *Atonement Theories*, 130. Scholars now often call this "Treatise on the Errors of Abelard."
53. On the ruthless efficiency of narcissists, see Ben Bursten, *The Manipulator: A Psychoanalytic View* (New Haven: Yale University Press, 1973); Stephen Finlan, *Bullying in the Churches* (Eugene, OR: Cascade, 2015), 15–19, 27–31, 65, 70–73.

The Thomasine Synthesis

In the thirteenth century, the Dominican Thomas Aquinas spells out the rational and legal reasons he sees for atonement. Both God's mercy and justice are operative "because by his passion Christ made satisfaction for the sin of the human race."[55] His theory can be made to fit within satisfaction theory, and also within the subcategory called penal substitution; he even says that God was "placated" by Christ's death.[56] Actually, Aquinas synthesizes many previous ideas of atonement (although ignoring Abelard). Within just one article in his master work, I find strong suggestions of moral influence, vicarious "merit," justification, and cosmic battle (in that order): "Man ... would be aroused to love him.... He gave us an example of obedience.... By his passion Christ not only freed man from sin but merited for him the grace of justification.... Man has been overcome and deceived by the devil. But it is a man also who overcomes the devil."[57]

Aquinas seems to want to unify most of the prior doctrines, at least those that contain a sufficient sense of guilt and gravity: "Now because Christ's Passion was the sufficient and super-abundant satisfaction for human guilt and the consequent debt of punishment, his Passion was a kind of price, which paid the cost of freeing us from both obligations."[58]

Philip Quinn says it is not surprising that a medieval thinker should "think of suffering as a kind of currency that can used to pay" for a moral debt, but in our society, our "intuitions ... are tutored by a very different legal picture," where innocent people cannot pay for serious crimes committed by others.[59]

---

54. Rita Nakashima Brock, "Life in My Hand: Rita's Story," in Rita Nakashima Brock and R. A. Parker, *Proverbs of Ashes: Violence, Redemptive Suffering, and the Search for What Saves Us* (Boston: Beacon, 2001), 156–57.
55. Thomas Aquinas, *Summa Theologiae* 3a, q. 46, a. 2; quoted in Gorringe, *God's Just Vengeance*, 120.
56. Thomas Aquinas, *Summa Theologiae*, 3a, q. 49, a. 4, quoted in Rashdall, *The Idea of the Atonement*, 375.
57. Thomas Aquinas, *Summa Theologiae* 3a, q. 46, a. 3; quoted in Romanus Cessario, *Christian Satisfaction in Aquinas: Toward a Personalist Understanding* (Washington, DC: University Presses of America, 1982), 193.
58. Thomas Aquinas, *Summa Theologiae* 3a, q. 48, a. 4; quoted in Thomas Gilby, *St. Thomas Aquinas: Theological Texts* (London: Oxford University Press, 1955), 333.
59. Philip L. Quinn, "Aquinas on Atonement," in *Trinity, Incarnation, and Atonement: Philosophical and Theological Essays*, ed. Ronald J. Feenstra and Cornelius Plantinga Jr. (Notre Dame: University of Notre Dame Press, 1989), 172.

Chronologically, I come now to the edge of the Reformation, but here I want to take the opportunity to look at the psychological essay by Paul Pruyser. There is no harm in putting off Luther and Calvin until after this section.

Anxiety, Guilt, and Shame

As mentioned above, books analyzing Christian atonement doctrines often posit three fundamental theories of atonement: the ransom theory, the satisfaction theory, and the moral influence theory. This threefold schema (or fourfold, if penal substitution is considered separately from satisfaction) is an oversimplification, but nevertheless does reflect a sequence of debates within the ancient and medieval church.

These three theories are so influential that some people read their favorite theory "back into the biblical texts"; for instance, scholars who believe in substitutionary atonement often read that concept back into Leviticus, which is to misread the latter.[60]

Pruyser offers a fascinating analysis in which he argues that each theory is an attempt to resolve a different underlying conflict. In each case, the Ego is in conflict with some other aspect of the mind. He uses the terms of Freudian theory, in which there are three basic "structures" to the individual human mind. The "Ego" is the self-conscious, self-interested part of the mind. The "Id" refers to the unconscious, powerful instinctive drives, mainly the will to survive and the sex drive. The "Super-Ego" is the voice of conscience, restraint, and morality—the cultural values and standards that the individual has learned and internalized. Another term, "Ego Ideal," comes from an earlier stage of Freud's thought; it refers to the sum total of aspirations and ideals for which one believes one is supposed to strive.

Pruyser starts with that the ransom theory, claiming it has to do with "Ego-Id conflicts, in which the Ego feels in captivity to strange symptoms"; it sees "new life in terms of *deliverance* and *adoption*."[61]

---

60. Brondos, *Paul on the Cross*, 19.
61. Paul W. Pruyser, "Anxiety, Guilt, and Shame in the Atonement," *Theology Today* 21 (1964): 24.

The explosive power of the Id and its unconscious nature make it seem "strange," and its power over us makes us feel like captives. This generates anxiety. In restating Pruyser's theory, I wanted to change "anxiety" to "fear," which is a simpler and more basic term, but on reflection I recognized why "anxiety" is the better term. Anxiety refers to a kind of fear in which one is unaware or partially unaware of the source of the fear. Anxiety is gnawing, persistent, deeply unsettling, and suggests levels of worry and frustration that go beyond the more basic "fear." This is appropriate, since we are talking here about unconscious drives that the Ego does not sponsor and the Super-Ego does not approve. These unexpected upwellings, urges, and storms of feeling contribute to nervous apprehension, disquiet, *anxiety*. With this kind of conflict, a person yearns to be *rescued* from what seem like demonic forces.

Satisfaction theories, Pruyser argues, have to do with conflicts between Ego and Super-Ego: with guilt feelings, with "the horror of transgressions.... To the relentless demands of the Super-Ego, sacrifices must be made ... penalties paid.... The goal of salvation ... is stated as *justification*."[62] Luther's theories have much to do with guilt, substitution, and "penalties paid." Anselm also demonstrates the horror of transgression, the focus on guilt.

Finally, feelings of shame "play a large part in the moral influence" theory, where the basic conflict is between the Ego and the Ego Ideal; the Ego knows itself to be wounded, and to have fallen short.[63] People who have been shamed often feel a need to be transformed, even to become a different person. Sometimes, the higher our ideals, the more crushing is the sense of falling short. "Conscience doth make cowards of us all."[64] But it is liberating to hear that the damaged "old self" can be destroyed and we can "walk in newness of life" (Rom. 6:6, 4; cf. Eph. 4:22–24). Pruyser is surprisingly optimistic about this theory; it sees humanity as "educable"; this approach "lives from hope."[65]

---

62. Ibid., 24–25.
63. Ibid., 25.
64. Shakespeare, *Hamlet* III.1.
65. Pruyser, "Anxiety, Guilt," 25.

Pruyser sees some practical but temporary usefulness to each theory. "God's image [needs to] be continually purged of the traces of hostility, cruelty, pride" that these theories embody; a mature and "therapeutic" approach to atonement theories sees "each as an interesting, but, in its one-sidedness, quite fallacious metaphor."[66]

One need not accept all the Freudian categories of thought in order to appreciate Pruyser's analysis. One could equally well say that ransom theories correspond to a mind beset with threatening unconscious emotions, that satisfaction responds to the problem of religious guilt, and that the moral influence theory answers the need for relief from shame about falling short. It should not surprise us, in this psychological age, to discover that our doctrines may unconsciously express our woundedness from anxiety, guilt, or shame.

We can generate a simple chart from Pruyser's article.

	Ransom Theory	Satisfaction Theory	Moral Influence Theory
Troubled Psychic State	Anxiety	Guilt	Shame
Area of Personality	Emotions, Id	Moral nature, Super-Ego	Self-concept, Ego Ideal

Pruyser's analysis cannot be proved. He found it to be a useful tool in therapy. One way for us to test its usefulness would be to try to locate Paul within Pruyser's scheme, despite Paul's preceding the emergence of the three theories. If Pruyser is describing a basic structure of psychological needs, then it should have a certain timelessness. If the ransom theory is a response to anxiety produced by upwellings from the Id, then a person may feel that their body is rebelling, as though there were "another law at war with the law of my mind.... Who will rescue me from this body of death?" (Rom. 7:23–24). Christ rescues us from the domain of death, and brings us into the reign of grace (Rom. 6:9, 14). The ransom-and-rescue category seems to fit Paul, but might there be features in the other categories that fit, as well?

66. Ibid., 29.

While the "body of death" suggests anxiety, the "body of sin" in Rom. 6:6 points to guilt, as do the pessimistic remarks earlier in the letter: "Everyone is a liar.... The whole world may be held accountable to God" (Rom. 3:4, 19). On balance, however, one can find many more images of enslavement and rescue, captivity and deliverance, than of guilt as such. Even the guilt passage I found in Rom. 6:6 is followed by the images of deliverance mentioned in the previous paragraph. Guilt seems to be secondary to anxiety for Paul. Anxiety is the principal characteristic, as we saw, in ambivalent attachment.

Now, let us consider shame as a possibility. Paul *does* feel stained or damaged, needing "the body of our humiliation" to be "transform[ed] ... conformed to the body of his glory" (Phil. 3:21). We saw in chapter 4 that Paul repeatedly faced the experience of being shamed, and that God's message to him was "My grace is sufficient for you, for power is made perfect in weakness" (2 Cor. 12:9). Is it possible that Paul could fit in all three categories, but with an emphasis on the first and third, where salvation is rescue or transformation respectively?

Or should it be argued that the three models are actually different aspects of the same experience of salvation? Perhaps the difference is one of time and focus, either a rescue from guilt (a focus on *past* failings), from anxiety (one's *present* subjection to an evil "law in my members"), or from shame (one's humiliating inability to achieve the *future* ideal)? I *have been* guilty; I *am* anxious; and I *am heading into* an abyss of shame. Who will rescue me from this body of death and give me a body of glory?

I will leave the final analysis of Pruyser's theory to the reader. It is a useful tool for thinking, but not a perfect analysis of atonement, especially since atonement concepts were around for at least two thousand years before the formulation of the three "basic" concepts.

Different individuals feel drawn to one or another of these theories, or to none of them. It is not right to impose any of these theories on young people or to claim that one of them is the basic and original theory. Ideological pressure causes distress, fear, and a panicky approach to salvation. Speaking of distress, it is time to look at the theology of Luther.

Luther and Calvin

In the sixteenth century, Luther would object to the legalism and rationalism of Aquinas, would take an antirationalist approach that still had a taint of legalism, and that had his own psychology and autobiography written all over it.

Not Now an Innocent Person

Luther claimed to despise Anselm's doctrine of satisfaction, and yet he clearly builds on it: "The wrath of God . . . could be appeased" only by "the sacrifice of the Son of God. . . . Only . . . the shedding of his blood could make satisfaction."[67] Aulén admits that Luther uses the terms "substitution" and "merit," but insists that they do not fit into the "Latin theory" (Anselm's theory) because "the satisfaction is made *by* God, not merely *to* God."[68] But this is neither an idea unique to Luther, nor one that is utterly foreign to Anselm. It is probably only the rationalism of Anselm that Luther rejects, not the basic interpretation. Luther insists on a strongly paradoxical, even illogical, account of salvation. He hates human pride and intellectualism. Allowing salvation to be rationally understandable would, for Luther, stink of pride. Luther seems to have an anti-intellectual bias, many times saying that we have no right to be outraged at what seem like unfair actions by God. "You may be worried that it is hard to defend the mercy and equity of God in damning the undeserving. . . . If His justice were such as could be adjudged just by human reckoning, it clearly would not be Divine."[69] Thus, says Luther, divine justice *has* to seem unjust.

Paul Tillich is much more generous to Luther than I am, but perhaps

---

67. An Easter sermon in *The Sermons of Martin Luther*, ed. John Nicholas Lenker (Grand Rapids: Baker, 1983), 7:190–91.
68. Aulén, *Christus Victor*, 134–35.
69. Martin Luther, *Bondage of the Will* 19; in John Dillenberger, *Martin Luther: Selections from His Writings* (Garden City, NY: Doubleday, 1961), 200.

he rescues Luther from the accusation of anti-intellectualism when he says, "Luther was not an irrationalist. What he fought against was that the categories of reason should transform the substance of faith. Reason is not able to save but must be saved itself."[70] Fair enough, but one could say *that* without making so many extremist antirational statements.

Pugh sharply distinguishes Anselm's theory from Luther's, arguing that, in the former, "punishment is *averted*. In penal substitution, punishment is *absorbed*,"[71] but in both cases, Jesus endured violence and paid a debt that humanity could not pay, although Luther greatly heightens the focus on punishment. Pugh insists that, in Anselm's theory, guilt is never transferred to Christ, while in Luther's it is,[72] and this is indeed a difference in their "mechanics" of atonement. Luther takes the metaphor of sin-transfer very literally, while Anselm never has Christ becoming "dirtied" with sin. In both cases, a transaction takes place at the crucifixion, with Christ's death functioning as a debt payment on humanity's behalf. While Anselm describes this with intellectual coolness, Luther brings out the heat of divine wrath, the shame of guilt-transfer, the terror of penalty-bearing.

Luther's anthropology is as pessimistic as Augustine's. He said that, even after salvation, "a man ought to hate himself."[73] He wrote, "Apart from God's grace all is sin. Man has not even the power to respond to God's call to freedom."[74] Luther's theology can be described as an exaggeration of Augustine's, which itself is "an exaggeration of one particular side in the many-sided theology of St. Paul."[75]

Luther even builds on the ransom theory, although he applies to the law what earlier theologians had said about the devil: the law thought it captured Christ, but it exceeded its rights and lost him.[76] Aulén argues that "the presupposition of the Latin theory was the

---

70. Tillich, *A History of Christian Thought*, 278.
71. Pugh, *Atonement Theories*, 56.
72. Ibid., 57.
73. Paraphrasing Martin Luther, *Commentary on Romans* 100.9 is Rashdall, *Idea of the Atonement*, 401.
74. Luther, *Bondage of the Will*, quoted from WA 17:777 by Grensted, *Short History*, 195.
75. Rashdall, *Idea of the Atonement*, 397.
76. Aulén, *Christus Victor*, 127–28.

moralistic idea of penance; but that was for Luther an abomination. The Latin doctrine .... is rational throughout," so it must be rejected.[77] Luther cannot tolerate that human acts of repentance are to be taken seriously. But what Aulén is establishing is not so much Luther's distance from "the Latin theory" as his hostility to any positive attitude toward human capabilities or conscience.

Luther's extremism reaches bizarre levels. He said that God *rightly* punished Christ: "All the prophets did foresee in spirit, that Christ should become the greatest transgressor, murderer ... rebel, blasphemer.... For he being made a sacrifice for the sins of the whole world, is not now an innocent person."[78] He makes a contrast between merciful Son and judgmental Father, who is "'placated' by the Son,"[79] which is certainly not found in Paul. It is really a contradiction of the doctrine of the Trinity to teach such a difference of natures between Father and Son.

Despite Luther's criticism of Catholic legalism, his teaching sounds legalistic. He assumes a legal charge against all humanity, and the Son's bearing of all human guilt certainly seems like a *legal* settlement, despite Luther's insistence that we are now "beyond the law," "dead to the law."[80] The divine Son "did bear in his body my sin, the law, death, the devil," yet "I am a sinner, and most worthy of God's wrath and indignation.... Therefore it is necessary that we should have imputation of righteousness"[81]—an *appearance* of legal innocence. Luther has been rightly criticized for imagining "a merely imputed—that is, a fictitious, juridical, pretended—righteousness," since a person is "incapable of any real righteousness at all."[82] This is unprecedented in its negativism. Justification is really very weak if *no actual goodness* is imparted by salvation. It certainly goes against the teachings of Paul, for whom salvation was truly transformative,

---

77. Ibid., 137.
78. Martin Luther, *Commentary on Galatians* 3.13 in Dillenberger, *Martin Luther*, 135; see also Grensted, *Short History*, 200; Rashdall, *Idea of the Atonement*, 399; Bartlett, *Cross Purposes*, 89–90.
79. Citing Luther, *Commentary on Galatians* 4.19 is Rashdall, *Idea of the Atonement*, 411.
80. Luther, *Commentary on Galatians*, in Dillenberger, *Martin Luther*, 119.
81. Luther, *Commentary on Galatians*, in Dillenberger, *Martin Luther*, 122, 133.
82. Referring to Martin Luther, *Commentary on Psalms* 51.1 is Rashdall, *Idea of the Atonement*, 404.

enabling one to know the will of God (Rom. 12:2), even to be "blameless and innocent" (Phil. 2:15). Luther attacked the linkage of love and faith that Thomas Aquinas made; "he definitely denies that saving faith includes any love at all."[83]

I think Luther's pessimism about humanity is rooted in his family history. Luther never won his father's approval, not when he had become a professor of biblical studies, and not even when he became the most talked-about intellectual in all of Europe. Luther's father was a "prohibitory presence," and Luther lived in constant "anticipation of his punishment."[84] His suffering at the hands of his father is entwined with the concept of a wrathful God that was common at the time. But Luther's experience seems darker and bleaker than that of his contemporaries. He felt rejected by God. "He could not love God because He suspected God is not lovable."[85] He came to feel that God and Christ were "revengers"; he describes being "terror-stricken when I heard the name of Christ."[86] Any hint of rebelliousness was punished, and Erik Erikson thinks that this created a deep-seated rebelliousness in him.[87]

Erikson sounds very much like the later writer Alice Miller when he says: "Parents are dangerous who thus take revenge on their child for what circumstances and inner compulsion have done to them."[88] "The child . . . is left to anticipate the date when he will have the brute power to make others more moral than he ever intends to be himself."[89]

None of this is to deny that Luther did a permanent service to Christendom when he fought the corruption of the clergy, the cruel greediness of the system of indulgences, the nonbiblical doctrine of papal authority, and the non-Christian nature of a priesthood that claimed control over salvation. The Reformation was a necessary and

---

83. Rashdall, *Idea of the Atonement*, 408; he cites *Commentary on Galatians* 4.8 and 5.9–10.
84. Erik H. Erikson, *Young Man Luther: A Study in Psychoanalysis and History* (New York: Norton, 1962), 122–23.
85. Roland H. Bainton, *The Reformation of the Sixteenth Century* (Boston: Beacon, 1952), 32.
86. Erikson, *Young Man Luther*, 70–71.
87. Ibid., 58, 65–66.
88. Ibid., 66.
89. Ibid., 70.

SACRIFICE AND ATONEMENT

useful event in human history. But the two most influential Reformers held some extraordinarily harsh concepts of God.

Armed for Vengeance

The height of sacrificial and substitutionary thinking, with accompanying pessimism about human nature, is reached by John Calvin, who goes on at great length with comments such as this: "The heart is so steeped in the poison of sin that it can breathe forth nothing but fetid corruption."[90] Although we inherited sin from Adam, it is also *our* sin, and we are "deservedly condemned by God.... Hence, even infants bringing their condemnation with them from their mother's womb, suffer not for another's but for their own defect.... Their whole nature is, as it were, a seed-bed of sin."[91] God "has barred the door of life to those whom he has given over to damnation."[92] In fact, only fear of damnation could reach man's heart.[93] This stands in direct contradiction to Jesus' teachings about some people being "pure of heart" or "peacemakers" (Matt. 5:8–9), able to "make the tree good" and to obtain the pearl of great price (Matt. 12:33; 13:46), able to "do the will of God" (Mark 3:35; John 7:17), "the will of my Father in heaven" (Matt 12:50).

Calvin offers an interpretation of Rom. 3:25 that has become, in some quarters, the standard understanding: "Paul commends the grace of God, in that he gave the price of redemption in the death of Christ.... By this price made satisfaction for sins.... Blood serves the purpose of satisfaction.... These words denote the payment ... which acquits us from guilt."[94] Although quite narrow, and leaving out the essential transformative core of Paul's theology, it does describe—and exaggerate—a Pauline theme.

---

90. John Calvin, *Institutes of the Christian Religion* 2.5.19, quoted by Grensted, *Short History*, 196.
91. Calvin, *Institutes* 2.1.8; trans. Henry Beveridge (Grand Rapids: Eerdmans, 1975), 1:217; this passage is summarized by Brondos, *Fortress Introduction to Salvation*, 105.
92. Calvin, *Institutes* 3.21.7, quoted by Brondos, *Fortress Introduction to Salvation*, 106.
93. Grensted, *Short History*, 213.
94. Calvin, *Institutes of the Christian Religion* 2.17.5 Beveridge 1:457.

But I wonder how long before more Christians will start to detect that Calvin is speaking from a place of deep, personal injury?

> No man can descend into himself, and seriously consider what he is, without feeling that God is angry and at enmity with him, and therefore anxiously longing for the means of regaining his favour (this cannot be without satisfaction) ... being always liable to the wrath and curse of God, who, as he is a just judge, cannot permit his law to be violated with impunity, but is armed for vengeance.[95]

Fear of a merciless authority who needs "satisfaction" and is armed for vengeance bespeaks the damage suffered in childhood from abusive parents. And the belief that God *has* to punish sin is not rooted in the teachings of Jesus. It makes the kindness and free will of God secondary to the stern demands of justice.

The psychological effects can be devastating. Believers are told that they are still *really* guilty, and should not relax their self-judgment. The idea of undeserved forgiveness does not dispel guilt. In fact, the idea of someone being tortured to death for me only increases my sense of guilt. If it stimulates any gratitude, it is a very nervous gratitude. Atonement appeals to emotions of fear, guilt, and self-doubt. Some Christians are locked into a mentality of shame about the "purchased" release; their gratitude is guilty-minded and joyless. For others, the liturgy brings a temporary respite from feelings of guilt. And then there are those who have learned not to feel guilt, since they believe that salvation by faith means not having to worry about "works" at all, even behavior that may be hurtful to others. Atonement tends to distort the consciousness of guilt into becoming either excessive or insufficient.

Any version of atonement creates problems for a monotheistic philosophy if it limits the power of God, if God has to go through a ritual of justice that is actually *unjust*: letting an innocent victim suffer the penalty.

Luther fits within Pruyser's scheme largely in the "satisfaction" area, where one's need is for resolution of guilt. But Luther also shows

---

95. *Institutes* 2.16.1 Beveridge 1:434.

anxiety (needing for rescue) and shame (needing to become a different person). I wonder if Luther's strong sense of guilt sums up his past life, while his anxiety in the present bespeaks the strong *present* power of his sensual drives, and his sense of shame reveals his distress about never living up to the ideal for the true Christian.

Calvin shows guilt and shame, but almost no present-tense awareness of his proud and lustful drives. Both men seem to have very little ability to restrain their own aggression; they compensate with theories about the unlimited pride of *all* humans—which partially lets *them* off the hook! The doctrine of total depravity[96] is often said to be "morally serious," but really it is morally evasive, pointing to the supposed wickedness of everyone, while averting attention from one's own violent temper. We need less of a *generalizing* doctrine about human sinfulness and more honest taking of responsibility for one's own *particular* sins. If Luther had done that, he might not have advised the nobles to "stab, smite, and slay all you can" of the peasants who had revolted, ignoring or not "realizing the effect of [his] violent language upon simple minds."[97] If Calvin had recognized and condemned his own lust for power, he would not have indulged in such vicious attacks on other Protestants, or helped to convict and execute Michael Servetus.[98]

The doctrines of Luther and Calvin present us with a seriously troubling antihumanistic version of Christian belief. If we disparage all human works and deny that humans have the ability to discern truth, to make an effective decision about God, then we undercut human freedom, dignity, and responsibility altogether. Many of the sayings of Jesus then become incomprehensible: "If anyone's will is to do God's will, he will know whether the teaching is from God or whether I am speaking on my own authority" (John 7:17 ESV). What is it to "know,"

---

96. Tillich says this doctrine of Luther's and Calvin's is often misunderstood. It "does not mean that there is nothing good in man. . . . It means that there are no special parts of man which are exempt from existential distortion" (Tillich, *A History of Christian Thought*, 245).
97. Owen Chadwick, *The Reformation*, Pelican History of the Church 3 (Harmondsworth, UK: Penguin, 1964), 60–61.
98. Will Durant, *The Story of Civilization*, vol. 6, *The Reformation: A History of European Civilization from Wyclif to Calvin: 1300–1564* (New York: Simon & Schuster, 1957), 482–84.

ATONEMENT PLAYED OUT

except to discern religious truth in the mind? And what is the "will to do God's will," if not an effective and life-changing choice?

Spirituality is linked with choice. If moral character matters, then the decisions we make *matter*. But if God drew up the lists of the saved and the damned before time began, then every decision is meaningless, and every moral effort is pointless. What good is religion if it crushes freedom and pours contempt on intellect?

Ritual Murder

I come now to the flood of popular antisemitism among Christians in the Middle Ages. I treat it out of chronological order because it is not part of the sequence of theological debates, but it is still very much a part of reflection on atonement, and it reveals something that the intellectual debates do not.

In the twelfth and thirteenth centuries, a time of Christian militarism and fanaticism, there was a sudden increase in antisemitic rumors and panics. This was the time of the Crusades, ostensibly directed at freeing the Holy Land from the Muslims but in fact involving many attacks on Jews in European cities.[99] There was a peculiar fear of Jews by Christians all across Europe.

Like the rapid spread of a disease, there grew up a narrative about Jews committing ritual murder and making use of Christian blood.[100] There are eight known cases of ritual-murder accusations in twelfth-century England, France, Germany, and Bohemia.[101] The myth itself may have literary origins before the twelfth century.[102] The spread of ritual-murder tales was facilitated by the printing press. Many small

---

99. Léon Poliakov, *The History of Anti-Semitism*, trans. Richard Howard, 2nd ed. (1965; repr., New York: Schocken: 1976), 42–49; Magdalene Schultz, "The Blood Libel: A Motif in the History of Childhood," in *The Blood Libel Legend: A Casebook in Anti-Semitic Folklore*, ed. Alan Dundes (Madison: University of Wisconsin Press, 1991), 286–87.
100. R. po-chia Hsia, *The Myth of Ritual Murder* (New Haven: Yale University Press, 1988), 2.
101. Ibid., 2–3; Colin Holmes, "The Ritual Murder Accusation in Britain," in Dundes, *Blood Libel Legend*, 101–2.
102. The fiction was "widely disseminated before and during the twelfth century by monastery and cathedral schools," according to Theresa Tinkle, "Exegesis Reconsidered: The Fleury *Slaughter of the Innocents* and the Myth of Ritual Murder," *Journal of English and Germanic Philology* 102 (2003): 242.

books and broadsheets were produced, some with lurid covers, such as the one illustrating an alleged murder in Sappenfeld: "The title page depicts a child tied to a pillar with cut wounds all over his body; a long-bearded Jew . . . holding a knife and a dish, approaches."[103] With some local variations, the accusation develops a standard plotline everywhere from England to (eventually) Russia (where the myth is still very much alive[104]): it claims that Jews are kidnapping and killing Christian children, draining their blood for various magical purposes, to perform healings from special Jewish afflictions (children born with bloodstained hands, males who menstruate),[105] or to perform evil rituals around Passover, meant to mock the Christian holidays.[106]

The persecution intensified in the thirteenth century. Many Jews were arrested, tortured, and killed as a result of the accusations. In a British case, Jews were accused of disemboweling a boy for purposes of black magic.[107] Nineteen Jews in the town of Lincoln were hanged.[108]

Ritual-murder discourse is a kind of martyrology, and it repeats a theme often found in martyrologies: innocent victims are subjected to monstrous cruelty from a band of heartless persecutors.[109] But in reality, the persecutors were Christian. The accusations aroused public hysteria, and the magistrates then arrested local Jews and tortured them, forcing confessions that fit perfectly well with what the accusers already believed was happening: the kidnapping and blood-draining of Christian children.[110] If the accusers had additional fears, such as well-poisoning, which was feared in Freiburg, the torture produced "evidence" of well-poisoning as well.[111] The myth of ritual murder

---

103. Hsia, *Myth of Ritual Murder*, 61.
104. Information taken from "Blood Libel," Wikipedia, last updated Jan. 17, 2016, https://en.wikipedia.org/wiki/Blood_libel, where footnotes 41–46 cite the Russian-language sources, regarding ritual murder accusations made by Russian nationalist parties in 2005.
105. Joshua Trachtenberg, *The Devil and the Jews* (New Haven: Yale University Press, 1943), 50–51; Holmes, "Ritual Murder Accusation in Britain," 100.
106. Hsia, *Myth of Ritual Murder*, 130–31.
107. Trachtenberg, *Devil and the Jews*, 143–44.
108. Holmes, "Ritual Murder Accusation in Britain," 102; Ernest A. Rappaport, "The Ritual Murder Accusation: The Persistence of Doubt and the Repetition Compulsion," in Dundes, *Blood Libel Legend*, 307–8; Tinkle, "Exegesis Reconsidered," 215.
109. Hsia, *Myth of Ritual Murder*, 61–62.
110. Ibid., 21–30, 34, 43, 50–51.
111. Ibid., 88.

is sometimes called the blood libel, and it *is* a libel, a series of false accusations arising out of Christian fear and superstition.

Why did this happen? Observers of social behavior know that an insecure group can shore up its identity through hatred and vilification of enemies. Hatred and disgust help an insecure group to define itself ("we are not like *those* people"). But why should Christianity, a powerful religion spread across three continents, feel so insecure?

I have heard people try to explain antisemitism as deriving from political competition or economic envy, but I find these totally inadequate for explaining the intense superstition that was manifested. Only a deep psychological panic can cause such extreme reactions. I think the problem was built into Christianity from New Testament times, when incompatible God concepts were forcibly combined, when Jesus' God of love was blended with the sacrifice-demanding God of atonement. This created an inward doubt about the nature of God, a doubt that persists to this day. Theologians have tried to make atonement beliefs seem rational and consistent with the idea of a God of love, but the idea of salvation being bought through a murder implies some frightening things about God, and the common believer has not been able to suppress these implications the way that some theologians have. The doctrine is bound to create psychological disturbances, as was dramatically demonstrated in the Middle Ages.

The linkage of the violence to atonement beliefs becomes clearer when we look at the acceleration of anxiety caused by the promulgation in 1215 CE of a very literal-minded interpretation of eating the body and drinking the blood of Christ.

Host Magic

In 1215, the strident and authoritarian Pope Innocent III called the Fourth Lateran Council and articulated the doctrine of transubstantiation, which proclaimed that the bread and wine were actually transformed into the body and blood of Christ.[112] The

---

112. Technically, it is the underlying "substance" of the bread and wine that are changed, while to the

sacrament was no longer to be treated as symbolic, but as literal. Catholics were told "that in the communion by drinking wine and eating a wafer, i.e., the Host, the communicant was drinking the blood of Christ and eating the actual flesh of Christ. Again the doubt crept in whether the communicant should with his teeth and tongue masticate the flesh of Christ."[113] I myself was raised Catholic, and was told not to chew the wafer, since that would be chewing Christ's flesh.

Not surprisingly, the transubstantiation teaching provoked intense confusion and guilt among thirteenth-century Christians, who were now *literally* consuming the Lord's flesh, engaging in a kind of God cannibalism![114] The doctrine seems to have triggered a collective panic, although it was a distress that could not be uttered or discussed. People were ill-equipped to understand the psychology of what was happening to them. There was a heightened focus on the suffering of Christ in church art and sermons; "there were masses ... 'of the wounds of Christ,' 'of the Five Wounds,' 'of the crown of thorns.'"[115] The believer had to eat the broken body of Christ every Sunday. I think this evoked a silent horror and disgust in Christians. But something that *could* be uttered was hatred for the "enemies of Christ." Preachers stoked the fires of resentment against the "Christ killers." Christians transferred their feelings of disgust to the Jews. The ritual-murder accusation is really a projection of Christian anxiety about the *Christian* blood ritual. A Christian cannot admit to feeling disgust with the Christian sacrament, so disgust is projected onto the enemy religion.

Hatred and accusation of the *other* enabled Christians to suppress their unconscious resentment of the God who arranged the ritual murder of Jesus and required Christians to reenact it every Sunday. Unconsciously, Christians were fearing and hating their own God, but this was too terrible to admit. At the bottom of the religious terror was

---

eye and mouth no change will be noticed. This is a fine philosophic detail that the common people did not appreciate.
113. Rappaport, "Ritual Murder Accusation," 309.
114. It "is at the very least symbolic cannibalism" (Alan Dundes, "The Ritual Murder or Blood Libel Legend," in Dundes, *Blood Libel Legend*, 354).
115. Hsia, *Myth of Ritual Murder*, 11.

a literal-minded sacramentalism based on blood-atonement teachings. Atonement is at the basis of this religious hysteria.

The doctrine of transubstantiation caused the worship of the consecrated Host (already a part of Catholic worship) to become more central, more intense, and more dangerous. Special saving power was attributed to the elevation of the Host in the Mass. "Preachers and bishops condemned the disorder during the reading of Mass: the elevation of the Host often degenerated into a moment of commotion as the people scrambled into the choir to behold the Eucharist, hoping to reap benefits from beholding the sacred."[116] The elevation of the Host is like a magical gesture, and is one of the primitive elements in the Catholic Mass. Even the term *host* has sacrificial origins: it derives from the Latin feminine noun *hostia*, which means sacrificial animal or sacrificial virgin.[117]

The thirteenth and fourteenth centuries became a time of Host mysticism, Host magic, and Host legends, reflected in the literature of the period, in the Grail poems with their bleeding lances, drops of blood in the snow, and visions of a man bleeding in the Host.[118] Martyrology extended to the Hosts as well. One of the crimes the Jews were said to perpetrate was theft or purchase of eucharistic Hosts, for the purpose of subjecting the Host to torture, in a kind of Satanic reenactment of the crucifixion. Preachers riled up crowds with reports of the terrible tortures inflicted on stolen Hosts.[119] One confession extracted under torture spoke of the Jews stabbing stolen Hosts "with a knife until blood flowed and the Eucharist turned itself into a young boy. The Jews then allegedly threw the Hosts into an oven from which two angels and doves flew out of the flames."[120]

These stories can be recognized as examples of a "Host-desecration narrative," which follows a familiar pattern, always ending in the exposure, punishment, and killing of many Jews, at least three

---

116. Ibid., 9.
117. Rappaport, "Ritual Murder Accusation," 333.
118. Charles Williams, *Arthurian Torso* (Oxford: Oxford University Press, 1948), 75–78.
119. Trachtenberg, *Devil and the Jews*, 113.
120. Hsia, *Myth of Ritual Murder*, 50–51; see the similar story, from Bavaria, on p. 58.

thousand Jews in one wave of accusations and punishments in Franconia, in Bavaria.[121]

The mythology of tortured and bleeding Hosts echoes Christian atonement ideas, in paranoid and literal-minded fashion. The myth of Christian blood being drained for ritual usage grotesquely echoes the symbolic blood magic of the Christian Eucharist.

Projective Inversion

There is a term that describes the projection that took place. Alan Dundes says the explanation for the ritual murder accusation "lies in the Christian need for a Jewish scapegoat and in the psychological process I have termed 'projective inversion.'"[122] This term signifies the projecting of one's unadmitted shame onto others, which leads to blaming and hating the others. Christians could not face the shame and revulsion they felt as a result of a liturgy requiring them to relive a ritual murder, which created a knot of anxiety and guilt inside them.

Projective inversion enables Christians to say that only the *Jews* use blood for ritual purposes, when in fact it is the *Christian* ritual that talks about blood.[123] Underneath the medieval superstition and violence are the magical notions of believers being justified by the blood, sharing in the blood of Christ, drinking a cup of the new covenant in Christ's blood (Rom. 5:9; 1 Cor. 10:16; 11:25). And so it is not just the pathological reactions of medieval Christians, but also the atonement beliefs of rational Christians, that are based on the notion of a sacrifice-demanding God and of salvation through a ritual bloodletting.

Christian atonement doctrine is a poison well that will continue to issue toxic results, even though most Christians manage to keep the lid of repression on top of the well, preventing most pathological eruptions. Unfortunately, another wave of scapegoating and violence was destined to sweep over Europe like a plague in the twentieth

---

121. Miri Rubin, "Desecration of the Host: The Birth of an Accusation," in *Christianity and Judaism: Papers Read at the 1991 Summer Meeting and the 1992 Winter Meeting of the Ecclesiastical History Society*, ed. Diana Wood (Oxford: Blackwell, 1992), 177.
122. Dundes, "Ritual Murder," 352.
123. Ibid., 354

century. It is high time that we recognize the psychological (and theological) roots of the disease. The hatred that Christians sometimes feel against the religion from which Christianity originated is really panic and rage aroused by their own religion's twisted teachings on atonement by blood.

What of our atonement intellectuals? Did they play a role in any of the paranoid narratives? First, there was considerable reflection by the church fathers on the Jewish role in the killing of Christ, with varying degrees of resentment and blame being expressed, but I am unaware of any early church father entertaining a Jewish ritual-murder narrative. Typical might be the remarks of Augustine and Aquinas; Augustine said the Jews acted against Christ because they were ignorant of his divine nature; Aquinas went further, saying that their ignorance arose from hostility, and their strong attraction to sin.[124]

Luther, on the other hand, heavily buys into the belief in Jewish black magic. Further, "Luther raises the charge of ritual murder many times in *On the Ineffable Name* and *On the Jews and Their Lies*"; he repeats what he has heard about Jews poisoning wells and stealing children; he says the Jews "deny this. That may or may not be [*Es sey oder nicht*], but I know well, that they do not lack the full, whole, and ready will, wherever they could come to do it, in secret or openly. They are the Devil's children."[125] R. po-chia Hsia claims that Luther is really engaging in an "antimagical discourse,"[126] arguing against the reality of magic, whether Jewish or Catholic. It is true that Luther's superstition does not approach that of his enemy, Johann Eck, who aggressively perpetuates the blood libel, claiming that Jews kidnap Christian children and mix their blood with their matzo bread.[127] But Luther can in no way be exonerated from the charge of participating in false rumors. Even though he is not sure whether the stories are true ("this may not be"), he does not hesitate to use the stories to back up his

---

124. Tinkle, "Exegesis Reconsidered," 221, 235.
125. Hsia, *Myth of Ritual Murder,* 133. He cites WA 52:482 and 53:530.
126. Hsia, *Myth of Ritual Murder,* 134.
127. Trachtenberg, *Devil and the Jews,* 146; see also Hsia, *Myth of Ritual Murder,* 127.

assertion that the Jews are children of the devil. He knowingly uses rumors to support his hatred!

It is to the credit of the popes (and to the education they received) that many of them worked against the anti-Jewish accusations and pogroms. In fact, Gregory X exposed the fact that Christians, in some cases, were hiding their own children in order to extort money from the Jews, and in other instances were imprisoning and torturing Jews to get money from them; Gregory ordered the release of all who were imprisoned in this way.[128] Other exceptions to the disgraceful tale of Christian antisemitism are the Dutchman Hugo Grotius and the German Andreas Osiander, who wrote books refuting the ritual-murder allegations, contributing to the eventual decline of the myth.[129]

By Calvin's time, the ritual-murder hysteria was subsiding. Still, it is to his credit that he gave no credence to it,[130] although he did engage in the usual polemics against "the Jews, on whom the Lord inflicted his severest judgments."[131]

Regarding the violent panic that has seized Christian communities over and over again, it is necessary to point out that there will always be recurrences of psychopathology among people who believe that access to God is through "the blood of Jesus" (Heb. 10:19), that "the blood of Jesus his Son cleanses us from all sin" (1 John 1:7). These need now to be recognized as morbid superstitions, more than likely (unconsciously) based on the experience of having to suffer pain in order to win back the love of angry parents. And those who have been hurt are often likely to hurt others.

Without Price

We have seen the depths to which atonement can sink, when fear and secret shame overwhelm the spiritual life. There may seem to have

---

128. Rappaport, "Ritual Murder Accusation," 327–28; also mentioned by Schultz, "Blood Libel," 282, but incorrectly attributed to Gregory VIII.
129. Hsia, *Myth of Ritual Murder*, 131, 136–43; Dundes, "Ritual Murder," 359.
130. Gary K. Waite, *Heresy, Magic and Witchcraft in Early Modern Europe* (London: Palgrave Macmillan, 2003), 98.
131. Calvin, *Institutes of the Christian Religion* 2.8.5 Beveridge 1:372.

been a certain inexorable momentum to the extremism that developed from the satisfaction theory. But we need not be controlled by that trend, and it is important to recognize that there has never been any standard doctrine of atonement. As Robert Cummings Neville points out, none of the ecumenical councils or early creeds spelled out an atonement teaching, "not the Apostles' Creed, not the Creed of Nicaea in 325, not the Creed of Constantinople of 381," and not six more creeds or councils up through 787; they all mention the death and resurrection of Jesus, "but the concerns about Jesus' suffering are not as to its redemptive powers but as to its marking Jesus' true humanity."[132]

And so, we can identify and then reject the blend of Augustinian, Anselmian, and Calvinist ideas that falsely claim to be the standard interpretation: the notion that all persons deserve eternal punishment, but salvation was purchased from the Father by the Son's sacrificial death. Many Christians are finding this idea to be no longer plausible. They are distressed by the toxicity of the teaching that people are depraved in all their faculties, and that the one and only innocent person had to be tortured and killed in order to purchase their salvation (or the salvation of *some*). This teaching assaults the idea of people having been created in the image of God, with a spirit within:

> Truly it is the spirit in a mortal,
> the breath of the Almighty, that makes for understanding. (Job 32:8)

Further, it is inconsistent with the experience and the teachings of Jesus himself.

The angry God that is assumed by Calvin and Luther does not fit well with the forgiving Father of the prodigal son parable, nor with the shepherd who diligently searches for one lost sheep, the comforting and available God of the beatitudes, or the God who honors the humble and persistent believer.[133] If the essence of humanity were depravity,

---

132. Robert Cummings Neville, *The Truth of Broken Symbols* (Albany: State University of New York Press, 1996), 211.
133. Prodigal, shepherd: Luke 15; shepherd: Matt. 18:10–14; Beatitudes: Matt. 5:3–12; humble, persistent: Matt. 23:11–12; Luke 18:1–17; 11:5–10; 14:10–11.

Jesus would hardly have called himself the "son of man" (or "son of humanity," since *anthrōpos* refers to humans of either gender), or used a child as an example of the kingdom of God (Matt. 19:14; Mark 9:35–37, 42; 10:14; Luke 18:16).

The depressing theology and disgraceful violence that we saw recounted above need not be perpetuated. We need not build our house on sand any more. We can build on a better foundation. The nonatonement theology that Jesus himself taught shows through in the Gospels. The open invitation to salvation is unlinked to the death: "It is your Father's good pleasure to give you the kingdom" (Luke 12:32); "the Father himself loves you" (John 16:27); "your Father knows what you need" (Matt. 6:8); "I have called you friends" (John 15:15). Salvation has always been freely offered. This idea was already present in Hosea ("I will heal their disloyalty; / I will love them freely," 14:4), and the Isaiahs ("The Lord waits to be gracious to you" [Isa. 30:18]; "Come, buy wine and milk / without money and without price" [Isa. 55:1]).

But it took the incarnated Son to show people they were freely accepted, which he did for many downcast and neglected individuals. But all of us are reminded: "You received without paying, give without pay" (Matt. 10:8 RSV).

Conclusion

I discuss three issues here. One is propitiation—the most problematic idea that atonement brings with it. Yet it is certainly necessary that we reflect on Christ's death, what led to it, and what we can learn from it. Finally, I look at the issue of manipulation.

Wrestling with Propitiation

A British theologian argues that the early church, "once cut from its Jewish roots, lost the Jewish outlook . . . and very naturally pagan ideas and explanations were imported. . . . Ideas of 'propitiation' and 'aversion' were introduced."[1] This is due to "converts from a pagan background in which propitiation was a presupposed understanding of sacrifice."[2] I think it is too convenient to attribute all propitiatory concepts to gentile contamination. Manipulative and propitiatory thinking was certainly *more* prevalent in Greco-Roman religion than in Hebrew religion, but it was present in the latter as well, enough to be attacked by prophets. The prophet of Nazareth, also, supported (Mark 12:33–34) and quoted antisacrificial passages (Matt. 9:13; 12:7; Mark 11:17). In its first few centuries, Christianity tolerated the coexistence of manipulative sacrificial ideas alongside advanced spiritual ideas. Both the manipulative notions and the more spiritual ideas have some Jewish roots and some gentile roots.

1. Frances M. Young, *Sacrifice and the Death of Christ* (Philadelphia: Westminster, 1975), 73.
2. Frances M. Young, *The Use of Sacrificial Ideas in Greek Christian Writers from the New Testament to John Chrysostom* (1979; repr., Eugene, OR: Wipf & Stock, 2004), 192.

SACRIFICE AND ATONEMENT

For two thousand years, Christians have been wrestling with the ideas of atonement, propitiation, forgiveness, moral character, and spiritual growth. Different thinkers saw different problems in the atonement mix. Anselm perceived an intolerable problem in the notion of God owing anything to the devil. Abelard saw a problem in the idea of God getting any kind of satisfaction or compensation out of an atrocity.

Often, I think, human reflection involves partial progress, which includes the partially unconscious rejection of certain ideas. In wrestling with atonement ideas over time, some thinkers have come up with what I call a *halfway concept*: a paradoxical restatement of a concept that is really (and unconsciously) on its way to being rejected, but which the thinker is not ready to reject outright. I find first Horace Bushnell, and then P. T. Forsyth, to be expressing halfway concepts about propitiation or atonement. After writing his *The Vicarious Sacrifice* (see 'The Problem with Atonement' in Chapter 4), Bushnell continued to think about forgiveness, and decided that he had left out a key truth: that *real* forgiveness involves a kind of self-propitiation. "I now assert a real propitiation of God, finding it in evidence from the propitiation we instinctively make ourselves, when we heartily forgive.... Truly a self-propitiation of God."[3] Real forgiveness is not just giving up revenge, he says, but taking on suffering for the sake of restoration of the relationship; this attitude "considers nothing to be really gained till it has gained a brother."[4] I think Bushnell is really halfway to rejecting the concept of propitiation altogether, but instead of taking such a radical step, he speaks of self-propitiation and of God's self-propitiation, by which he means wholly committed forgiveness.

A different version of this concept is expressed forty years later by a Scottish Congregationalist named P. T. Forsyth, who is interested in "the moralising of dogma."[5] To that end he wrote, "A holy God self-

---

3. Horace Bushnell, *Forgiveness and Law, Grounded in Principles Interpreted by Human Analogies* (New York: Scribner, Armstrong, 1872), 12, 59. (Later republished as volume 2 of *The Vicarious Sacrifice*, 1877.)
4. Ibid., 40.
5. The titles of chapters 8 and 9 in P. T. Forsyth, *The Person and Place of Jesus Christ: The Congregational Union Lecture for 1909* (Cincinnati: Jennings & Graham, 1909), 211–57.

atoned in Christ is the moral centre of the sinful world. . . . He gave his Son as a propitiation to His own holiness."[6]

Such a concept is, of course, paradoxical, even absurd. That does not mean these are useless ideas. Rather, they are verbal concepts that function as a halfway stage in an unconscious progress toward eventually letting go of propitiation or atonement altogether. They redefine the terms, mystify them, and transfer them to God's realm, as though in an unconscious prayer for divine help with an idea that has become embarrassing.

This paradoxical word game is parallel to the process by which believers learn to let go of vengeance. The statement "vengeance is mine . . . says the Lord" (Rom. 12:19; based on Deut. 32:35 and Lev. 19:18) represents an advance in human thought, when people learn to hand vengeance over to the Lord, not to seek it themselves. It is a halfway concept. The *next* stage would be the insight that God was never vengeful in the first place, even that *there is no vengeance on the divine level*, but neither the Pentateuch nor Paul is ready to say that, although Paul is moving in that direction, since there is no vengeance in his concept of the afterlife.[7] Likewise, *there is no propitiation or appeasement on the divine level*, but first somebody had to express the halfway concept of God being self-propitiating. Bushnell's and Forsyth's confusing statements represent the vector of human thought slowly liberating itself from the concept of propitiation.

What We Can Say about Christ's Death

We can certainly say "Christ died for all humanity," as long as we do not mean that God was thus paid off, soothed, mollified, or that sin was magically cleansed and deported. What it *can* mean is that Jesus died heroically, buying some time for his apostles and thus ensuring that

---

6. P. T. Forsyth, *The Justification of God: Lectures for War-Time on a Christian Theodicy* (New York: Charles Scribner's Sons, 1917), 93, 110.
7. I do not think Paul believed in hell. He says the general resurrection is only for believers (Rom 6:5; 1 Cor. 15:23; 1 Thess. 4:16–17; 5:10). As for sinners, "the wages of sin are death" (Rom. 6:23); "flesh and blood cannot inherit the kingdom of God, nor does the perishable inherit the imperishable" (1 Cor. 15:50). The strange remark in Rom. 12:20, "heap burning coals on their heads," quotes Prov. 25:22 to make a point against vengeance. It does not state his afterlife views.

the gospel would begin its rapid spread. He demonstrated the greatest love, "to lay down one's life for one's friends" (John 15:13). He founded his community on love *before* he died, but the death was a further demonstration of this love, and (colloquially speaking) it bought some time for his community "to go and bear fruit, fruit that will last" (John 15:16).

Further, Jesus really did die for the cause of spiritual freedom; he refused to compromise with the holders of coercive religious power, and exposed their pride and cruelty. The religious rulers' cruelty was linked with their spiritual blindness: "if you had known what this means, 'I desire mercy and not sacrifice,' you would not have condemned the guiltless" (Matt. 12:7). Jesus stood up for the "guiltless," the "meek," the pious widow, the respectful gentile, the humble publican. He won religious freedom for us, although we seem to want to domesticate and control his revelation with hierarchies and ritualism that resemble the old religious systems.

Because he never compromised with the corrupt authorities and because he spoke the truth, Jesus remains the source and the inspiration of perpetual reform and liberation, including liberation from supposedly Christian power structures, and from all forms of religious or ideological enslavement. We are not slaves but sons and daughters in God's household (John 8:35; Rom. 8:15–17; Gal. 3:26; Eph. 2:19). Whenever we rediscover Jesus, we get access to renewal and transformation. The truth can make us free indeed (John 8:32, 36; Gal. 5:1). It may take continual effort and self-critique to maintain this freedom and to avoid lethargy and reenslavement, but the opportunity for renewal is always there, if we "grow up in every way into him who is the head, into Christ" (Eph. 4:15).

Further, we can certainly say that Christ died to demonstrate how God can triumph through nonviolence. The centurion who said, "Truly this man was God's Son!" (Matt. 27:54; Mark 15:39) was just the first of many who had a change of heart after seeing the behavior of a nonviolent witness to the truth. We see a continuation of this in the

Acts of the Apostles, where the movement continued to grow, even after persecutions.

Jesus died "for us" in the same sense that he taught "for us"—to reveal truth about God and love and salvation. His death was part of his continuous revelation of God, so he died for us in the same way that he *lived* for us, and carried out healings for us, and offered comfort and inspiration for us.

But if we mean his death purchased or obtained something that could not be attained if he had not been killed, then we have sunk into magical and morbid thinking, based on the assumption that God is cruel or crazy and needs to be appeased. This reveals more about psychological damage suffered on the human level than about spiritual attitudes existing on the divine level.

The idea of God as judgmental and strict was probably an inevitable by-product of a serious monotheism struggling to survive in an immoral world, but it needs to be recognized as a phase of religious thinking that is inconsistent with what Jesus revealed about the loving Father, and it does not reflect Jesus' own attitude toward the Father, which is embodied in the sayings: "Do not fear, only believe" (Mark 5:36; Luke 8:50); "Serve him without fear" (Luke 1:74).

No Need to Manipulate

Most scholars and theologians nowadays recognize that the idea of manipulating God is repulsive, and almost all of them argue, in one way or another, against propitiation. Some say there is no propitiation in the Bible at all, some say that it is only present in an old layer of the Old Testament, others allow that it is present but only as a minor theme. Not many are willing to say what I say: sacrifice was a fundamentally selfish and manipulative phase of religious development; it needs to be outgrown. It is natural that there should be primitive phases, but we need to get beyond them. When the compensatory or magical power of sacrifice is retained, even in metaphorical form, it becomes unprogressive. This may sound like a radical position. I speak for myself, then.

SACRIFICE AND ATONEMENT

Despite the best intentions of thoughtful theologians, sacrifice and atonement will always carry problems with them. Atonement theology undermines monotheism in the following ways:

- The doctrine that God *had* to punish someone limits God's freedom.
- The idea that God would allow an unjust action to "pay" for all the other unjust actions undermines God's goodness.
- The notion that the Son embodies mercy while the Father embodies stern justice disintegrates unity of purpose within the Trinity. Genuine Trinitarian monotheism must have perfect unity of purpose between the persons of the Trinity. Without such unity, there is no Trinity, only polytheism.

Even while it claims to extol God's power and goodness, atonement theology pictures a sacrifice-demanding God who is not free to forgive. This is crazy-making theology. It makes for an admirable Son but a despicable (or pitiable) Father. It perpetuates the victimization of tenderhearted people by strict and judgmental people.

It is the primitive legacy of sacrificial theology that causes these problems. Inasmuch as sacrifice is part of a purification system, it is inherently exclusionary, and its underlying assumptions are magical. To the extent that sacrifice is payment in a system of exchange with the deity, it is manipulative and materialistic. Jesus understood this level of human religiosity, and he was remarkably patient with it, but he did try to raise people to a higher and more mature relationship with God, one where they grew up like children of healthy and loving parents. There is no need to manipulate such a parent: "Do not be afraid, little flock, for it is your Father's good pleasure to give you the kingdom" (Luke 12:32).

Any doctrine that has salvation depending on a sacrifice, a noble death, or a ritual cleansing is alien to the teachings of Jesus, for whom salvation and wholeness are freely available without any mediating *transaction* or *payment*, for whom faith itself saves people (Luke 7:50; 8:48; 17:19). "Faith" meaning trusting in the generosity of God, who already loves us (John 16:27), who fills the hungry, reveals divinity to the pure in heart (Matt. 5:6–8), and for whom forgiveness is conditioned only by one's willingness to repent and forgive others (Matt. 6:14–15; Mark 11:25). With Jesus, "there is not the slightest suggestion that anything else but repentance is necessary—the actual death of a Saviour, belief in the atoning efficacy of that death ... church membership—not a hint of any of these."[8]

It is contrary to the teachings and to the personal experience of Jesus to teach that God ever withheld love until a debt was satisfied. This notion has been a constant aggravation for Christian theology, and Herculean efforts have been made to salvage the lovingkindness of God in the face of God's (alleged) need for satisfaction. If we really trusted God, and truly obeyed the instruction "Do not fear" (Luke 8:50), we would recognize that God has never required ritual victims, animal or human. These are vestiges from the childhood of the race that have become increasingly embarrassing when defended.

And yet we allow sacrificial thinking to continue to dominate our liturgies and our hymns, often when the pastor no longer believes the concepts found in them. Do we want to continue rhapsodizing a bloody theology in our hymns? "Draw me nearer ... blessed Lord, to thy precious, bleeding side."[9] "O purest fountain, welling from out the Savior's side! We faint with thirst; revive us."[10] Such thinking is increasingly being exposed as ethically weak and psychologically immature.

Salvation needs to be detached from the crucifixion. We have gone on too long, covering up the message of Jesus with a mythology about his death, a death caused by his enemies. To some degree, we have allowed his enemies—the hypocrites, the power brokers, the conductors of sacrifice—to set the agenda.

---

8. Hastings Rashdall, *The Idea of the Atonement in Christian Theology* (London: Macmillan, 1919), 26.
9. Fanny Crosby, "I Am Thine, O Lord," in *The United Methodist Hymnal* (Nashville: United Methodist Publishing House, 1989), hymn 419.
10. Seventeenth-century German hymn, "O Food to Pilgrims Given," in *United Methodist Hymnal*, hymn 631.

We need to be saved from cruel doctrine. God saves us *in spite of* the crucifixion, not because of it.

Bibliography

Primary Sources

Calvin, John. *Institutes of the Christian Religion*. Translated by Henry Beveridge. Grand Rapids: Eerdmans, 1975.

Diogenes Laertius II. Edited and translated by Jeffrey Henderson. LCL. Cambridge, MA: Harvard University Press, 1931.

Euripides. *Ten Plays by Euripides*. Translated by Moses Hadas and John McLean. New York: Bantam, 1960.

Isaac, E., trans. "1 (Ethiopic Apocalypse of) Enoch." In *OTP* 1:5–90.

Kee, Howard Clark, trans. "The Testament of Levi, the Third Son of Jacob and Leah." In *OTP* 1:788–95.

Luther, Martin. *D. Martin Luthers Werke. Kritische Gesamtausgabe*. (Known as the Weimarer Ausgabe [WA].) Weimar: Herman Böhlau; H. Böhlaus Nachfolger, 1883–2009.

——. *Martin Luther: Selections from His Writings*. Edited by John Dillenberger. Garden City, NY: Doubleday, 1961.

——. *The Sermons of Martin Luther*. Vol. 7. Edited by John Nicholas Lenker. Grand Rapids: Baker, 1983.

Plato. *Euthyphro*. In *Plato: The Last Days of Socrates*. Translated by Hugh Tredennick. Harmondsworth, UK: Penguin, revised 1969.

——. *Plato: The Laws*. Translated by Trevor J. Saunders. Harmondsworth, UK: Penguin, 1975.

Plutarch. *Pompey*. Translated by Bernadotte Perrin. Vol. 5 of *Plutarch's Lives*. LCL. Cambridge, MA: Harvard University Press, 1917.

"The Teaching of the Twelve Apostles, Commonly Called the Didache." In *Early Christian Fathers*, edited and translated by Cyril C. Richardson, 161–82. New York: Touchstone, 1996.

Staniforth, Maxwell, ed. and trans. *Early Christian Writings*. Revised by Andrew Louth. London: Penguin, 1987.

Thomas Aquinas. *St. Thomas Aquinas: Theological Texts*. Selected and translated by Thomas Gilby. London: Oxford University Press, 1955.

Secondary Sources

Ainsworth, Mary D. Salter. "Attachment: Retrospect and Prospect." In *The Place of Attachment in Human Behavior*, edited by Colin Murray Parkes and Joan Stevenson-Hinde, 3–30. New York: Basic, 1982.

Albertz, Rainer. *A History of Israelite Religion in the Old Testament Period; Volume I: From the Beginnings to the End of the Monarchy*. Translated by John Bowden. OTL. Louisville: Westminster John Knox, 1994.

———. *A History of Israelite Religion in the Old Testament Period; Volume II: From the Exile to the Maccabees*. Translated by John Bowden. OTL. Louisville: Westminster John Knox, 1994.

Anderson, Gary. "Sacrifice and Sacrificial Offerings (OT)." In *ABD* 5:870–86.

Aulén, Gustaf. *Christus Victor: An Historical Study of the Three Main Types of the Idea of the Atonement*. London: SPCK, 1931.

Bailey, Daniel P. "Jesus as the Mercy Seat: The Semantics and Theology of Paul's Use of *Hilasterion* in Romans 3:25." PhD dissertation, Cambridge University, 1999.

———. "Jesus as the Mercy Seat: The Semantics and Theology of Paul's Use of *Hilasterion* in Romans 3:25." *TynBul* 51 (2000): 155–58.

Bainton, Roland H. *The Reformation of the Sixteenth Century*. Boston: Beacon, 1952.

Baker, Sharon L. *Executing God: Rethinking Everything You've Been Taught about Salvation and the Cross*. Louisville: Westminster John Knox, 2013.

Bartlett, Anthony W. *Cross Purposes: The Violent Grammar of Christian Atonement*. Harrisburg: Trinity Press International, 2001.

Beck, Richard. *Unclean: Meditations on Purity, Hospitality, and Mortality*. Eugene, OR: Cascade, 2011.

Bermann, Eric. *Scapegoat: The Impact of Death-Fear on an American Family*. Ann Arbor: University of Michigan Press, 1973.

Boersma, Hans. *Violence, Hospitality, and the Cross: Reappropriating the Atonement Tradition*. Grand Rapids: Baker Academic, 2004.

Boring, M. Eugene, Klaus Berger, and Carsten Colpe. *Hellenistic Commentary to the New Testament*. Nashville: Abingdon, 1995.

Bowen, John R. *Muslims through Discourse: Religion and Ritual in Gayo Society*. Princeton: Princeton University Press, 1993.

Bowlby, John. "Attachment." In *The Oxford Companion to the Mind*, edited by R. L. Gregory, 57–58. Oxford: Oxford University Press, 1987.

_____. *Attachment and Loss*. Vol. 2, *Separation: Anxiety and Anger*. New York: Basic, 1973.

_____. *The Making and Breaking of Affectional Bonds*. 1956. Reprint, London: Routledge, 1979.

Breytenbach, Cilliers. "Versöhnung, Stellvertretung und Sühne: Semantische und traditionseschichtliche Bemerkungen am Beispiel der paulinischen Briefe." *NTS* 39 (1993): 59–79.

Brock, Rita Nakashima, and Rebecca Ann Parker. *Proverbs of Ashes: Violence, Redemptive Suffering, and the Search for What Saves Us*. Boston: Beacon, 2001.

Brondos, David A. *Fortress Introduction to Salvation and the Cross*. Minneapolis: Fortress Press, 2007.

_____. *Paul on the Cross: Reconstructing the Apostle's Story of Redemption*. Minneapolis: Fortress Press, 2006.

Browning, Don S. *Atonement and Psychotherapy*. Philadelphia: Westminster, 1966.

Büchner, Dirk. "Ἐξιλάσασθαι: Appeasing God in the Septuagint Pentateuch." *JBL* 129 (2010): 237–60.

Burkert, Walter. *Greek Religion: Archaic and Classical*. Translated by John Raffan. Oxford: Blackwell, 1985.

Bursten, Ben. *The Manipulator: A Psychoanalytic View*. New Haven: Yale University Press, 1973.

Bushnell, Horace. *Christ and His Salvation: In Sermons Variously Related Thereto*. New York: Charles Scribner, 1864.

_____. *Forgiveness and Law, Grounded in Principles Interpreted by Human Analogies*.

New York: Scribner, Armstrong, 1872. (Later republished as vol. 2 of *The Vicarious Sacrifice*, 1877.)

———. *The Vicarious Sacrifice: Grounded in Principles of Universal Obligation*. New York: Charles Scribner, 1871.

Campbell, Douglas A. *The Deliverance of God: An Apocalyptic Rereading of Justification in Paul*. Grand Rapids: Eerdmans, 2009.

Capps, Donald, *The Child's Song: The Religious Abuse of Children*. Louisville: Westminster John Knox, 1995.

———. "Religion and Child Abuse: Perfect Together." *JSSR* 31 (1992): 1–14.

Cessario, Romanus. *Christian Satisfaction in Aquinas: Toward a Personalist Understanding*. Washington, DC: University Press of America, 1982.

Chadwick, Owen. *The Reformation*. Pelican History of the Church 3. Harmondsworth, UK: 1964.

Chalke, Steve. "The Redemption of the Cross." In *The Atonement Debate: Papers from the London Symposium on the Theology of Atonement*, edited by Derek Tidball, David Hilborn, and Justin Thacker, 34–45. Grand Rapids: Zondervan, 2008.

Clabeaux, John J. "The Ritual Meal in Didache 9–10: Progress in Understanding." In *The Didache: A Missing Piece of the Puzzle in Early Christianity*, edited by Jonathan A. Draper and Clayton N. Jefford, 209–30. SBLECL 14. Atlanta: SBL, 2015.

Cortez, Felix H. "From the Holy to the Most Holy Place: The Period of Hebrews 9:6-10 and the Day of Atonement as a Metaphor of Transition." *JBL* 125 (2006): 527–47.

Cory, Catherine A., and David T. Landry, eds. *The Christian Theological Tradition*. Englewood Cliffs, NJ: Prentice-Hall, 2000.

Crook, Zeba A. *Reconceptualising Conversion: Patronage, Loyalty, and Conversion in the Religions of the Ancient Mediterranean*. BZNW 130. Berlin: de Gruyter, 2004.

Crosby, Fanny. "I Am Thine, O Lord." Hymn 419 in *The United Methodist Hymnal*. Nashville: United Methodist Publishing House, 1989.

Crysdale, Cynthia S. W. *Embracing Travail: Retrieving the Cross Today*. New York: Continuum, 1999.

Cummins, Stephen Anthony. *Paul and the Crucified Christ in Antioch: Maccabean*

Martyrdom and Galatians 1 and 2. SNTSMS 114. Cambridge: Cambridge University Press, 2001.

Davies, W. D. *Paul and Rabbinic Judaism: Some Rabbinic Elements in Pauline Theology.* Rev. ed. New York: Harper, 1948.

Dawson, David. *Flesh Becomes Word: A Lexicography of the Scapegoat or, the History of an Idea.* East Lansing: Michigan State University Press, 2013.

de Jong, Albert. "Animal Sacrifice in Ancient Zoroastrianism: A Ritual and Its Interpretation." In *Sacrifice in Religious Experience.* Edited by Albert I. Baumgarten. SHR 93. Leiden: Brill, 2002.

De Roos, Simone A., et al. "Influence of Maternal Denomination, God Concepts, and Child-Rearing Practices on Young Children's God Concepts." *JSSR* 43 (2004): 519–35.

DeLozier, Pauline P. "Attachment Theory and Child Abuse." In *The Place of Attachment in Human Behavior*, edited by Colin Murray Parkes and Joan Stevenson-Hinde, 95–117. New York: Basic, 1982.

DeSilva, David A. *The Letter to the Hebrews in Social-Scientific Perspective.* Eugene, OR: Cascade, 2012.

———. *Perseverance in Gratitude: A Socio-political Commentary on the Epistle to the Hebrews.* Grand Rapids: Eerdmans, 2000.

Dickie, Jane R., Amy K. Eshleman, Dawn M. Merasco, Amy Shepard, Michael Vander Wilt, and Melissa Johnson. "Parent-Child Relationships and Children's Images of God." *JSSR* 36 (1997): 25–43.

Dickie, Jane R., Lindsey V. Ajega, Joy R. Kobylak, and Kathryn M. Nixon, "Mother, Father, and Self: Sources of Young Adults' God Concepts." *JSSR* 45 (2006): 57–71.

Dodd, C. H. *The Meaning of Paul for Today.* London: Fontana, 1920, 1958.

Douglas, Mary. *In the Active Voice.* London: Routledge & Kegan Paul, 1982.

———. *Natural Symbols: Explorations in Cosmology.* New York: Pantheon, 1982.

———. *Purity and Danger: An Analysis of Concepts of Pollution and Taboo.* 1966. Reprint, New York: Routledge, 1991.

Dozier, Mary, Melissa Manni, and Oliver Lindhiem. "Lessons from the Longitudinal Studies of Attachment." In *Attachment from Infancy to Adulthood: The Major Longitudinal Studies*, edited by Klaus Grossman, Karin Grossmann, and Everett Waters, 305–19. New York: Guilford, 2005.

Draper, Jonathan A. "Conclusion: Missing Pieces in the Puzzle or Wild Goose Chase? A Retrospect and Prospect." In *The Didache: A Missing Piece of the Puzzle in Early Christianity*, edited by Jonathan A. Draper and Clayton N. Jefford, 529–43. SBLECL 14. Atlanta: SBL, 2015.

Dundes, Alan. "The Ritual Murder or Blood Libel Legend." In *The Blood Libel Legend: A Casebook in Anti-Semitic Folklore*, edited by Alan Dundes, 336–76. Madison: University of Wisconsin Press, 1991.

Dunn, James D. G. *Romans 1–8*. WBC 38A. Dallas: Word, 1988.

———. *The Theology of Paul the Apostle*. Grand Rapids: Eerdmans, 1998.

Durant, Will. *The Story of Civilization*. Vol. 6, *The Reformation: A History of European Civilization from Wyclif to Calvin: 1300–1564*. New York: Simon & Schuster, 1957.

Eaton, John. *The Psalms: A Historical and Spiritual Commentary with an Introduction and New Translation*. London: T&T Clark, 2003.

Eberhart, Christian A. Review of *Cult and Character: Purification Offerings, Day of Atonement, and Theodicy*, by Roy E. Gane. *Review of Biblical Literature*, July 1, 2006, http://www.bookreviews.org/pdf/5068_5341.pdf.

———. "Sacrifice? Holy Smokes! Reflections on Cult Terminology for Understanding Sacrifice in the Hebrew Bible." In *Ritual and Metaphor: Sacrifice in the Bible*, edited by Christian A. Eberhart, 17–32. RBS 68. Atlanta: SBL, 2011.

———. *The Sacrifice of Jesus: Understanding Atonement Biblically*. Facets. Minneapolis: Fortress Press, 2011.

Ehrman, Bart D. *Misquoting Jesus: The Story behind Who Changed the Bible and Why*. San Francisco: HarperSanFrancisco, 2005.

Elliott, Neil. *Liberating Paul: The Justice of God and the Politics of the Apostle*. Maryknoll, NY: Orbis, 1994.

Erikson, Erik H. *Childhood and Society*. 2nd ed. New York: Norton, 1963.

———. *Young Man Luther: A Study in Psychoanalysis and History*. New York: Norton, 1962.

Fee, Gordon D. *The First Epistle to the Corinthians*. NICNT. Grand Rapids: Eerdmans, 1987.

———. "Paul and the Metaphors for Salvation: Some Reflections on Pauline Soteriology." In *The Redemption: An Interdisciplinary Symposium*, edited by

Stephen T. Davis, Daniel Kendall, and Gerald O'Collins, 43–67. Oxford: Oxford University Press, 2004.

Ferguson, Everett. "Spiritual Sacrifice in Early Christianity and Its Environment." In *ANRW* 23.2:1151–89.

Finlan, Stephen. *The Background and Content of Paul's Cultic Atonement Metaphors*. AcBib 19. Atlanta: SBL, 2004.

———. *Bullying in the Churches*. Eugene, OR: Cascade, 2015.

———. "Can We Speak of Theōsis in Paul?" In *Partakers of the Divine Nature: The History and Development of Deification in the Christian Traditions*, edited by Michael J. Christensen and Jeffery A. Wittung, 68–80. Grand Rapids: Baker Academic, 2007.

———. "Deification in Jesus' Teachings." In *Theōsis: Deification in Christian Theology*, edited by Vladimir Kharlamov, 2:21–41. PTMS 156. Eugene, OR: Wipf & Stock, 2011.

———. *Problems with Atonement: The Origins of, and Controversy about, the Atonement Doctrine*. Collegeville, MN: Liturgical, 2005.

———. "Spiritualization of Sacrifice in Paul and Hebrews." In *Ritual and Metaphor: Sacrifice in the Bible*, edited by Christian A. Eberhart, 83–97. RBS 68. Atlanta: SBL, 2011.

Finlan, Stephen, and Vladimir Kharlamov, eds. *Theōsis: Deification in Christian Theology*. PTMS 52. Eugene, OR: Wipf & Stock, 2006.

Forsyth, P. T. *The Justification of God: Lectures for War-Time on a Christian Theodicy*. New York: Charles Scribner's Sons, 1917.

———. *The Person and Place of Jesus Christ: The Congregational Union Lecture for 1909*. Cincinnati: Jennings & Graham, 1909.

Frymer-Kensky, Tikva. "Pollution, Purification, and Purgation in Biblical Israel." In *The Word of the Lord Shall Go Forth*, edited by Carol L. Meyers and M. O'Connor, 399–414. Winona Lake, IN: Eisenbrauns, 1983.

Furley, William P. "Prayers and Hymns." In *A Companion to Greek Religion*, edited by Daniel Ogden, 117–31. Oxford: Wiley-Blackwell, 2010.

Gaiser, Frederick J. "The David of Psalm 51: Reading 51 in Light of Psalm 50." *WW* 23 (2003): 382–93.

Gammie, John G. *Holiness in Israel*. 1989. Reprint, Eugene, OR: Wipf & Stock, 2005.

Gane, Roy E. *Cult and Character: Purification Offerings, Day of Atonement, and Theodicy*. Winona Lake, IN: Eisenbrauns, 2005.

Gathercole, Simon. *Defending Substitution: An Essay on Atonement in Paul*. Grand Rapids: Baker Academic, 2015.

Gelardini, Gabreiella. "The Inauguration of Yom Kippur according to the LXX and Its Cessation or Perpetuation according to the Book of Hebrews." In *The Day of Atonement: Its Interpretations in Early Jewish and Christian Traditions*, edited by Thomas Hieke and Tobias Nicklas, 225–54. Leiden: Brill, 2012.

Gerstenberger, Erhard S. *Psalms, Part 1, with an Introduction to Cultic Poetry*. FOTL 14. Grand Rapids: Eerdmans, 1988.

———. *Psalms, Part 2, and Lamentations*. FOTL 15. Grand Rapids: Eerdmans, 2001.

Gilders, William K. *Blood Ritual in the Hebrew Bible: Meaning and Power*. Baltimore: Johns Hopkins University Press, 2004.

Girard, René. *I See Satan Fall Like Lightning*. Translated by James G. Williams. Maryknoll, NY: Orbis, 2001.

Goldingay, John. "Old Testament Sacrifice and the Death of Christ." In *Atonement Today*, edited by John Goldingay, 3–20. London: SPCK, 1995.

Gorman, Frank H., Jr. *The Ideology of Ritual: Space, Time and Status in the Priestly Theology*. JSOTSup 91. Sheffield: Sheffield Academic, 1990.

Gorman, Michael J. *The Death of the Messiah and the Birth of the New Covenant: A (Not-So) New Model of the Atonement*. Eugene, OR: Wipf & Stock, 2014.

Gorringe, Timothy. *God's Just Vengeance: Crime, Violence and the Rhetoric of Salvation*. Cambridge Studies in Ideology and Religion 9. Cambridge: Cambridge University Press, 1996.

Green, Joel B. "Death of Jesus." In *Dictionary of Jesus and the Gospels: A Compendium of Contemporary Biblical Scholarship*, edited by Joel B. Green, Scot McKnight, and I. Howard Marshall, 146–63. Downers Grove, IL: InterVarsity Press, 1992.

———. Speech given at Pacific School of Religion, March 24, 1997.

Green, Joel B., and Mark D. Baker. *Recovering the Scandal of the Cross: Atonement in New Testament and Contemporary Contexts*. Downers Grove, IL: InterVarsity Press, 2000.

Grensted, L. W. *A Short History of the Doctrine of the Atonement*. Manchester: Longmans, Green, 1920.

Greven, Philip. *Spare the Child: The Religious Roots of Punishment and the Psychological Impact of Physical Abuse*. New York: Knopf, 1991.

Grimsrud, Ted. *Instead of Atonement: The Bible's Salvation Story and Our Hope for Wholeness*. Eugene, OR: Cascade, 2013.

Gunton, Colin. "The Sacrifice and the Sacrifices: From Metaphor to Transcendental?" In *Trinity, Incarnation, and Atonement: Philosophical and Theological Essays*, edited by Ronald J. Feenstra and Cornelius Plantinga Jr., 210–20. Notre Dame: University of Notre Dame Press, 1989.

Haber, Susan. *"They Shall Purify Themselves": Essays on Purity in Early Judaism*. Edited by Adele Reinhartz. EJL 24. Atlanta: SBL, 2008.

Halbertal, Moshe. *On Sacrifice*. Princeton: Princeton University Press, 2012.

Harnack, Adolph. *History of Dogma*. Vol. 5. Translated from the 3rd German ed. by Neil Buchanan. 1900. Reprint, New York: Dover, 1961.

Harrington, Hannah K. "Clean and Unclean." In *The New Interpreter's Dictionary of the Bible*, edited by Katharine Doob Sakenfeld, 1:681–89. Nashville: Abingdon, 2006.

Hays, Richard B. "'Here We Have No Lasting City': New Covenantalism in Hebrews." In *The Epistle to the Hebrews and Christian Theology*, edited by Richard Bauckham, Daniel R. Driver, Trevor A. Hart, and Nathan MacDonald, 151–73. Grand Rapids: Eerdmans, 2009.

Heesterman, J. C. *The Broken World of Sacrifice: An Essay in Ancient Indian Ritual*. Chicago: University of Chicago Press, 1993.

———. *The Inner Conflict of Tradition: Essays in Indian Ritual, Kingship, and Society*. Chicago: University of Chicago Press, 1985.

Heim, S. Mark. *Saved from Sacrifice: A Theology of the Cross*. Grand Rapids: Eerdmans, 2006.

Hengel, Martin. *The Atonement: The Origins of the Doctrine in the New Testament*. London: SCM, 1981.

Hilber, John W. *Cultic Prophecy in the Psalms*. BZAW 352. Berlin: de Gruyter, 2005.

Hill, David. *Greek Words and Hebrew Meanings: Studies in the Semantics of Soteriological Terms*. Cambridge: Cambridge University Press, 1967.

Hinde, Robert A. "Ethology and Attachment Theory." In *Attachment from Infancy to Adulthood: The Major Longitudinal Studies*, edited by Klaus Grossman, Karin Grossmann, and Everett Waters, 1–12. New York: Guilford, 2005.

Holmes, Colin. "The Ritual Murder Accusation in Britain." In *The Blood Libel Legend: A Casebook in Anti-Semitic Folklore*, edited by Alan Dundes, 99–134. Madison: University of Wisconsin Press, 1991.

Holmes, Stephen R. "Death in the Afternoon: Hebrews, Sacrifice, and Soteriology." In *The Epistle to the Hebrews and Christian Theology*, edited by Richard Bauckham, Daniel R. Driver, Trevor A. Hart, and Nathan MacDonald, 229–52. Grand Rapids: Eerdmans, 2009.

Hooke, S. H. "The Theory and Practice of Substitution." *VT* 2 (1952): 2–17.

Hooker, Morna D. "Christ, the 'End' of the Cult." In *The Epistle to the Hebrews and Christian Theology*, edited by Richard Bauckham, Daniel R. Driver, Trevor A. Hart, and Nathan MacDonald, 189–212. Grand Rapids: Eerdmans, 2009.

———. *Not Ashamed of the Gospel: New Testament Interpretations of the Death of Christ*. Grand Rapids: Eerdmans, 1994.

Horvath, Tibor. *The Sacrificial Interpretation of Jesus' Achievement in the New Testament: Historical Development and Its Reasons*. New York: Philosophical Library, 1979.

Houston, Walter J. *Purity and Monotheism: Clean and Unclean Animals in Biblical Law*. JSOTSup 140. Sheffield: Sheffield Academic, 1993.

———. Review of *Impurity and Sin in Ancient Judaism*, by Jonathan Klawans. *JTS* 52 (2001): 722–25.

Hsia, R. po-chia. *The Myth of Ritual Murder*. New Haven: Yale University Press, 1988.

Janzen, David. *The Social Meanings of Sacrifice in the Hebrew Bible: A Study of Four Writings*. BZAW 344. Berlin: de Gruyter, 2004.

Jay, Nancy. *Throughout Your Generations Forever: Sacrifice, Religion, and Paternity*. Chicago: University of Chicago Press, 1992.

Jennings, Theodore W., Jr., *Transforming Atonement: A Political Theology of the Cross*. Minneapolis: Fortress Press, 2009.

Jewett, Robert. *Romans: A Commentary*. Hermeneia. Minneapolis: Fortress Press, 2007.

Johnson, Luke Timothy. *Hebrews: A Commentary*. NTL. Louisville: Westminster John Knox, 2006.

Jones, Michael Owen. "What's Disgusting, Why, and What Does It Matter?" *Journal of Folklore Research* 37 (2000): 53–71.

Kazen, Thomas. *Issues of Impurity in Early Judaism*. ConBNT 45. Winona Lake, IN: Eisenbrauns, 2010.

Keenan, Dennis King. *The Question of Sacrifice*. Bloomington: Indiana University Press, 2005.

Kelly, J. N. D. *Early Christian Doctrines*. Rev. ed. New York: Harper & Row, 1978.

Kirkpatrick, Lee A. *Attachment, Evolution, and the Psychology of Religion*. New York: Guilford, 2005.

Klawans, Jonathan. *Impurity and Sin in Ancient Judaism*. Oxford: Oxford University Press, 2000.

_____. *Purity, Sacrifice, and the Temple: Symbolism and Supersessionism in the Study of Ancient Judaism*. Oxford: Oxford University Press, 2006.

Kraus, Hans-Joachim. *Psalms 1-59*. CC. Translated by Hilton C. Oswald. Minneapolis: Fortress Press, 1993.

_____. *Theology of the Psalms*. Translated by Keith Crim. Minneapolis: Fortress Press, 1992.

Lee, J. A. L. *A Lexical Study of the Septuagint Version of the Pentateuch*. SBLSCS 14. Chico, CA: Scholars Press, 1983.

Levine, Baruch A. *Leviticus: The Traditional Hebrew Text with the New JPS Translation*. Philadelphia: Jewish Publication Society, 1989.

Lightfoot, J. B. *St. Paul's Epistle to the Galatians: A Revised Text with Introduction, Notes, and Dissertations*. London: Macmillan, 1869.

Lyonnet, Stanislas. "The Terminology of Redemption." In *Sin, Redemption and Sacrifice: A Biblical and Patristic Study*, by Stanislas Lyonnet and Léopold Sabourin, 61–184. AnBib 48. Rome: Biblical Institute, 1970.

Main, Mary. "The Adult Attachment Interview: Fear, Attention, Safety and Discourse Processes." *JAPA* 48 (2000): 1055–96.

Main, Mary, Erik Hesse, and Nancy Kaplan. "Predictability of Attachment Behavior and Representational Processes at 1, 6, and 19 Years of Age: The Berkeley Longitudinal Study." In *Attachment from Infancy to Adulthood: The Major Longitudinal Studies*, edited by Klaus Grossman, Karin Grossmann, and Everett Waters, 245–304. New York: Guilford, 2005.

Malherbe, Abraham J. *Paul and the Thessalonians: The Philosophic Tradition of Pastoral Care*. Philadelphia: Fortress, 1987.

Manson, T. W. "ΙΛΑΣΤΗΡΙΟΝ." *JTS* o.s. 46 (1945): 1–10.

Marshall, I. Howard. "Soteriology in Hebrews." In *The Epistle to the Hebrews and Christian Theology*, edited by Richard Bauckham, Daniel R. Driver, Trevor A. Hart, and Nathan MacDonald, 253–77. Grand Rapids: Eerdmans, 2009.

———. "The Theology of Atonement." Society of Evangelical Arminians. Posted March 29, 2013. evangelicalarminians.org/wp-content/uploads/2013/03/Marshall.-The-Theology-of-the-Atonement.pdf .

Martin, Dale. *Slavery as Salvation: The Metaphor of Slavery in Pauline Christianity*. New Haven: Yale University Press, 1990.

Matera, Frank J. *Romans*. Paideia. Grand Rapids: Baker Academic, 2010.

McCarthy, Dennis J. "Further Notes on the Symbolism of Blood and Sacrifice." *JBL* 92 (1973): 205–10.

McClymond, Kathryn. *Beyond Sacred Violence: A Comparative Study of Sacrifice*. Baltimore: Johns Hopkins University Press, 2008.

McIntosh, Mark A. *An Introduction to Christian Theology*. Malden, MA: Blackwell, 2008.

McKnight, Scot. *A Community Called Atonement*. Living Theology. Nashville: Abingdon, 2007.

McNish, Jill L. "The Bible and the Psychology of Shame." In *Psychology and the Bible: A New Way to Read the Scriptures*. Vol. 3, *From Gospel to Gnostics*, edited by J. Harold Ellens and Wayne G. Rollins, 239–64. Westport, CT: Praeger, 2004.

Mendelson, Myer. *Psychoanalytic Concepts of Depression*. 2nd ed. Flushing, NY: Spectrum, 1974.

Milavec, Aaron. "When, Why, and for Whom Was the *Didache* Created? Insights into the Social and Historical Setting of the *Didache* Communities." In *Matthew and the Didache: Two Documents from the Same Jewish-Christian Milieu?*, edited by Huub van de Sandt, 63–84. Minneapolis: Fortress Press, 2005.

Milgrom, Jacob. "Further on the Expiatory Sacrifices." *JBL* 115 (1996): 511–14.

———. "Kipper." Pages 1039–44 in *Encyclopaedia Judaica*, volume 10. New York: Macmillan, 1971.

———. *Leviticus 1–16*. AB 3. Garden City, NY: Doubleday, 1991.

———. *Studies in Cultic Theology and Terminology*. SJLA 36. Leiden: Brill, 1983.

Miller, Alice. *For Your Own Good: Hidden Cruelty in Child-Rearing and the Roots of Violence*. Translated by Hildegarde and Hunter Hannum. New York: Farrar, Straus & Giroux, 1983.

———. *Paths of Life: Seven Scenarios*. New York: Vintage, 1998.

———. *Thou Shalt Not Be Aware: Society's Betrayal of the Child*. Translated by Hildegarde Hannum and Hunter Hannum. New York: Farrar, Straus & Giroux, 1984.

Mody, Rohintan K. "Penal Substitutionary Atonement in Paul: An Exegetical Study of Romans 3:25–26." In *The Atonement Debate: Papers from the London Symposium on the Theology of Atonement*, edited by Derek Tidball, David Hilborn, and Justin Thacker, 115–35. Grand Rapids: Zondervan, 2008.

Moffitt, David M. *Atonement and the Logic of Resurrection in the Epistle to the Hebrews*. NovTSup 141. Leiden: Brill, 2011.

———. "Blood, Life, and Atonement: Reassessing Hebrews' Christological Appropriation of Yom Kippur." In *The Day of Atonement: Its Interpretations in Early Jewish and Christian Traditions*, edited by Thomas Hieke and Tobias Nicklas, 211–24. Leiden: Brill, 2012.

Mowinckel, Sigmund. *The Psalms in Israel's Worship*. Translated by D. R. Ap-Thomas. 2 vols. 1962. Reprint, Grand Rapids: Eerdmans, 2004.

Murray-Swank, Aaron, Annette Mahoney, and Kenneth I. Pargament. "Sanctification of Parenting: Links to Corporal Punishment and Parental Warmth among Biblically Conservative and Liberal Mothers." *International Journal for the Psychology of Religion* 16 (2006): 271–87.

Nelson-Pallmeyer, Jack. *Jesus against Christianity: Reclaiming the Missing Jesus*. Harrisburg, PA: Trinity Press International, 2001.

Neville, Robert Cummings. *The Truth of Broken Symbols*. Albany: State University of New York Press, 1996.

The New Century Hymnal. Cleveland: Pilgrim, 1995.

Parker, Robert. "Pleasing Thighs: Reciprocity in Greek Religion." In *Reciprocity in Ancient Greece*, edited by Christopher Gill, Norman Postlethwaite, and Richard Seaford, 105–25. Oxford: Oxford University Press, 1998.

Pattison, Stephen. "Shame and the Unwanted Self." In *The Shame Factor: How Shame Shapes Society*, edited by Robert Jewett, with Wayne L. Alloway Jr. and John G. Lacey, 9–29. Eugene, OR: Cascade, 2011.

Polen, Nehemia. "Leviticus and Hebrews . . . and Leviticus." In *The Epistle to the Hebrews and Christian Theology*, edited by Richard Bauckham, Daniel R.

Driver, Trevor A. Hart, and Nathan MacDonald, 213–25. Grand Rapids: Eerdmans, 2009.

Poliakov, Léon. *The History of Anti-Semitism*. Translated by Richard Howard. 2nd ed. 1965. Reprint, New York: Schocken: 1976.

Pruyser, Paul W. "Anxiety, Guilt, and Shame in the Atonement." *Theology Today* 21 (1964): 15–33.

———. *Religion in Psychodynamic Perspective: The Contributions of Paul W. Pruyser*. Edited by H. Newton Malony and Bernard Spilka. New York: Oxford University Press, 1991.

Pugh, Ben. *Atonement Theories: A Way through the Maze*. Eugene, OR: Cascade, 2014.

Quinn, Philip L. "Aquinas on Atonement." In *Trinity, Incarnation, and Atonement: Philosophical and Theological Essays*, edited by Ronald J. Feenstra and Cornelius Plantinga Jr., 153–77. Notre Dame: University of Notre Dame Press, 1989.

Rado, Sandor. "The Automatic Motivating System of Depressive Behavior." In *Psychoanalysis of Behavior: The Collected Papers of Sandor Rado*. Vol. 2, 1956–1961, 163–77. New York: Grune & Stratton, 1962.

———. "Contribution to a Discussion on Masochism." In *Psychoanalysis of Behavior: The Collected Papers of Sandor Rado*. Vol. 2, 1956–1961, 84–86. New York: Grune & Stratton, 1962.

———. "Hedonic Control, Action-Self, and the Depressive Spell." 286–311 in *Psychoanalysis of Behavior; Collected Papers*, vol. 1: 1922–1956. New York and London: Grune & Stratton, 1956.

———. "The Problem of Melancholia." In *Psychoanalysis of Behavior: The Collected Papers of Sandor Rado*. Vol. 1, 1922–1956, 47–63. New York: Grune & Stratton, 1956.

———. "Rage, Violence, and Conscience." In *Psychoanalysis of Behavior: The Collected Papers of Sandor Rado*. Vol. 2, 1956–1961, 147–51. New York: Grune & Stratton, 1962.

Rappaport, Ernest A. "The Ritual Murder Accusation: The Persistence of Doubt and the Repetition Compulsion." In *The Blood Libel Legend: A Casebook in Anti-Semitic Folklore*, edited by Alan Dundes, 304–35. Madison: University of Wisconsin Press, 1991.

Rashdall, Hastings. *The Idea of the Atonement in Christian Theology*. London: Macmillan, 1919.

Reid, Barbara E. *Taking Up the Cross: New Testament Interpretations through Latina and Feminist Eyes*. Minneapolis: Fortress Press, 2007.

Rhoads, David M., and Sandra Roberts Rhoads. "Justification by Grace: Shame and Acceptance in a County Jail." In *The Shame Factor: How Shame Shapes Society*, edited by Robert Jewett, with Wayne L. Alloway Jr. and John G. Lacey, 86–102. Eugene, OR: Cascade, 2011.

Ribbens, Benjamin J. "Forensic-Retributive Justification in Romans 3:21-26: Paul's Doctrine of Justification in Dialogue with Hebrews." *CBQ* 74 (2012): 548–67.

Roetzel, Calvin. *Paul: The Man and the Myth*. Edinburgh: T&T Clark, 1999.

Rosen, Irwin C. "The Atonement-Forgiveness Dyad: Identification with the Aggressed." *Psychoanalytic Inquiry* 29 (2009): 411–25.

Rozin, Paul, Jonathan Haidt, and Clark R. McCauley. "Disgust." In *Handbook of Emotions*, edited by Michael Lewis, Jeannette M. Haviland-Jones, and Lisa Feldman Barrett, 757–76. 3rd ed. New York: Guilford, 2008.

Rozin, Paul, Jonathan Haidt, Clark McCauley, and Sumio Imada. "Disgust: Preadaptation and the Cultural Evolution of a Food-Based Emotion." In *Food Preferences and Taste: Continuity and Change*, edited by Helen Macbeth, 65–82. The Anthropology of Food and Nutrition 2. Oxford: Berghahn, 1997.

Rubin, Miri. "Desecration of the Host: The Birth of an Accusation." In *Christianity and Judaism: Papers Read at the 1991 Summer Meeting and the 1992 Winter Meeting of the Ecclesiastical History Society*, edited by Diana Wood, 169–85. Oxford: Blackwell, 1992.

Sabourin, Leopold. *The Psalms: Their Origin and Meaning*. 2nd ed. New York: Alba House, 1974.

Sanders, E. P. *Paul and Palestinian Judaism*. Philadelphia: Fortress Press, 1977.

_____. *Paul, the Law, and the Jewish People*. Minneapolis: Fortress Press, 1983.

Schmitt, Mary. "Restructuring Views on Law in Hebrews 7:12." *JBL* 128 (2009): 189–201.

Schneider, Carl D. *Shame, Exposure and Privacy*. Boston: Beacon, 1977.

Schreiber, Stefan. "Weitergedacht: Das versöhnende Weihegeschenk Gottes in Röm 3,25." *ZNW* 106 (2015): 201–15.

Schultz, Magdalene. "The Blood Libel: A Motif in the History of Childhood." In *The Blood Libel Legend: A Casebook in Anti-Semitic Folklore*, edited by Alan Dundes, 273–303. Madison: University of Wisconsin Press, 1991.

Schwartz, Seth. *Were the Jews a Mediterranean Society? Reciprocity and Solidarity in Ancient Judaism*. Princeton: Princeton University Press, 2010.

Siegel, Daniel J. *The Developing Mind: Toward a Neurobiology of Interpersonal Experience*. New York: Guilford, 1999.

Skarsaune, Oskar. "Does the Letter to the Hebrews Articulate a Supersessionist Theology? A Response to Richard Hays." In *The Epistle to the Hebrews and Christian Theology*, edited by Richard Bauckham, Daniel R. Driver, Trevor A. Hart, and Nathan MacDonald, 174–82. Grand Rapids: Eerdmans, 2009.

Sklar, Jay. *Sin, Impurity, Sacrifice, Atonement: The Priestly Conceptions*. HBM 2. Sheffield: Sheffield Phoenix, 2005.

Souter, Alexander. *The Text and Canon of the New Testament*. New York: Charles Scribner's Sons, 1913.

Sroufe, L. Alan, Byron Egeland, Elizabeth Carlson, and W. Andrew Collins. "Placing Early Attachment Experiences in Developmental Context." In *Attachment from Infancy to Adulthood: The Major Longitudinal Studies*, edited by Klaus Grossman, Karin Grossmann, and Everett Waters, 48–70. New York: Guilford, 2005.

Stählin, Gustav. "Περίψημα."In *TDNT* 6:84–93.

Stockitt, Robin. *Restoring the Shamed: Towards a Theology of Shame*. Eugene, OR: Cascade, 2012.

Stökl Ben Ezra, Daniel. "Atonement. Judaism: Second Temple Period." In *Encyclopedia of the Bible and its Reception*. Vol. 3, *Athena–Birkat ha-Minim*, edited by Hans-Josef Klauck, Bernard McGinn, Choon-Leong Seow, Hermann Spieckermann, and Barry Dov Walfish, 43–46. Berlin: de Gruyter, 2011.

―――. "Fasting with Jews, Thinking with Scapegoats: Some Remarks on Yom Kippur in Early Judaism and Christianity, in Particular 4Q541, *Barnabas* 7, Matthew 27 and Acts 27." In *The Day of Atonement: Its Interpretations in Early Jewish and Christian Traditions*, edited by Thomas Hieke and Tobias Nicklas, 165–87. Leiden: Brill, 2012.

―――. *The Impact of Yom Kippur on Early Christianity: The Day of Atonement from*

Second Temple Judaism to the Fifth Century. WUNT 163. Tübingen: Mohr Siebeck, 2003.

Stott, John. *Basic Christianity*. 1958. Reprint, Downers Grove, IL: InterVarsity Press, 2008.

_____. *The Cross of Christ*. Downers Grove, IL: InterVarsity Press, 1986.

Stowers, Stanley K. "Does Pauline Christianity Resemble a Hellenistic Philosophy?" In *Paul beyond the Judaism/Hellenism Divide*, edited by Troels Engberg-Pedersen, 81–102. Louisville: Westminster John Knox, 2001.

_____. "Greeks Who Sacrifice and Those Who Do Not: Toward an Anthropology of Greek Religion." In *The Social World of the First Christians: Essays in Honor of Wayne A Meeks*, edited by L. Michael White and O. Larry Yarbrough, 293–333. Minneapolis: Fortress Press, 1995.

_____. "The Religion of Plant and Animal Offerings versus the Religion of Meanings, Essences, and Textual Mysteries." In *Ancient Mediterranean Sacrifice*, edited by Jennifer Wright Knust and Zsuzsanna Várhelyi, 35–56. Oxford: Oxford University Press, 2011.

_____. *A Rereading of Romans: Justice, Jews, and Gentiles*. New Haven: Yale University Press, 1994.

Stuhlmacher, Peter. *Reconciliation, Law and Righteousness: Essays in Biblical Theology*. Philadelphia: Fortress Press, 1986.

Swartley, Willard M. *Covenant of Peace: The Missing Peace in New Testament Theology and Ethics*. Grand Rapids: Eerdmans, 2006.

Tamminen, Kalevi, Renzo Vianello, Jean-Marie Jaspard, and Donald Ratcliff. "The Religious Concepts of Preschoolers." In *Handbook of Preschool Religious Education*, edited by Donald Ratcliff, 59–81. Birmingham, AL: Religious Education Press, 1988.

Tatlock, Jason. "The Place of Human Sacrifice in the Israelite Cult." In *Ritual and Metaphor: Sacrifice in the Bible*, edited by Christian A. Eberhart, 33–48. RBS 68. Atlanta: SBL, 2011.

Theissen, Gerd. *Psychological Aspects of Pauline Theology*. Translated by John P. Galvin. Philadelphia: Fortress Press, 1987.

Tillich, Paul. *A History of Christian Thought from Its Judaic and Hellenistic Origins to Existentialism*. Edited by Carl E. Braaten. New York: Simon & Schuster, 1967.

Tinkle, Theresa. "Exegesis Reconsidered: The Fleury *Slaughter of the Innocents* and the Myth of Ritual Murder." *Journal of English and Germanic Philology* 102 (2003): 211–43.

Tiwald, Markus. "Christ as Hilasterion (Rom 3:25). Pauline Theology on the Day of Atonement in the Mirror of Early Jewish Thought." In *The Day of Atonement: Its Interpretations in Early Jewish and Christian Traditions*, edited by Thomas Hieke and Tobias Nicklas, 189–209. Leiden: Brill, 2012.

Trachtenberg, Joshua. *The Devil and the Jews*. New Haven: Yale University Press, 1943.

Tylor, Edward Burnett. *Primitive Culture*. Vol. 2, *Religion in Primitive Culture*. 1874. Reprint, New York: Harper & Bros., 1958.

Voegelin, Eric. *Order and History*. Vol. 4, *The Ecumenic Age*. Baton Rouge: Louisiana State University Press, 1974.

Waite, Gary K. *Heresy, Magic and Witchcraft in Early Modern Europe*. London: Palgrave Macmillan, 2003.

Warner, Rex. *The Greek Philosophers*. New York: Mentor, 1958.

Weaver, J. Denny. "Narrative *Christus Victor*: The Answer to Anselmian Atonement Violence." In *Atonement and Violence: A Theological Conversation*, edited by John Sanders, 1–29. Nashville: Abingdon, 2006.

———. *The Nonviolent Atonement*. Rev. ed. Grand Rapids: Eerdmans, 2011.

———. "Violence in Christian Theology." *Cross Currents* 51 (2001): 150–76.

Wedderburn, Alexander J. M. *The Death of Jesus: Some Reflections on Jesus-Traditions and Paul*. WUNT 299. Tübingen: Mohr Siebeck, 2013.

Weingart, Richard E. *The Logic of Divine Love: A Critical Analysis of the Soteriology of Peter Abailard*. Oxford: Clarendon, 1970.

Weiss, Alexander. "Christus Jesus als Weihegeschenk oder Sühnemal? Anmerkungen zu einer neueren Deutung von *hilasterion* (Röm 3,25) samt einer Liste der epigraphischen Belege." *ZNW* 105 (2014): 294–302.

Westcott, B. F., and F. J. A. Hort. *Introduction to the New Testament in the Original Greek with Notes on Selected Readings*. 1882. Reprint, Peabody, MA: Hendrickson, 1988.

Whale, J. S. *Victor and Victim: The Christian Doctrine of Redemption*. Cambridge: Cambridge University Press, 1960.

Whitlark, Jason A. *Enabling Fidelity to God: Perseverance in Hebrews in Light of the*

Reciprocity Systems of the Ancient Mediterranean World. Paternoster Biblical Monographs. Milton Keynes, UK: Paternoster, 2008.

Williams, Charles. *Arthurian Torso.* Oxford: Oxford University Press, 1948.

Williams, Jarvis J. *Christ Died for Our Sins: Representation and Substitution in Romans and Their Jewish Martyrological Background.* Eugene, OR: Pickwick, 2015.

———. *Maccabean Martyr Traditions in Paul's Theology of Atonement: Did Martyr Theology Shape Paul's Conception of Jesus' Death?* Eugene, OR: Wipf & Stock, 2010.

Wright, David P. "Day of Atonement." In *ABD* 2:72–76.

Wright, N. T. *The Climax of the Covenant: Christ and the Law in Pauline Theology.* Edinburgh: T&T Clark, 1991.

Young, Frances M. *Sacrifice and the Death of Christ.* Philadelphia: Westminster, 1975.

———. *The Use of Sacrificial Ideas in Greek Christian Writers from the New Testament to John Chrysostom.* 1979. Reprint, Eugene: Wipf & Stock, 2004.

Index of Names

Abelard, Peter, 159–61, 184
Adam, 104, 152, 156, 170
Ainsworth, Mary D. Salter, 61
Ajega, Lindsey, 65
Albertz, Rainer, 46, 52, 54
Amos (re: the prophet), 46, 51, 54
Anderson, Gary, 46
Anselm, 157–59, 163, 166–67, 181, 184
anti-sacrificial sayings, xiv, 45–54, 57, 116, 130–31
antisemitism, 173–80
anxiety, xv, xvii–xviii, 2–3, 17, 41, 61–64, 66, 74, 104, 108–9, 162–65, 171–72, 175–78
appeasing, xiii, 25, 27–29, 31, 33, 37, 69–70, 83, 85, 99–100, 115–16, 142, 161, 165–66, 185, 187
Aquinas, Thomas, 161, 166, 169, 179
ark of the covenant, 8–9, 17, 81
Athanasius, 94, 154–55
attachment theory, xix, 59–66, 68–69, 71, 73–74, 104, 108–9, 142–43, 145

atonement: In New Testament. *See* chapters 4–6; In Old Testament. *See* chapters 1–2; Traditional theories of. *See* chapter 7
Augustine, 87, 99, 152, 156–57, 167, 179
Aulén, Gustaf, 155, 157, 166–68

Bailey, Daniel, 8, 81–84
Bainton, Roland, 169
Baker, Mark, 158
Baker, Sharon, 11, 117
Bartlett, Anthony, 156, 168
BAG, 96
Beck, Richard, 14–16, 18–21
Berger, Klaus, 96
Bermann, Eric, 70
blood, xii–xii, xvii, 5–6, 8–10, 12–13, 17, 20, 25, 30–31, 46, 48, 52, 70, 73, 75–78, 80–82, 85, 93, 97–101, 109, 124–27, 130–32, 135–37, 140–42, 145, 150, 159, 166, 170, 173–80, 185, 189
Boersma, Hans, 94

211

Boring, M. Eugene, 96
Bowen, John, 28
Bowlby, John, 62
Brock, Rita Nakashima, 161
Brondos, David, 88, 152–53, 162, 170
Browning, Don, 158
Büchner, Dirk, 83
Burkert, Walter, 1–2, 91
Bursten, Ben, 160
Bushnell, Horace, 109–11, 184–85

Calvin, Jean, 94, 99, 110, 162, 166, 170–72, 180–81
Campbell, Douglas, 79, 85
Capps, Donald, 37, 67, 118, 141, 143, 157
Carlson, Elizabeth, 63
Cessario, Romanus, 161
Chadwick, Owen, 172
Chalke, Steve, 89
Clabeaux, John, 127
Clement of Alexandria, 135
Collins, W. Andrew, 63
Colpe, Carsten, 96
compensation or reparation, xix, 5–6, 23–25, 29, 34–36, 40, 59, 65, 70, 76, 80, 106, 158–59, 184, 187
Cortez, Felix, 144
Cory, Catherine, 157
covenant, 4, 13, 82, 100, 113, 117–18, 121, 124, 127, 132–37, 140, 142, 145, 178
Crook, Zeba, 39, 55
Crosby, Fanny, 189

cruelty, xiv, xvii–xviii, 30, 34, 59, 61, 66–68, 106, 156–59, 164, 169, 171, 174, 177–78, 181, 186–87, 190
Crysdale, Cynthia, 158
Cummins, Stephen Anthony, 151
"cut off." *See kereth*
Cynicism, 55

David, xvi, 25–26, 30–31, 52, 119, 126
Davies, W. D., 77
Dawson, David, 94
de Jong, Albert, 25
De Roos, Simone, 65
DeLozier, Pauline, 61–62
DeSilva, David, 139
Deuteronomistic historian, editor, 31, 52, 137
developmental psychology, 5, 48, 60, 63–65, 187
Dickie, Jane, 65
Diogenes of Sinope, 55
Dittenberger, Wilhelm, 96
Dodd, C. H.,
disgust, 14–20, 45, 59–60, 75, 77, 93, 102–8, 140, 175–76
disorder, 1, 16–17, 177
Dostoyevsky, Fyodor, 35
Douglas, Mary, 1–2, 46
Dozier, Mary, 60
Draper, Jonathan, 127
Dundes, Alan, 176, 178, 180
Dunn, James, 92, 95, 102, 104
Durant, Will, 172

INDEX OF NAMES

Eaton, John, 45
Eberhart, Christian, 10, 27, 30, 53
Egeland, Byron, 63
Ehrman, Bart, 124
Elliott, Neil, 80
Erikson, Erik, 32–33, 169
Eshleman, Amy, 65
Eucharist, 12, 19–20, 38, 77, 79–80, 117, 124–27, 177–78
expiation, 1, 8, 18, 29–30, 35–36, 50, 78, 80, 83, 85, 88, 113, 159
Ezekiel (re: the prophet), 51–52, 54, 140

favor, favoritism, xiii–xiv, 28, 31, 38, 40–41, 44–47, 51, 55–56, 60, 87, 100, 106
fear, xi, xv–xviii, 2, 14–19, 31, 33–36, 42, 60–63, 73, 79, 84, 100, 105, 108–9, 129, 137–38, 140, 142, 144, 156, 160, 163, 165, 170–71, 173–77, 180, 187, 189
Fee, Gordon, 83–84, 96
Ferguson, Everett, 77
Finlan, Stephen, 53, 94, 153, 155, 160
First Peter (aside from specific passages), 116, 122, 151
forgiveness, xvii, 6, 9–11, 13, 24, 35–36, 70, 72, 78–80, 87, 89, 98, 100–101, 109, 118–20, 122, 129, 133, 137, 147, 159–60, 171, 181, 184, 188–89
Forsyth, P. T., 184–85

Frazer, James, 94
Freud, Sigmund, 32, 34, 162, 164
Frymer-Kensky, Tikva, 7

Gaiser, Frederick, 52
Gammie, John, 4
Gane, Roy, 10
Gathercole, Simon, 88
Gerstenberger, Erhard, 43, 49
Gilby, Thomas, 161
Girard, René, 94
Goldingay, John, xi
Gorman, Michael, 117–18, 121–22
Gorringe, Timothy, 29, 157–61
Gouldner, A., 38
Green, Joel, 124–25, 158
Gregory of Nazianzus, 94, 152, 155
Gregory of Nyssa, 94, 152–53
Gregory the Great, xvii, 99, 152, 157–58
Grensted, L. W., xvii, 153–56, 158, 160, 167–68, 170
Greven, Philip, 143
Grimsrud, Ted, 115–16, 118, 121
Grotius, Hugo, 180
guilt, xvii–xviii, 5–6, 21, 23, 26, 30, 32–33, 35–37, 73, 104, 106, 110, 156–57, 160–65, 167–68, 170–72, 176, 178, 186
Gunton, Colin, 77

Haber, Susan, 7, 132
Haggai (re: the prophet), 54
Haidt, Jonathan, 15–16

213

Harnack, Adolph, 156
Halbertal, Moshe, 2-3
Harrington, Hannah, 7
Hays, Richard, 85, 133-34
Heesterman, J. C., 32
Heim, S. Mark, 94
Hengel, Martin, 91
Hesse, Erik, 61-63
Hilber, John, 52
Hill, David, 95
Hinde, Robert, 62
Hitler, Adolf, 16, 68
Holmes, Colin, 173
Holmes, Stephen, 129
Hooke, S. H., 91
Hooker, Morna, 87-88, 95, 134, 153
Hort, F. J. A., 124
Horvath, Tibor, 151
Hosea (re: the prophet), 51-52, 54, 138, 182
Houston, Walter, 6, 77
Hsia, R. po-chia, 173-74, 176-77, 179-80

Ignatius of Antioch, 80, 150-51
Imada, Sumio, 15-16
impurity, 1-3, 5-10, 12-19, 21, 30, 82, 90-91, 99, 101, 103, 105-6, 132
Indian and Vedic religion, 32, 50
Innocent III, Pope, 175
Irenaeus, 152
Isaiah (re: the prophet[s]), 46, 51, 53, 77, 140, 182

Janzen, David, 2, 4, 31
Jaspard, Jean-Marie, 65
Jay, Nancy, 5
Jennings, Theodore, Jr., 101
Jeremiah (re: the prophet), 52-53, 137, 140
Jewett, Robert, 85
Joel (re: the prophet), 54
John (aside from specific passages), 122-23, 147, 151
Johnson, Luke Timothy, 135, 140
Johnson, Melissa, 65
Jones, Michael Owen, 16
Joubert, S., 38

Kaplan, Nancy, 61-63
Kazen, Thomas, 2, 14, 16-17, 60, 105
Keenan, Dennis King, 38
Kelly, J. N. D., 156
kereth, 4, 7, 17
Kharlamov, Vladimir, 94, 155
kipper, 7-8, 10-11, 26-27, 29-30
Kirkpatrick, Lee, 61, 69, 74
Klawans, Jonathan, 6-7, 26, 53-54
Kobylak, Joy, 65
Kraus, Hans-Joachim, 52
Kümmel, Werner, 104

Landry, David, 157
Lao Tse, 51
Lee, J. A. L., 83
Levine, Baruch, 28
LSJ, 84
Lightfoot, J. B., 96

INDEX OF NAMES

Lindhiem, Oliver, 60
Luke (aside from specific passages), 118, 121–25, 151
Luther, Martin, xix, 8, 81, 99, 162–63, 166–69, 171–72, 179–81
Lyonnet, Stanislas, 98

magic, magical thinking, 9, 15–16, 21, 29, 33–34, 48, 53–54, 56, 76, 97, 100–101, 120, 138, 144–45, 174–80, 185, 187–88
Mahoney, Annette, 64
Main, Mary, 61–63
Malachi (re: the prophet), 52, 54
Malherbe, Abraham, 102
manipulation, xiv, 24–26, 33–34, 36, 44–45, 47–48, 50, 52, 56–57, 59–60, 69–70, 79, 85, 98, 100–102, 106, 109, 111, 159–60, 180, 183, 187–88. *See also* psychology
Manni, Melissa, 60
Manson, T. W., 83
Mark (aside from specific passages), 118, 122–23, 151
Marshall, I. Howard, 87, 130
Martin, Dale, 96
martyrdom, 11, 18, 35, 75–76, 78–80, 89, 97, 100, 150–51, 154, 174, 177
Matera, Frank, 82
Maximus the Confessor, 94
McCarthy, Dennis, 25
McCauley, Clark, 15–16
McClymond, Kathryn, 24
McIntosh, Mark, 152

McKnight, Scot, 101
McNish, Jill, 106–7
Mendelson, Myer, 34, 36
Merasco, Dawn, 65
mercy seat, 8–9, 17, 76, 81–84
metaphors, xiii, xviii, 2, 6, 9–14, 18, 25, 50–51, 53–54, 76–85, 87, 89–91, 96–99, 101–2, 109, 115, 129, 131, 134, 138, 140, 164, 167, 187
Micah (re: the prophet), 46, 52, 138
Milavec, Aaron, 127
Milgrom, Jacob, 7–11, 23–24, 27
Miller, Alice, 66–68, 143–44, 169
Mody, Rohintan, 86, 89
Moffitt, David, 135–36
Mowinckel, Sigmund, 43
Murray-Swank, Aaron, 64
myth of ritual murder. *See* ritual murder accusation

Nelson-Pallmeyer, Jack, 156
Neville, Robert Cummings,
Nixon, Kathryn, 65

order, 1–2, 4, 14, 40, 125
Origen, 154
Osiander, Andreas, 180

P (priestly author), 2, 7, 9, 31
parental rage. *See* rage
Pargament, Kenneth, 64
Parker, Rebecca Ann, 161
Parker, Robert, 28, 38

215

participationist, 88, 92–93, 113–15
patrilineal, 5
Pattison, Stephen, 72, 107
patronage, 37, 39, 43, 47, 55–56, 84, 138–39
payback, 24, 29–31, 41, 47, 140, 142
payment, xvi–xvii, xx, 23–29, 43–44, 47–48, 56, 59, 69–70, 72, 78, 84–85, 87, 89, 94–102, 106, 109–11, 120–21, 138–39, 141–42, 152–53, 155, 157–59, 161, 167, 170–71, 175, 181–82, 184, 187–88
Plato, 38–40, 45, 47–48, 78, 134–35
Polen, Nehemia, 9
Poliakov, Léon, 173
propitiation, 25, 28–31, 36, 83–85, 88, 113, 121, 154, 183–85, 187
Pruyser, Paul, 151, 162–65, 171
psychology, xi–xiv, 14–21. More specifically: *See* anxiety, attachment theory, developmental psychology, disgust, fear, guilt, manipulation, selfishness
Pugh, Ben, 152–54, 158–60, 167
purchase. *See* payment
purity, purification, xii–xii, xviii–xix, 1–21, 27, 30–31, 54, 59–60, 75–78, 80–81, 85, 90–91, 98–100, 105–6, 109, 130, 132, 134–37, 142, 188

Quinn, Philip, 161

Rado, Sandor, 34–36, 69, 79, 159
rage, xviii, 33–36, 48, 107, 119, 142, 179
ransom. *See* redemption
the ransom theory, 151–55, 157, 162–64, 167
Rappaport, Ernest, 176–77, 180
Rashdall, Hastings, 8, 92, 153–54, 157, 159, 161, 167–69, 189
Ratcliff, Donald, 65
Redemption, xii–xiii, xviii, 6, 27, 29, 78, 81–82, 84–86, 89, 90, 93–100, 109, 118, 123, 131, 135–37, 150, 152–56, 158–59, 170, 181
reciprocity, 23, 28, 37–39, 41, 47, 55–57, 138–39
Reid, Barbara, 78
reparation. *See* compensation or reparation
revelation, xv, 18, 115, 118, 121, 126, 129, 132, 137, 144, 154, 160, 186–87, 189
Revelation (aside from specific passages), xii, 12, 122, 151
Rhoads, David, 72
Rhoads, Sandra Roberts, 72
Ribbens, Benjamin, 95
ritual, xi, xviii, 1–14, 17–18, 25, 27–30, 32–33, 42, 44–46, 49–54, 57, 60, 69–70, 75, 81–82, 90–91, 96–97, 99–101, 109, 120, 126, 129, 131–32, 123, 135, 141–42, 144–47,

171, 174, 176, 178, 186, 188–89. *See* also ritual murder accusation
ritual murder accusation, 173–80
Rosen, Irwin, 33–34
Rozin, Paul, 14–16
Rubin, Miri, 178

Sabourin, Leopold, 42
sacrifice, xi–xix, 1–14, 17–19, 21, 23–59, 69–70, 74–85, 87, 89–92, 94, 96–102, 105, 109–10, 113, 115–16, 118–19, 125–26, 129–42, 145–47, 149–51, 154–57, 163, 166, 168, 170, 175, 177–78, 181, 183–84, 186–89
Sanders, E. P., 11, 113–14
scapegoat, scapegoating, 12, 68, 70, 89–94, 97, 99–102, 106, 108, 178–79
Schmitt, Mary, 133
Schneider, Carl, 106–7
Schreiber, Stefan, 84
Schultz, Magdalene, 173, 180
Schwartz, Seth, 55–56
self-punishment, 34–36, 79, 159
selfishness, xiii, 39, 45, 47–48, 59, 72, 105–6, 120, 123, 128, 138, 156, 162, 187
sexual behaviors, rules, 4, 7, 15, 17, 105–7, 162
shame, 21, 72–73, 75, 103, 106–9, 120, 143, 162–65, 167, 171–72, 178, 180

Shepard, Amy, 65
Siegel, Daniel, 62, 64
Skarsaune, Oskar, 134
Sklar, Jay, 27
Socrates, 39–40, 51, 78
Sophocles, 78
Souter, Alexander, 125
spiritual growth or progress, xiv, 51–52, 56, 59, 67, 80, 100, 106–7, 118–19, 121, 147, 184–87
spiritualizing, xviii, 12–14, 53, 76–77, 97, 100–101, 105
Sroufe, L. Alan, 63
Stählin, Gustav, 90, 92
Stockitt, Robin, 75
Stoic, Stoicism, 55, 102
Stökl Ben Ezra, Daiel, 8, 11, 91
Stott, John, 87, 137
Stowers, Stanley, 2, 11, 37–38, 104
Stuhlmacher, Peter, 151
substitution, xvii–xix, 9, 21, 65, 70, 78–79, 86–90, 103, 113, 118, 146, 161–63, 166–67, 170
Sulzer, J., 66
supersessionism, 76, 133–34
Swartley, Willard, 118
symbols, xvi–xvii, 1, 6, 25–26, 38, 46, 53, 59, 75, 80, 93, 99–100, 120, 125–26, 131, 133, 136, 176, 178, 181

Tamminen, Kalevi, 65
Tatlock, Jason, 30
Theissen, Gerd, 104

theōsis, transformation into Christlikeness, xix, 89, 93–94, 102, 105, 108, 144, 147, 154–55, 160, 165
Thomas Aquinas. *See* Aquinas, Thomas
Tillich, Paul, 160, 167, 172
Tinkle, Theresa, 173, 179
Trachtenberg, Joshua, 174, 177, 179
Transubstantiation, 175–77
Tylor, Edward Burnett, 24
Tyndale, William, 8, 81
typology, 26, 79, 132–36

Vedic religion. *See* Indian and Vedic religion
Vianello, Renzo, 65
violence, divine, xiv, xvi–xix, 2–4, 18, 29, 31, 69–70, 85, 89, 100–101, 116, 140, 142, 159–61, 166–69, 171, 175
violence, human, xiv, xvi–xvii, xx, 6, 29–33, 66–69, 90, 94, 97, 99, 115–16, 120, 141–44, 156–58, 169, 171–74, 177–78, 180–82

Voegelin, Eric, 94

Waite, Gary, 180
Warner, Rex, 55
Weaver, J. Denny, 155, 158–59
Webster's New Collegiate Dictionary, 23
Wedderburn, Alexander, 123
Weingart, Richard, 157
Weiss, Alexander, 84
Westcott, B. F., 124
Whale, J. S., 28
Whitlark, Jason, 37, 39, 47, 138–40
Wikipedia, 174
Williams, Charles, 177
Williams, Jarvis, 11, 79, 92, 95
Wilt, Michael Vander, 65
Wright, David, 8–9
Wright, N. T., 13

Young, Frances, 18, 25–26, 154–55, 183

Zarathustra, Zoroastrianism, 25, 51

Index of Scripture and Pre-Modern Sources

Old Testament

Genesis
4:3–5......3
8:21......25
32:20......27

Exodus
19:6......50
21:8......95
21:30......27
23:15......26
23:23......26
24:8......132
25:21......81
25:22......9
30:10......27
30:12–16......27
30:15......27
30:15–16......27
32:12......83
33:16......40
34:9–11......40
34:19......40

Leviticus
1–16......2
1:9......23, 25
1:13......25
1:17......25
2:2......25
2:9......25
4:17–18......10
4:19......10
4:20......6, 10
4:20–35......10
4:25......10
4:26......10
4:30......10
4:31......10
4:34......10
5:4......154
5:5–6......10
5:9......10
5:10......6, 10
5:10–18......10
6:4–5......17
6:15–18......5

SACRIFICE AND ATONEMENT

7:1–7......6, 23
7:2......154
10:1–2......3
10:10......4
11......17
13:45–46......17
15:31......17
16:2......9, 17
16:10......91
16:14–19......8
16:21......90
16:22......12
16:29–34......8
17:4......4
17:9......4
18......7
18–21......4
18:13–28......4
18:24......17
18:25......140
18:28......7
18:29......4
19:10......4
19:18......185
20......7
20:2......4
20:6......4
20:13......4
20:18......4, 17
20:22......7
20:22–26......4
20:25–26......3
20:27......4
23:13......25
23:22......4
24:16–17......4
24:21......4
25:24......95
26:2–3......40
26:9......40
26:14......40
26:16......40

Numbers
7:89......9
13:23......126
15:10......25
16:23–25......4
25......29
25:7–8......29
25:11......29
25:13......29
28:2......25
28:6......23
35......27
35:31–33......27
35:33......4

Deuteronomy
10:5......81
12:27–28......31–32
13:13–15......30
13:16......30
21:8......11, 83
32:22......xiv
32:35......185
32:41......140
33:16–17......31

INDEX OF SCRIPTURE AND PRE-MODERN SOURCES

1 Samuel
12:1–5......27
15:22......xiv, 50
15:33......30
24:1......31
24:15......31
26:19......25

2 Samuel
6:6–7......xvi
6:9......xvi
21......6
21:1......30
21:6......30
21:14......30
24:24......25–26
24:25......26

2 Kings
8:8–9......28
23:20......30

1 Chronicles
21:24......25
21:26......26
22:12......4

Job
3:14......xvii
32:8......181

Psalms
4......44
4:4–5......44

4:5......45
4:7–8......44
5:12......41
20......xiii
20:3–4......xiii
26......41
26:1......41
26:5–6......41
26:6......42
26:7......42
26:8......42
26:9......41
26:11–12......42
26:12......42
27......42
27:3......42
27:4......42
27:6......42
27:6–7......xiii
27:9......xiii
35:18......41, 43
35:28......43
39:11......49
40......48–49
40:14......49
41:10–11......41
43......42
43:1–2......42
43:3–4......42
43:5......42
50......48–49, 52
50:13......52
50:16......49
50:22......49

51......48–49, 52
51:6......49
51:10......49
51:12......49
51:13......49
51:15–17......49
51:16......52
51:16–17......49
51:17......49, 57
51:19......49
52:9......43
53:5–6......49
53:6–8......49
54......42
54:3......42
54:5–7......6
54:6......42
54:7......42
57:2......55
65:3......11
65:4 [MT]......11
66......43
66:13......43
66:13–14......43
66:15......43
66:18......43
68:30......28
69......49
69:4......49
69:6–12......49
69:18–28......49
69:30–32......49
71:24......43
77:7......41

78:38......11
79:9......11
80:8......126
89:15–17......41
103:4......56
106......29
106:38......4
107:15......44
107:20–21......44
107:22......44
111:1......41
116:6–8......44
116:12......44
116:14......44
116:16......44
116:16–17......44
116:17......44
116:18......44
119:58......40
141......6
141:2......49

Proverbs
2:5......126
6:35......27
13:24......144
22:15......144
25:22......185
28:4......4

Isaiah
1......46
1:13......52
1:17......53

INDEX OF SCRIPTURE AND PRE-MODERN SOURCES

1:18......xiv, 140
2......118
6:9......56
8:19......50
9......118
11:9......126
18:7......28
20:2–3......53
30:18......182
32......118
32:15–16......50
35:5......56
35:5–8......140
42:1......126
42:6......19
42:7......56
43:10......126
49:1......51
54:10......117
54:13......56
55:1......182
56:7......56
61:1–2......56

Jeremiah
1:5......51
7:11......56
7:22......52
7:22–23......46
9:24......126
26:15–23......150
27:2......53
31—32......140
31:31–34......140
31:33......137
31:34......137
32:38–41......140
32:40......140
33:8......140

Ezekiel
16:63......11
20:41......25
36:25–27......140
36:25–32......51
40:5—47:14......51

Hosea
4:1......126
4:2......47
4:6......126
4:8......47
6:6......56, 126, 131
8:11......50
8:12......47
8:13......47
10:1......126
10:12......50
14:4......182

Joel
1:13–14......51
2:13–16......51
2:28......51

Amos
5:4......56
5:10–11......53

223

5:12......27
5:21–22......45
5:25–26......45
7:2......83
7:10–13......150

Micah
3:11......xiv
6:6–7......46
6:7......xiv, 131
6:8......xiv, 56
7:6......56

Zephaniah
1:18......140

Zechariah
9:9......119
12:10......150
13:7......150

Malachi
1:8 MT......26
1:10......26

New Testament

Matthew
5:3–12......181
5:5–9......21
5:6–8......189
5:8......138
5:8–9......170
5:48......155
6:8......182
6:14–15......189
6:26–30......105
6:30–33......xiv
7:7–11......xiv
7:9......xiv
7:11......xv
7:17......105
8:10......77
9......72
9:12–13......19, 72
9:13......56, 131, 183
9:22......20
10:8......182
10:32......147
10:35–36......56
12:7......56, 131, 186
12:33......170
12:33–36......21
12:35......138
12:50......138, 170
13:44......96
13:46......96, 170
15:1–20......3
18:5......144
18:6......144
18:10......144
18:10–14......181
19:14......182
20:28......95, 123
21:5......119
21:13......56
21:34......119
21:37......119
22:2......119

INDEX OF SCRIPTURE AND PRE-MODERN SOURCES

22:6–7......119
22:45......119
23:11–12......181
23:16–22......120
23:23......56, 120
23:23–27......3
26:28......12
27......91
27:54......186

Mark
2:15......3
2:22......xv
3:35......138, 170
5:34......20–21
5:36......187
7:1–21......3
8:31–33......119
9:30–32......119
9:35–37......182
9:42......182
10:14......182
10:32–34......119
10:45......95, 123
10:52......21
11:15–17......3
11:17......56, 183
11:25......189
12:2......119
12:6......119
12:32–34......16
12:33–34......183
12:37......119
14:22–25......127

14:24......12
15:39......186
15:46......96

Luke
1:2–3......123
1:68......95
1:74......187
4:18–19......56
5:14......12
6:45......21, 138
7:50......21, 117, 137, 188
8:21......21, 138
8:47–48......73
8:48......73
8:48......21, 188
8:50......137–38, 187, 189
9:6......89
9:13......96
9:22......123–24
9:44......123–24
9:50......19
10:27–28......21
10:37......21
11:5–10......181
11:13......xv
11:42......21
11:49......124
12:32......56, 182, 188
13:33–34......124
14:10–11......181
15......181
16:10......21, 138
17:14......12

225

17:19......21, 188
17:21......138, 155
18:1–17......181
18:13......83
18:16......182
18:31......123–24
18:33......124
18:42......21
19:8......72
19:42......119
19:44......119
20:10......119
21:28......95
22:17–18......124
22:19a......125
22:19b–20......124
22:20......124
22:24–27......123
23:50......16
24:21......95

John
1:3......47
2:14–19......3
3:1......16
6:37......19
6:45......56
7:17......138, 170, 172–73
8:1......147
8:32......144, 186
8:35......186
8:36......186
8:58......146
10:12......147
10:18......147
12:2......147
12:15......119
15:13......186
15:15......182
15:16......186
16:27......182, 188–89
17:3......147
17:4–5......146

Acts
2:33......125
2:38......149–50
2:40......149–50
3:13......150
3:18......150
3:19......147
5:30......125
6:5......151
7:52......124
10......121
10:35–36......122
10:36......122
10:38......122
10:39–43......122
10:43......125
11:18......147
13:39......147, 150
15:5......4
16:31......147
20......149
20:28......124–25, 147, 150
20:35......147, 150
27......91

Romans
1:16......77
1:18......18
1:19......102
2:8......85
2:27......4
3......79, 86–87, 114
3—4......89
3:4......165
3:7......74
3:19......165
3:19–26......159
3:21......86
3:21–22......86
3:22......85
3:23–25a......81
3:24......86, 94–95, 97
3:24–25a......82
3:24–25......96
3:25......8, 11, 76, 80, 82–84, 115, 170
3:25a......82
3:25b......86
3:25b–26......86
3:26......86
3:27......86, 107
3:29......77
3:30......86
4......114
4:25......80, 86
5—7......89
5—8......104
5:2......55, 85
5:3–5......102
5:5......108, 115

5:5–8......101
5:5–11......115
5:6......115
5:6–8......85
5:8......76, 115
5:8–10......xii
5:9......14, 80, 85, 101, 115, 178
5:10......80, 90, 115
5:15......55
5:19......93
5:20......55
5:21......89
6:4......103, 163
6:4–8......74
6:4–11......144
6:5......93
6:6......89, 92, 103, 108, 165
6:6–8......103
6:8......93
6:9......164
6:11......92
6:12......93, 103
6:14......89, 92, 164
6:17......55
6:17–18......93
6:22......89
6:23......185
7—8......104
7:4......74, 97, 103
7:5......74, 102, 108
7:6......144
7:7–25......104
7:11......74
7:17......103

7:18......74, 102–3
7:23......74, 103
7:23–24......164
7:24......103
7:25......55, 104
8:1–4......86, 103
8:2......74, 104
8:3......13, 76, 86, 92, 97
8:4......86
8:5–9......103
8:6......117
8:8......105
8:9......105
8:10......93, 103, 105
8:10–24......89
8:11......93
8:13......93, 105
8:14......109
8:15......108
8:15–17......186
8:17......93, 103, 114
8:23......109
8:29......89, 144, 155
8:29–30......xix
8:32......90
8:33......97
8:33–34......84, 86
10:9......147
12......xix, 115
12:1......77, 105
12:2......89, 105, 115, 144, 169
12:3–13:10......89–90
12:19......185
12:20......185

13:14......103
14:17......117
14:23......106
15:16......51
16:20......117

1 Corinthians
1:30......95
3:16......76
4:7......107–8
4:9......92
4:13......91
4:18......107–8
5:1......105
5:1–8......114
5:7......xii, 76
5:7–8......51
5:9......105
6:9–10......105
6:14......80
6:15......98
6:18......106
6:20......96–98, 101, 106, 109
7:23......96–98, 109
8:11......76
10:16......80, 93, 178
11......80
11:21......80
11:25......117, 124, 127, 178
11:27–30......79–80
11:25–27......80
12:3......147
13:4......107–8
15:3......88, 100

15:3–4......xii
15:4......80
15:23......185
15:50......185

2 Corinthians
1:22......93
2:15......53
3:6......82
3:10......82
3:17–18......144
3:18......155
4:4......154
5......114
5:6–7......109
5:14......76, 88, 113
5:15......120
5:17......105, 114
5:18......114
5:18–20......101
5:21......93, 101, 114, 160
6:6......13
6:16–17......103
7:1......109
12:9......107, 165
12:9–10......108
12:10......107

Galatians
1:4......82, 154
1:15......51
2......114
2:11–16......151
3:13......xii, xix, 86, 96–97, 106, 168

3:25......82
3:26......186
4:8......169
4:19......168
5:1......186
5:9–10......169
5:19......13
5:24......92

Ephesians
1:7......95
1:14......95
2:19......186
4:15......186
4:22–24......163
4:30......195
5:2......26
5:26–27......12
6:15......117

Philippians
1:19......105
2:5......xix
2:8......85
2:12......73
2:13......73
2:15......169
2:17......50
3:4......108
3:7–8......74
3:9......160
3:10–11......114
3:21......165
4:18......25, 53

SACRIFICE AND ATONEMENT

Colossians
1:14......95

1 Thessalonians
1:6......xix
1:10......85
2:9–12......102
4:16–17......185
5:10......76, 185
5:23......117

1 Timothy
2:5–6......xii
2:6......xiii
6:12......73

Titus
2:14......12, 95–96, 98

Hebrews
1:1–3......129–30, 139
1:3......xii, 13, 18, 142, 147
2:3......xvi, 139, 144
2:9......139, 143
2:10......142, 145–46
2:10–11......139
2:11......143
2:14......145–46
2:16......133
2:17......137, 146
3:6......145
3:14......145
3:17–18......143
4:3......143

4:6......143
4:11......143
4:12......143
5:7–8......147
5:7–9......145
5:8–9......142
5:9......14
6:1......142, 145
6:4–6......139
7—10......133
7:11......132–33, 142
7:12......133
7:18–19......133
7:19......142
7:25–27......14
7:27......130, 132
7:28......142
8:1......147
8:4......136
8:5......130, 134, 136
8:6......133
8:8–9......136
8:10......137
8:13......133
9:1......137
9:2–8......136
9:6–10......144
9:6–15......11
9:7–14......141
9:9......130, 136, 142
9:10......130
9:10–14......136
9:11......136, 142
9:11–12......131, 136

9:11–15......136–37
9:12......13, 95, 137
9:13......130
9:13–14......xii, 18, 130
9:14......12–13, 133, 140, 142, 144
9:15......95
9:18......141
9:19–20......132
9:21–22......132
9:21–10:3......11
9:22......137
9:22–23......13–14, 18, 137
9:23......133–35
9:23–25......136
9:24......136
9:26......xiii, xvii, 13, 133
10:1......130, 133, 135, 142
10:1–11......131
10:3......130
10:4......133
10:5......130
10:9......133
10:10......xvii, 137
10:11......130
10:12......13, 130, 135, 147
10:14......142
10:16......137
10:18......133
10:19......135, 180
10:19–22......141
10:20......13, 136
10:21......137
10:22......18, 142
10:23–25......xvi
10:24......142
10:26......144
10:26–27......xvi, 142
10:26–29......139
10:27......140
10:29......140, 142
10:29–30......142
10:30......140
10:31......18, 144
11:1......139
11:28......141
11:40......142
12:2......139, 142, 147
12:5......141
12:5–10......147
12:6–7......141
12:7–9......139
12:8......141
12:9–10......141
12:11......141
12:23......142
12:24......140–41
12:25–29......139
12:28......139
12:28–29......xvi, 18
12:29......69
13:12–21......141
13:13......141
13:16......139

James
1:21......123
2:24–26......123
3:17–18......123

4:8–10......123
5:15–16......123

1 Peter
1:18......xiii
1:18–19......96, 99

1 John
1:7......12, 180
4:18......xv

Revelation
5:9......96

Other Jewish Literature

First Enoch
46.4......19
48.4......19
48.8......19

4 Maccabees
6:28–29......78
17:20–22......78
17:22......83–84

Josephus
Antiquities of the Jews
16.182......84

Mishnah
Yoma
6.4......91

Sirach (Ecclesiasticus)
35:1......50

Testament of Levi
3.6......77

Wisdom of Solomon
2:10–20......150

Ancient Greek Literature

Aeschylus
Choephoroi
255–57......28
791–93......28

Aristotle
Nicomachean Ethics
1123 B17–21......39

Corpus Hermeticum
13.19......77

Diogenes Laertius
6.63......55

Euripides
Iphigenia at Aulis
1389–99......78
1555......78

Plato
Crito
50A–52E......78

Euthyphro
12E–13B......39
15A......39

Laws
10.885C......45
10.909B......48
10.910A......48
12.948C......45

Republic
390E–391A......45

Papyrus Oxyrhynchus
1149......5, 96

Plutarch
Pompey
24.4......95

Theophrastus
Περὶ εὐσέβειας
24.1–5......39

Early Christian and Patristic Literature

Augustine
Contra Faustum Manichaeum
14.4......156

Athansius
On the Incarnation
11–16......155
54......154

Barnabas
7......91
7.6–8......91

The Didache
9.2......125–26
9.2–3......126
9.3......126
9.4......126
10.2......126
10.5......126

Ignatius of Antioch
Ephesians
20.2......80

Smyrnaeans
6.1......80

Irenaeus
Adv. haer.
2.22.4......152
5......preface, 153

Gregory of Nazianzus
Oration
45.22......155

Gregory of Nyssa
Great Catechism
24......153

Gregory the Great
Moralia on Job

233

3.14......xvii
17.46......157
33.7.14......157

Origen
Contra Celsus
1.1......154
1.31......18
3.28......154

Tertullian
Adversus Marcionem
3.7.7......91

Medieval and Reformation Literature

Abelard
Commentary on Romans
2......159

Epitome of Theology......160

Aquinas, Thomas
Summa Theologiae
3a, q. 46, a. 2......161
3a, q. 46, a. 3......161
3a, q. 49, a. 4......161
3a, q. 48, a. 4......161

Bernard of Clairvaux
Epistle (or "Treatise on the Errors of Abelard")
190.7......160

Calvin, Jean
Institutes of the Christian Religion
2.1.8......170
2.5.19......170
2.8.5......180
2.16.1......171
2.17.5......170
3.21.7......170

Luther, Martin
Bondage of the Will......167

Commentary on Galatians......168
3.13......xix, 168
4.19......168

Commentary on Psalms
51.1......168

Commentary on Romans
100.9......167

On the Ineffable Name......179

On the Jews and Their Lies......179

Shakespeare
Hamlet
III.1......163

Other Religions

Zoroastrianism
Yasht
8.58......25

www.ingramcontent.com/pod-product-compliance
Lightning Source LLC
Chambersburg PA
CBHW071155070526
44584CB00019B/2802